UNDERSTANDING
JOURNALISM

UNDERSTANDING JOURNALISM

Second edition

Lynette Sheridan Burns

Los Angeles | London | New Delhi
Singapore | Washington DC

Los Angeles | London | New Delhi
Singapore | Washington DC

SAGE Publications Ltd
1 Oliver's Yard
55 City Road
London EC1Y 1SP

SAGE Publications Inc.
2455 Teller Road
Thousand Oaks, California 91320

SAGE Publications India Pvt Ltd
B 1/I 1 Mohan Cooperative Industrial Area
Mathura Road
New Delhi 110 044

SAGE Publications Asia-Pacific Pte Ltd
3 Church Street
#10-04 Samsung Hub
Singapore 049483

Editor: Mila Steele
Editorial assistant: James Piper
Production editor: Imogen Roome
Marketing manager: Michael Ainsley
Cover design: Jennifer Crisp
Typeset by: C&M Digitals (p) Ltd, Chennai, India
Printed by MPG Books Group, Bodmin, Cornwall

© Lynette Sheridan Burns 2013

First published 2013

First edition published 2002, reprinted 2009

Library of Congress Control Number: 2012934262

British Library Cataloguing in Publication data

A catalogue record for this book is available from the British Library

Mixed Sources
Product group from well-managed forests and other controlled sources
www.fsc.org Cert no. SA-COC-1565
© 1996 Forest Stewardship Council
FSC

ISBN 978-1-4462-0738-3
ISBN 978-1-4462-0739-0 (pbk)

For
Warren Thomas Burns (1955–2004)
Thomas Riley Sheridan Burns
Anna Grace Sheridan Burns

CONTENTS

ABOUT THE AUTHOR

Lynette Sheridan Burns has been a journalist for more than 30 years, first on Sydney metropolitan newspapers. She won three consecutive journalism awards after moving to regional New South Wales in 1985. In 1989 she moved to the University of Newcastle, Australia, where she established its journalism programme in 1992. Today she is Professor of Journalism and Deputy Dean of Humanities and Communication Arts at the University of Western Sydney. In addition, she continues her award-winning research into media representation of minorities through problem-based curriculum design. She divides her time between Sydney and the 'splendid isolation' of the family home in a rural village outside Newcastle.

ABOUT THE BOOK

'Where to begin?' is a crucial question for new journalists, whether they are trying to apply information from lectures or 'learning journalism' on the job. Journalism is always created in a complex cultural context that is evolving all the time. A focus on the practices or skills used by journalists cannot keep up with changing definitions of journalism or offer broad advice in a global context.

This book starts with what Schön (1983) called 'the conversations we have with ourselves'. It guides beginners through the thinking processes used by journalists to produce thoughtful, quality journalism that is also attractive to the market. It is not so much a critique of media practice but a means to negotiate the challenges.

PREFACE

'I love to learn but I hate being taught'

Winston Churchill

First and foremost, this book owes its genesis to the brilliant young, and not so young, minds I have encountered in more than two decades of teaching journalism in universities.

These beginning journalists have, individually and as a group, directly challenged everything I ever learned about journalism in years of professional practice. It was as a teacher, not as a journalist, that I found myself asking *how* I knew the things I knew to be true. These students forced me to find clear and reliable explanations of a practice considered by most practitioners to be intrinsic.

From the classroom, my thinking returned to the newsrooms I have worked in and the talented and generous peers and mentors who shared their knowledge and passion for journalism with me. I am also grateful to my colleagues in journalism education for stimulating and expanding my thinking.

Yet, the seeds of this book go back much further.

When I was seeking a journalism cadetship in the late 1970s, I turned to my father for help in phrasing the all-important application letter. He added a sentence that began 'Being *mindful* of the importance of on-the-job training...'.

Later, as a working journalist, I looked back on this turn of phrase as quaint, and considered *mindful* a word quite unsuited for a reporter. The word came back to me, during the preparation of the first edition. Visiting Laos, a colleague gave me Ellen Langer's 1989 book *Mindfulness*, and I realized that being mindful is exactly what good journalism is all about.

I thank my father, Gordon Sheridan, for that early insight into the difference between knowledge and understanding and for his continued interest in what I do.

There are others to whom I owe a great deal for their support during the preparation of the second edition, not least the remarkable Helen Johnson, whose encouragement and practical support made the many hours of writing and research possible. Then there are my journalism colleagues, Asha Chand, Milissa Deitz and Barbara Alysen, who were so generous with their insights. And Mila Steele and Imogen Roome from Sage for their support.

There are others whose support sustains me – Valmai Sheridan and Tracy Sheridan in particular. Above all, however, I remain indebted to Warren Thomas Burns (1955–2004), and our children, Riley and Grace.

Riley and Grace, now wonderful adults, have patiently and affectionately indulged my work for years despite the many inconveniences it has imposed. Their loving support of their mother brings a tear to my eye. And I am still grateful for unconditional faith in me that was their father's greatest gift.

This book is for journalists who want to be better at what they do, including those who are already working, and those who still aspire to their first job. You already know that journalism is a complex business. Journalists have to please the boss, his boss, the proprietor, and a myriad of groups formerly defined as the audience. The temptation to take the path of least resistance is strong, and many fail to resist it, but this book comes to praise journalism, not bury it.

It focuses on the practices of the everyday journalist and seeks to understand them. No one can tell you with certainty what you will encounter in your practice of journalism. For this reason, no one can tell you, with certainty, how to deal with the challenges that will inevitably arise. However, if you are able to encounter a new situation and understand *what* it is, *how* to make the decisions that journalism practice requires and you are *able* to do that ethically and with confidence, then this book has done its job.

LSB 2012

PART ONE

From Knowing How to Being Able

1

INTRODUCTION

In the years since the first edition of *Understanding Journalism* was published in 2002, the emergence of social media and mobile media has transformed the way millions of people communicate. Worldwide, SMS is used five times more than any other means of data communication – including telephone. These changes also raise important questions about the definition of journalism and its role in society. The emergence of user-generated content, distributed through social networks such as YouTube, Twitter and Facebook, challenges journalism practices that have been largely unchanged for decades. As Clay Shirky wrote in *Here Comes Everybody*:

> Television and radio changed the landscape in which the newspaper operated, but even then printed news had a monopoly on the written word – until the Web. The Web didn't introduce a new competitor into the old ecosystem ... the Web created a new ecosystem. (Shirky, 2008: 60)

There is no doubt that the Internet has transformed the way people access information. Search engine algorithms steer individual consumers through a mass of content so great that no individual will find and consume it all. Journalists need research systems to locate and evaluate the best secondary sources for their work.

The new era fundamentally shifts the journalist's relationship with the audience, who is now part of the process. User-generated content is both a source for professional journalists and a direct competitor for the interest of the audience. In this environment power resides in the individual's reputation and an ability to consistently draw an audience, rather than in privileged ownership of means of production.

Those in the pre-professional stage of their education need to think through new paradigms and graduates must be skilled in cross-platform delivery. This moves or eliminates the boundaries between communication and design, music and media production. Journalists must be visually literate and understand information design and media production.

The technical mastery required to negotiate the new environment continues to evolve and change at such a rate that books can't keep up but it is a mistake to focus on technical possibilities alone. With so many voices and so few louder than the rest, there is a renewed urgency for journalists to focus on the *writing* aspect of their craft. In this era of a multiplicity of voices, when *reputation* defines influence, it is more important than ever than journalists are able to write eloquently and persuasively. It is a return to a view of communication that pre-dates the idea of an objective truth. As Thomas Hobbes wrote in *Leviathan* in the seventeenth century:

> When we believe any saying, whatsoever it be, to be true, from arguments taken, not from the thing itself, or from the principles of natural reason, but from the authority and good opinion we have of him that hath said it; then is the speaker, or person we believe in, or trust in, and whose word we take, the object of our faith; and the honour done in believing is done to him only.

Without the power to impose a particular view of the truth, the writer must return to persuading the audience through reasoned argument and deft use of language. The second edition of *Understanding Journalism* includes a renewed focus on professional writing and editing across a variety of genres from the most abbreviated forms of communication, such as Twitter and SMS, to longer formats such magazine articles. The second core focus is the development of a clearly defined ethical framework. A reasoned individual framework for evaluating information and acting ethically is more important than ever before because it is increasingly difficult to codify practice. The importance of mindful research and the development of processes for evaluating the appropriateness of sources are equally important.

The role of the journalist in society has changed too. For almost 200 years, newspapers were the dominant medium by which society 'spoke to itself'. The newspaper seemed to be a ubiquitous and fixed part of the communication landscape and those who prepared the news were seen as similarly integral. Access to self-publishing technology changed that irrevocably.

> The pattern here is simple – what seems like a fixed and abiding category like journalist turns out to be tied to an accidental scarcity created by the expense of publishing apparatus. Sometimes this scarcity is decades old (as with photographers) or even centuries old (as with journalists), but that doesn't stop it from being accidental, and when that scarcity gets undone, the seemingly stable categories turn out to be unsupportable. This is not to say that professional journalists and photographers do not exist, but it does mean that the primary distinction between the two groups is gone. What once was a chasm has now become a mere slope. (Shirky, 2008: 76)

The loss of exclusive access to the means of production and the advertising revenue stream attached to it has threatened the viability mainstream news media as never before. In Australia, the newspaper industry changed as it never has before.

In June 2012, Fairfax Media announced it would shed 1900 jobs, convert its broadsheet papers to tabloid and move to being a 'digital first' news provider. The first jobs lost were primarily for printers and sub-editors as production services were aggregated and in some cases moved off-shore.

Days later, News Limited announced has it would shrink its divisions in eastern Australia from 19 to five as part of a restructure that will 'centralize' operations in each state and cause large job losses.

'This single-newsroom concept will transform our existing metro newsrooms. ... It doesn't mean that everyone will physically move to a single location. But it does mean that we will manage our editorial operation in each state as a single news network,' said Chief Executive Kim Williams at the time.

A downside of the single-newsroom is that it inevitably leads to aggregation of content. And greater aggregation of news content will, over time, hurt the quality of journalism as the editing and fact-checking takes place far from the community the news is produced.

There is already a centralized sub-editing facility at News Limited's Sydney headquarters, called News Central. The *Daily Telegraph* and *Sunday Telegraph*, always separate mastheads, will be merged into a single state-focused offering.

Consumers can expect more generalized news coverage, because there are fewer reporters on the ground in the communities. With these changes, it's most likely that that the journalistic workforce will be younger, with less experience. That might be expected to have a negative impact on quality. It's very much a 'wrong but not for long' approach.

In sub-editing, what we're seeing across the sector is the end of a move that began some years ago to change the role of a sub-editor from someone who actually edits and improves work to someone who's a process worker, who really just formats and processes copy in a pre-designed template. The level of expertise that used to be applied as quality control – improving the work of reporters – has gone from most newsrooms.

In September 2012, it was announced that Australian Consolidated Press, publishers of iconic Australian magazines, had been sold to the German Bauer group, which has a number of global mastheads, with country-specific editions. While Bauer has been praised for allowing each version of a masthead to operate independently, in other Bauer publications there is regular sharing of journalistic content. For example, the magazine article discussed in Chapter 10 was published first in Australia by Emap (owned by Bauer). The camera-ready pages were then on-sold to the same publication in Malaysia and then Singapore. With space for feature length articles severely restricted in many magazines to one or two articles, this on-selling reduces the opportunities for feature writers.

For mainstream media around the world, the pressures created by the rise of self-publishing are exacerbated by a decline in public confidence in journalism as a source of truth.

Today's (mostly) tertiary-educated journalists are more likely to be denigrated as 'cappuccino sippers' of the middle class, promulgating a politically correct point of view remote from that of their audience. Modern Western journalists are criticized as peddlers of a commodity called 'information' that is marketed to commercial advantage, without reference to the individual's 'own reason, sensitivity and commitment' (McManus, 1994: 203). Underwood (1993) and Nichol and McChesney

(2008) support the view that as newsgathering became more explicitly directed by market concerns, the focus of journalism became softer and real political coverage suffered. Unfortunately, this did not stem the outward tide in readership and market share:

> The issues that News workers are facing today stem directly from the changes that have occurred in the real age of mass media – that is, from the time when the contours of the 20th century mediascape were formed: the age of radio, television and the mass circulation modern newspaper. It was also in this period that the fourth estate became the dominant way of thinking about the news media even though the term itself comes from the 18th century. (Nichol and McChesney, 2008: 69)

Journalism experienced a fundamental shift in the 1970s, with the emphasis on market-driven journalism, where return to shareholders became a guiding priority. That meant news organizations were weakened when the onslaught of self-publishing came.

> Even before that decline, newspaper owners were choosing short-term profits over long-term viability. … Corporate newspaper owners abandoned any responsibility to maintain the franchise. When the Internet came along, newspapers were already heading due south. Even then journalism suffered from a generally agreed-upon professional code that relied far too heavily on official sources to set the news agenda and decide the range of debate in our political culture. That weakness of journalism has been magnified in the era of corporate control. (Nichols and McChesney, 2011)

Journalism as we know it today has been evolving continuously, sometimes as a result of developing technology, sometimes as a reflection of changes in society. For example, the invention of telegraph technology changed the language of journalism. Instead of reports taking a form more like a letter from a correspondent, pay-per-word telegraph technology deemed that reporters 'stick to the facts' and deliver them in the most economical language possible. When journalism was produced by hot-metal linotype, the technology dictated that all stories could be cut from the end up because the technology did not allow for last-minute cuts within sentences. Today, digital technologies affect the way that journalism is presented to audiences and new forms of journalism are emerging. In some ways, the new forms draw on old techniques, for example, there are parallels between telegraphic writing and writing for Twitter.

The expanding uses of increasingly advanced media technology have fundamentally changed media *content* as well as its production. Some argue this has led to a victory of style over substance (Grattan, 1998). For news providers seeking to win back audiences drawn to niche magazines, technological advances have made it easier for daily publications to adopt the presentation of less frequent publications. Over time, media presentation techniques, which began as artists' illustrations, or humble graphics on the screen behind a news reader, have been transformed into seamless 're-enactments', hidden camera scoops, and digitally altered photographs, sounds and television images purporting to represent 'truth'. Marshall and Kingsbury found that media techniques also profoundly affect content:

> In terms of production of media content, as distinct from the technology itself, the activities of the American Cable News Network (CNN) have been steadily transforming ideas of what news can and should be. ... Not least there was the generation of the 'mega' event in which the media's reporting of its own activities is virtually as important as the news itself. (Marshall and Kingsbury, 1996: 87)

JOURNALISTS AND THEIR AUDIENCES

The all-important mass audience was once considered to be homogeneous. A reporter could simply be instructed to 'write for Mrs Smith down the street'. Residents of today's streets are known to be diverse in their culture, interests and values. As journalists in the 1970s, we saw our job as telling the people 'the facts' about what they needed to know. We felt confident that we knew what that was because the readers were exactly like us. We did not consider our news sense to be subjective, just 'professional'. As Australian journalist and author Craig McGregor recalled in *Soundtrack for the Eighties*:

> When I was a cadet reporter on the *Sydney Morning Herald*, we were lectured on the virtues of objectivity, detachment and lack of bias (unless you were writing about a subject in which your proprietor was involved, in which case you were expected to show a certain pragmatic common sense). (McGregor, 1983: 135)

The prioritization of news values from industrialization to near the end of the twentieth century were very directly tied to the demographic profile of the target audience. These profiles were on-sold to advertisers as likely consumers of their goods and services. The more 'eyeballs' you could sell to an advertisers, the more you could charge. Lord Northcliffe, founder of the popular press in the UK, described huge circulations as 'having the whip hand over advertisers' and it was a model that largely worked until social media fractured audiences into constantly changing groupings. The definition of news and the role of journalism have always been much more complex activities than simply providing 'a window on the world' because 'the view through the window depends upon whether the window is large or small, has many panes or few, whether the glass is opaque or clear' (Koch, 1990: 20). It was once said that the role of journalism is to 'comfort the afflicted and afflict the comfortable', but the trend towards market-driven journalism means that the perceived interests of the audience and the advertisers take priority. In an online article in *The Nation*, Nichols and McChesney (2011) described the effect on American journalism:

> The news media blew the coverage of the Iraq invasion, spoon-feeding us lies masquerading as fact-checked verities. They missed the past decade of corporate scandals. They cheered on the housing bubble and genuflected before the financial sector (and Gilded Age levels of wealth and inequality) as it blasted debt and speculation far beyond what the real economy could sustain. Today they do almost no investigation into where the trillions of public dollars being spent by the Federal Reserve and Treasury are going but spare not a moment to update us on the 'Octomom'. They trade in trivia and reduce everything to spin, even matters of life and death.

Critics such as Hall (1992) and Chomsky and Herman (1988) argued that twentieth-century media aimed at 'production of consent' not 'reflection of consensus'. According to this view, the media plays a crucial role, for example, in whether industrial action is represented as a defence of workers' rights or as a minority group holding the public to ransom. The position from which the journalist observes the 'facts' unfold determines the presentation of the 'truth'. This truth is, in turn, a calculated reinforcement of the position thought to be held by the audience. The effect is that stories are often written from only one, often narrow, point of view. Alternative outlooks are ignored or dismissed. Those who challenge or confront the preferred image of society are marginalized or not heard. Some media critics see these failings are the reasons for the mainstream media's decline:

> Some observers, confident of the blessings of technology, refused to shed any tears for the traditional giants of journalism on the grounds that their troubles are of their own making and of little consequence to the general welfare. In this view, regardless of whether newspapers successfully adapt to the Internet, new and better sources of news will continue developing online, and they will fill whatever the week newspapers leave. Others are so angry at the mainstream media – the reviled MSM – that they see the economic misery of the press as a deserved comeuppance. (Starr, 2009: 19)

But Starr argues that social media are no substitute for mainstream journalism. The profusion of opinion online, but there is little fact-based reporting and even less reporting that subject to any rigourous fact-checking or editorial scrutiny. He also argues that apart from news aggregators such as Google News – which link to articles from publications that still derive most of their revenue from print – the most successful news sites are oriented to specialized audiences. Hedges (2011) supports this gloomy view:

The world will not be a better place when bees in fact-based news organisations die. We will be propelled into a culture where facts and opinions will be interchangeable, where lives will become true, and where fantasy will be peddled as news. I will lament the loss of traditional news. It will unmoor us from reality. The tragedy is that the moral void of the news business contributed as much to its own annihilation as the proto-fascists who feed on its carcass. (Hedges, 2011: 213)

Others take a much more positive view of the impact of Internet-based communication in all its forms. Deitz (2010) sees much to anticipate as social media becomes ubiquitous in the communication landscape and a wider range of media platforms are used to identify and disseminate news:

People of all ages are getting news: it's just not the news as we think we know it. The contemporary media scape has been referred to as 'networked journalism' – and networked practice of producing, editing, forwarding, sharing and debasing – and media were intermediation, mediamorphosis and hybridisation. The now outmoded concepts of Web 2.0, often simply referred to as social media – Facebook and others, and photo sharing site Flickr – showcases possibilities of mass participation in collaborative work.

These entities, including Facebook, YouTube and Twitter, are media platforms. They are not replacing journalism or journalists, but through their very existence are questioning the conventions of traditional news and current affairs, including how such conventions may constrain what and who is regarded as newsworthy. (Deitz, 2010: 7)

So the challenge for modern journalists is to find a way to negotiate the often-competing professional, commercial and ethical considerations involved in finding and presenting news, while adhering to the responsibility of journalism as an important role in society. The work of journalists has never been more important – as a means of guiding citizens through the clamour of communication to the information they need to know. Andrew Keen (2007) laments the relegation of the professional as a reliable source:

Before the Web 2.0, our collective intellectual history has been one driven by the careful aggregation of truth – through professionally edited books and reference materials, newspapers, radio and television. But as all information becomes digitalised and democratised, and is made universally and permanently available, the media of record becomes an Internet on which misinformation never goes away. As a result, our banks have collected information becomes infected by mistakes and fraud blogs are connected through a single link or series of links, to countless other blogs, and MySpace pages are connected to countless other MySpace pages which link to countless YouTube videos, Wikipedia entries, and websites with various origins and purposes. It's impossible to stop the spread of misinformation, let alone identify its source. Future readers often inherit and repeat this misinformation, compounding the problem, creating a collective memory that is deeply flawed. (Keen, 2007: 75)

JOURNALISTS AND SOCIETY

Splichal and Sparks (1994) conducted a study of first-year journalism students from 22 countries. They sought to identify professional attitudes about the power and responsibility of journalism in society among those undertaking journalism education. Splichal and Sparks concluded that journalism occupied a difficult position when it came to protecting freedom and avoiding marginalization of the media's power for good.

> The dilemma for journalism is that it is an occupation whose proper discharge is fundamental to a theory of democracy and that must, therefore, at one and the same time, avoid the dangers of elitism inherent in professionalization and of amateurism inherent in the free press. It must avoid the dependent relation upon established power that follows from the exercise of self-regulation while at the same time avoiding the marginalization that can follow complete deregulation. (Splichal and Sparks, 1994: 86)

Another outcome of the Splichal and Sparks study was further evidence of the extent to which journalism is a cultural practice. What may appear to be the internationally dominant perception of journalists' goals is not always the dominant opinion or ethical standard within particular countries (Splichal and Sparks, 1994: 167). The culture of the newsroom is every bit as influential on the work of journalists as the broader social culture. In fact, the 'reality' of any journalist's working life is most likely to be shaped by the images held by the individual and the organizations for which he or she works. On an individual level, the role and image of the journalist is affected by the details of their own experience – their training, the size, type and culture of organization(s) worked for, editorial pressures and personal idiosyncrasies.

> Journalists' view of themselves, as disseminators, interpreters, investigators or adversaries, depends on 'the society they live in, the image of the press in general, and the image of the organization in which they work. (Gaunt, 1990: 142)

A survey in 2000, by the Pew Research Center for the People and the Press and *Columbia Journalism Review*, reinforces this view. The study, which surveyed almost 300 journalists in the United States, found that four out of 10 journalists purposely avoid or soften stories to preserve the interests of their news organization (Associated Press, 2000). The poll found that most journalists blamed market pressure for the tendency to steer clear of stories considered too complicated or too boring. About one-third of the journalists surveyed conceded that they avoided stories that might harm the financial interests of the news organization or embarrass advertisers, but few said such censorship was common. Hall (1992) and others argue that while journalists always give some 'spin', conscious or otherwise, to the news of the day, they always retain some control in this process. Their activities are not determined by hegemonic influences but are a reflection of the way they respond to often-competing commercial, professional and ethical pressures of professional practice.

One way in which the 'realities' of journalism impact on the daily lives of journalists is in their ability to give the degree of attention to their reporting that they professionally consider necessary. The reality is that smaller staffs and earlier production deadlines mean that journalists are less independent in their research than ever before. Newsroom influences, such as deadlines, space and staffing, place heavy constraints on those journalists who are responsible for news selection. As a result, journalists tend to take the line of least resistance and select those news items that are the easiest to find and edit. Underwood describes the temptations:

> By tradition, albeit a shaky one, daily newspapers do much of the work extracting the information on which our Information Age depends – at least the information that is hard to extract. At the same time, legions of public relations agents and corporate and government image-makers are standing by, eager to be the brokers of information that is easy to gather. (Underwood, 1993: 147)

The dual rhetorics of commercial imperative and journalistic idealism can combine to support a culture of rationalization, which ultimately 'exonerates' journalists who succumb to the market. For example, a metropolitan TV news editor who tailors the evening bulletin to fit a pattern of 'hard' and 'soft' news that has been unchanged for 30 years, hotly denies that the news is 'constructed' or manipulated to reflect a certain worldview. But he is happy to acknowledge his preoccupation with the audience's 'comfort zone'. 'You don't want to be putting the viewers off their dinners', he tells young journalists. Altschull (1984) describes how some journalists reconcile the contrast between what they might do and what they most often do by assigning the first with the romantic qualities of an heroic but impossible dream. He says that while it is possible for journalism to induce positive changes in society, political and economic realities severely circumscribe the potential of journalists to do so.

Gaunt (1990) also ponders the dilemma facing journalists who aspire to live up to the definition of journalism as 'not just another business' (Schultz, 1994). Bacon agrees that it is increasingly harder for journalists to reconcile their professional ideologies with the disenchantment of increasingly sophisticated audiences. She found that journalists are openly troubled about many aspects of journalism:

> Journalists constantly talk about which stories get a run and which do not; or what the likely impact of a new owner or editor is likely to be. They question the way news agendas are influenced by marketing research. (Bacon, 1999: 90)

This ongoing conversation among media practitioners may be described as 'shop talk' – a form of reflection on practice. This book argues that every individual journalist at some point chooses the words they use to describe the world. Each is empowered to be part of the problem or part of the solution. Each has the power to resist the 'easy' story that is fed to them by obliging media relations personnel. Each has the power to choose a different interviewee, to seek another point of view before writing. Each has the power to choose their own words to describe events, rather than duplicate what is provided to them in a media release. Today's journalists, either with their editors or despite them, must find ways to fit challenging ideas into conservative news agendas. The same newsroom culture that can limit the potential of journalism can work to a journalist's advantage. The crucial factors are determination, a sound understanding of the organization's news values, and a willingness to accept responsibility for the kind of journalism you write, and therefore the kind of journalist you are.

NEGOTIATING THE CHALLENGES

Sometimes beginners think that knowing *how* to write journalism is the same as being *able* to do it. In truth, the second is the most difficult of the two because it requires applying conceptual knowledge and understanding to new and unfamiliar situations. This book provides a methodology to guide beginning practitioners through the process required to produce thoughtful, quality journalism that is also attractive in the marketplace. This text is aimed at students of journalism, but is equally relevant to those who have come to journalism without formal training. For those making the transition from students of journalism to active practitioners, information learned in lectures can be hard to put into action under the pressure of new and exacting circumstances. For those who are 'learning journalism' in the workplace, the question 'Where to begin?' is equally crucial whether tracking down an interviewee or undertaking a report based on archive files.

The book's premise is that journalism practice consists of a series of ill-structured problems that are resolved by a series of decisions. Modern journalists resolve these problems in a context where 'every decision is at once an ethical decision, a professional decision and a commercial decision' (Sheridan Burns, 1996a). The book contends that while the answers a journalist reaches will depend on contextual factors, the questions he or she asks are the same around the globe. In 2000, the author tested this hypothesis at a workshop of journalism educators from nine countries. Some of these countries were poor or developing, others were rich developed nations. Some of the countries were communist, some capitalist. As the workshop progressed, it quickly became apparent that all the journalists were using the same framework to take on the tasks assigned to them. This book therefore focuses on what Schön (1983) called 'the conversations we have with ourselves' – the processes used by journalists to define, identify, evaluate and create journalism.

This book sets out to show that no matter how much natural talent as a writer you bring to it, journalism is not an organic or intrinsic practice but an approach to writing that can be taken apart and understood. The answers journalists find to their questions may depend on the sensitivities of the individuals, and the rhythm of the sentences may owe much to an intrinsic affinity with words; the questions the best journalists ask themselves and those asked by the least talented are the same. The answers will differ because each journalist's thinking processes and values are unique. This book offers questions to guide the way to reliable, consistent decisions.

The central proposition is that a journalist who is conscious of and understands the active decisions that make up daily practice is best prepared to negotiate the challenges involved.

The second major proposition in this book is that every journalist has some power to practise responsibly, thoughtfully and effectively. The power is literally within the individual and is demonstrated with every decision he or she makes about what news is, what questions to ask, what to include and omit, and so on. Every one of these decisions has professional, commercial and ethical dimensions that must be brought into balance in the context of the story. This applies to everything a journalist writes, no matter how 'small'. For example, a fair reported in the local newspaper responsibly and with flair can do real good in a small community. In the same way, a metropolitan daily's thoughtless wording from a police brief about a road death in a suburb of the city may cause lasting harm to those affected. It is not the owner of the news medium who has that power, however powerless an individual journalist feels in the newsroom. It is a complicated business and individual journalists are expected to bring many qualities to their decision making.

The third proposition is that every journalist should acknowledge and accept the responsibility that comes with the media's potential to affect people's lives. Professional integrity is not something you have when you are feeling a bit down at the end of a long week. It is a state of mindfulness that you bring to everything you write, no matter how humble the topic.

As a journalist, you face the unknown every day and make the best of it. The person who writes the story helps set the agenda. If this is done thoughtfully, mindful of the values brought to decision making and aware of the potential consequences of those decisions, then ethical journalism is more than feasible – it is a reasonable expectation. Put simply, given the power that you have to do good or harm by virtue of the decisions you make, under pressure each day, the least you can do is think about it. That is not the same thing as relinquishing control to the media consumer, it is reasserting your professional status. Hartley criticized journalism education as 'aspiring to produce architects while actually turning out real estate salesman' (Hartley, 1996: 35). In this statement he makes a distinction between the architect, who works in the best interest of the client, and the real estate agent, whose only priority is making a sale.

For some journalists, the concepts in this book may represent a writing-down of what is simply 'common sense'. The trouble with common sense, of course, is that it is not common to you until someone tells you. Everyday journalism consists of a series of decisions. These include decisions about what constitutes news; decisions about the nature and scope of the public interest; decisions about the accuracy of information and the reliability of sources; decisions about the ethical considerations applicable to the situation; and decisions about the best way to organize information into news. This text offers a process for decision making that centres on developing skills in critical self-reflection. Critical self-reflection has always been a feature of the work of a professional journalist:

> Critical self-reflection is a hallmark of good professional practice. When other groups, such as accountants or doctors, engage in debate about their professions, it is part of their practice, not a remote and separate intellectual discussion. ... Most journalists don't deny the power that the media has to define the 'taken-for-granted-world'. Instead they blend the development of professional writing skills with the ability to critically reflect on what they do and why. (Sheridan Burns, 1999: 4)

This book presents journalistic tasks, strips back the layers of the tasks and identifies and considers strategies for selecting and implementing resolutions. Then it reflects critically on the appropriateness of those choices. This approach integrates media, communication and cultural theory with the conscious development of writing skills. The book is not primarily a critique of media practices, but offers a means by which to negotiate the challenges.

In the rough-and-tumble of old-style learning 'on the job', if you made a mistake you were called to account for it, usually in no uncertain terms. In the newsrooms where I learned the craft, the only sin that was completely unforgivable was to not know *why* something had been done a certain way. Making mistakes was inevitable, but there was no excuse for a blank stare when asked 'Why?' If you could articulate the factors you prioritized, you were still wrong but at least you were 'being professional' in your approach to your work.

This book investigates the way that journalists work through consideration of news events commonly reported around the world. It reveals that while the context in which journalism is produced is defined by the culture of the society, the questions faced in making a journalistic decision are the same. For example, while reporting the death of a prominent individual is likely to have global news value, how that death is reported is a direct reflection of the society's attitudes about the privacy of public figures, community standards about reporting grief and any restrictions imposed by the society's laws.

You will notice that the book resists categorizing news as 'hard' or 'soft' and does not deal separately with, for example, sports stories or community news. This book does not set out to describe 'how to', but emphasizes the thinking processes involved in journalism. It may be argued that while a court story may illustrate different priorities to community news, the thinking processes used are the same. The book does not provide exemplars because 'best practice' is defined by the professional, social and cultural context in which the story is written. This complex context is constantly changing and evolving. Chapters 9 and 10 consider the editing process and so include first and final drafts of stories, but these are not intended to be definitive.

The first part of the book, 'From Knowing How to Being Able', considers how professional journalists develop their skills and understanding.

- Chapter 2 considers who can claim the title of journalist in an era of multiple journalisms and platforms. It argues that the changing and changeable nature of media practices is such that it makes no sense to teach it as a set of skills because the required skills are evolving all the time. It is through identifying and internalizing the underlying processes used in decision making that professional knowledge is realized in action.

- Chapter 3 explores the methodology underlying professional practice as a process of critical reflection, which Schön (1983), Adam (1993), Meadows (1997) and others have identified as central to media's professional role in society. The chapter explores professional ethics and provides a structure by which to make explicit what is implicit in the professional decision making and to consider these factors in relation to the media's ethical, professional and commercial obligations. Instead of relying on theoretical knowledge to explain everything, the reflective practitioner is constantly testing ideas against practical experience. Instead of making problems fit existing categories, the reflective practitioner constructs the categories that will enable him or her to find a suitable response.

The second part of the book, 'Journalism in Action', is specifically concerned with fundamental journalistic activities – identifying potential news; evaluating information and the reliability of sources; writing news; editing news for an audience; and the role of journalism in society. It uses working examples commonly experienced by journalists around the world.

- Chapter 4 explores the nature of news and the factors influencing the exercise of news judgement, particularly the role of the audience. It provides a methodology for identifying news and critically reflecting on processes through the consideration of a specified journalism task.

- Chapter 5 focuses on the way that journalists exercise power in choosing the information that will be presented as news. It offers a methodology for reliable ethical decision making in any circumstances.

- Chapter 6 looks at the ways that journalists source news and the challenges faced in judging the veracity and usefulness of information provided by a range of secondary sources, including those found on social media sites.

- Chapter 7 considers the processes used by journalists to gather information from human sources, focusing on the issues inherent in reporting on grief.

- Chapter 8 explores the processes used in transforming 'raw material' into journalism, through the creation of a piece of journalism and critical reflection on the processes underlying the inclusion and omission of information.

- Chapter 9 considers the editing process as applied to news. It also provides a methodology by which readers can strip their own writing back to its parts and critically reflect on the decisions underlying style, tone and content.

- Chapter 10 looks at a more complex editing process, as the final form of a news feature is negotiated between the writer and the commissioning editor.

As with any text, this book describes decision making in journalism in its own context. That the questions posed in this book might give rise to other questions not raised here is further evidence of 'the conversations we have with ourselves' in action. When you finish reading this book, you will have already made hundreds of professional journalistic decisions. If the book has done its job, you should also be confident you know how you made those decisions and the values that you brought to bear. This combination of active decision making and critical reflection is the most important thing a journalist needs. Since you will also know how to make a sound ethical decision in any circumstances, anything is possible.

2

WHO IS A JOURNALIST?

> You are checking the most clicked items on YouTube for story ideas and you find the most viewed item for the day is a piece titled 'Rid Yourself of Fear and Anxiety'. It appears to be a television journalism interview, but when you go the link, it is an infomercial for a self-help course. Is it news? What makes what you might write journalism?

Global communication is going through a transformation of a magnitude not seen since the Industrial Revolution ushered in the modern age. We have moved from an era of transmission to one of conversation. Media audiences are no longer content to simply receive information – they want to interact with it in real-time using mobile technology. Interactive social networks are the preferred means of communication and 'wisdom of many' is preferred over the wisdom of the 'expert'. This chapter considers the impact of these changes on journalism practice. YouTube is a great example of the way convergence has changed our experience of media. It is at once free to all and, in the right hands, a powerful tool for acquiring money and fame.

> YouTube understands the concept of the media ecosystem. One might say it embodies it. When the video sharing entity announced a new and free tool – one that allows news organisations to highlight newsworthy video footage from 'citizen journalists' on their websites – online news sites the *Huffington Post*, the *San Francisco Chronicle* and the *Washington Post* were amongst the first US outlets to sign on. YouTube Direct allows any media organisation to request, review and rebroadcast YouTube clips directly from YouTube users. The head of news and politics at YouTube, Steve Rose, said a post on YouTube was not only aimed at connecting citizen journalists with traditional news outlets but could also be used, for example, by businesses wishing to highlight promotional videos. (Deitz, 2010: 101)

What makes a writer a journalist? With the widespread emergence of self-publishing on the Internet, a working definition of 'journalist' has never been more complex.

Is everyone who publishes to an audience a journalist? Splichal and Sparks (1994) and others argue that journalism is a profession, the practitioners of which share common values and aspirations. Others argue that journalists are not professionals at all because they lack autonomy in making the judgements that guide their practice. Unlike professionals such as doctors, lawyers and architects, journalists are not paid by those who use their services. They are employees, whose primary function is to enhance the profitability of the employer.

Splichal and Sparks (1994) offer three definitions, drawn from consideration of not only 'whether all or most journalists possess a certain set of skills, but also about the kinds of behavior associated with journalists, the social cohesion of the group itself and its status relative to other groups' (Splichal and Sparks, 1994: 36). The differences in their definitions are partly semantic, but also profoundly affect the way that working journalists define their social responsibilities. The first definition describes a professional journalist as someone who earns his or her living from an activity of journalism, thereby defining journalism as a set of practices. The second definition is underpinned by the notion of technical mastery, which separates journalists from those who are merely published. By this definition, one is only a journalist if accepted as such by the occupational group. A member of a journalists' association is a journalist: a person who is unaccredited is not. Splichal and Sparks' third definition is couched in terms of social responsibility 'involving patterns of behavior which are rooted in that occupation but which have implications for the general deportment of the professional individual' (1994: 36).

These three definitions strike at the heart of the problems encountered in defining the social and ethical responsibilities of journalists. This chapter considers the appropriateness of professionalism as a model for journalism and offers reflective practice as an alternative framework.

JOURNALISM AS PRACTICES

Is anyone who publishes to an audience a journalist? Once a journalist could be simply defined as 'a person employed to write for a newspaper or magazine'. This definition separated journalists from other writers. Modern editions of Oxford and Cambridge dictionaries still define journalists in occupational terms that focus on the production of news:

- a person who writes news stories or articles for a newspaper or magazine or broadcasts them on radio or television. (Cambridge)

- a person who writes for newspapers or magazines or prepares news to be broadcast on radio or television. (Oxford)

There are abiding problems with this definition. If 'journalist' is applied to everyone whose writing is published in a newspaper or magazine, then a politician who submits a weekly column is a journalist, and so is the academic who contributes book reviews. The modern definition does not make explicit reference to employment, but does suggest an occupational activity.

Are public relations practitioners also journalists because they are employees whose work is published in newspapers and magazines? The occupational group that is journalism, as represented by unions and associations, argues that these writers are not journalists because their text is a form of advocacy, intended to persuade rather than inform. Yet much of what is written and published by those employed in mainstream media does not meet this test. As I.F. Stone is said to have remarked, 'News is what someone, somewhere, wants concealed. Everything else is advertising' (Jervis, 1987: 62). This raises pertinent questions about the perception that journalists, unlike other writers, deal in objective facts. Public confidence in the notion of 'truth' in reporting is declining. Once most journalism was published anonymously, on the understanding that the reader accepted the veracity of the publication as a whole, rather than putting faith in the integrity of an individual journalist. The perceived objectivity of the journalist – a 'fly on the wall' just reporting the facts – was seen to be a good thing.

Quite the contrary. Forde (1999) found that there is a large body of literature that cites the notion of objectivity as one of the principal reasons the mainstream media fail to present diverse information to the public. She proposes that objectivity leads journalists to prefer 'neutral' topics, like crime and natural disasters, at the expense of 'intelligent examinations into the cause of events' (Forde, 1999: 39). Patterson and Wilkins (1994: 3) note that the requirement for 'professional and objective' journalism forces news reporting to be driven by events rather than issues, which are not objective at all. Gurevitch (1990: 282) concluded that adherence to professional definitions of news act as a powerful force for conformity, explaining why journalists often reach a common answer, across an otherwise diverse set of news outlets, to the question 'What is the most significant news today?'

Clay Shirky argues that journalists were defined by their employment for important reasons to do with freedom of the press:

> This definition has worked for decades because the ties among journalists, publishers, and the means of production were strong. So long as publishing was expensive, publishers would be rare. So long as publishers were rare, it would be easy to list them and thus identify journalists as their employees. This definition, oblique as it is, served to provide the legal balance we want from journalistic privilege – we have a professional class of truth tellers who are given certain latitude to avoid cooperating with the law. We didn't have to worry, in defining those privileges, that they would somehow become general, because it wasn't like just anyone could become a publisher. And now it is like that. It's exactly like that. To a first approximation, anyone in the developed world can publish anything any time, and the instant it is published, it is globally available and is readily findable. If anyone can be a publisher, then anyone can be a journalist. And if anyone can be a journalist, then journalistic privilege suddenly becomes a loophole too large to be borne by society. Journalistic privilege has to be applied to a minority of people in order to preserve the law's ability to uncover and prosecute wrongdoing, while allowing a safety valve for investigative reporting. (Shirky, 2008: 71)

Some online dictionaries have dealt with the question of 'work' by expanding their definition of who may claim the title 'journalist' to include older definitions. Dictionary.com, which claims on its site to be the most trusted online dictionary, includes as a journalist those who make a daily record of their thoughts, whether or not these thoughts are published:

1. A person who practices the occupation or profession of journalism.

2. A person who keeps a journal, diary, or other record of daily events.

(Dictionary.com)

This definition would also include bloggers and other web diarists, many Facebook users and daily Tweeters. Some of these content generators may think of themselves as journalists, even though they don't meet the definitions for practising the occupation of journalism. The distinction was traditionally made between those who wrote for themselves (the journal keepers) and those who wrote for an audience. It is a distinction that cannot be routinely applied today. Many individuals reach global audiences on particular topics via social media and many 'professional' journalists share their personal thoughts with the audiences as freely as their 'professional' ones. Whether those who contribute to public debate are practising journalism is still hotly contested at the time of writing. Like Shirky, Andrew Keen argues that a journalist is defined by more than access to an audience:

> The simple ownership of a computer and Internet connection doesn't transform one into a serious journalist any more than having access to a kitchen makes one into a serious cook. (Keen, 2007: 46)

Kingsbury found that the Net was sometimes 'hailed as a return to old-fashioned participant democracy' (1998: 91), eliminating boundaries of news dissemination and providing uncensored freedom to share views and opinions. This unrestricted access has put further pressure on traditional definitions of journalism because only a fraction of those published have been accredited by the occupational group. Shirky argues this is a crucial part of the definition:

> It's tempting to regard the people taking pictures of the Indian Ocean tsunami as a new crop of journalists. The label has an obvious conceptual appeal. The problem, however, is that mass professionalisation is an oxymoron since a professional class implies a specialised function, minimum tests the confidence, and a minority of members. None of those conditions exists with political weblogs, photo sharing or a host of other self-publishing tools. The individual weblogs are not merely alternate sites of publishing; they are alternatives to publishing itself, in the sense of publishers as a minority and professional class. (Shirky, 2008: 66)

Many others agree that bloggers and other 'journal keepers' are not journalists, because they do not ascribe to the codes of ethics and practice set down for 'professional' journalists, nor are they affiliated with professional organizations. Lehmann (2006) is particularly sceptical.

Further, Pavlik (1998: 14) argues that the freedom to post ideas on the Internet comes without the ethical or social obligations usually associated with journalism. He argues that the price of media ownership and power is a legal requirement to act responsibly and serve the public interest, but this does not apply to self-publishers. This definition of journalists requires that they have some clear obligation to use their power and influence for social good rather than personal gain. Or as Andrew Keen put it:

> Bloggers don't go to jail for their work, journalists do. (Keen, 2007: 49)

CITIZEN JOURNALISM

According to a study published by the Pew Internet & American Life Project in 2006, there were 12 million bloggers in the United States, and 34 per cent of them consider blogging to be a form of journalism. The majority see their blogging as self-expression. Enthusiasts see 'citizen journalism', meaning sites that publish the contributions of people who don't have jobs with news organizations but are performing a similar function, as the bright new future of the media. Citizen journalists 'are supposedly inspired amateurs who find out what's going on in the places where they live and work, and who bring us a fuller, richer picture of the world than we get from familiar news organizations' (Lehmann, 2006). Usher (2011) sees citizen journalism as a way to shock conventional journalism into the twenty-first century:

> Citizen journalists need to violate, to shock, and to challenge the norms of traditional journalism; and as proponents of a vibrant democracy, we should encourage citizen journalism to flourish in all shapes and forms: trash inverted pyramids; offer a point of view; experiment visually and graphically; leave narrative behind; create stories as conversation. James Carey has said that the soul of democracy is conversation, and that conversation is journalism. The conversation carried out by the mainstream press can keep out some of the voices of this conversation, but the potential of citizen journalism serves to enrich the conversation by breaking down the walls between the public and the press as the public becomes the press. It is my hope that citizen journalism will prompt traditional journalists to stretch the definition of what counts as news. (Usher, 2011: 276)

If the definition of journalism is measured by practices, then it is true that unpaid people practise journalism on the Internet. These are the people who investigate and bring to public attention issues that they consider important to the public good. There is potential for such people to become a significant ongoing part of the media ecosystem, but limited evidence of the fact. Benkler (2011) points to the impact of citizen journalism on reporting of the 2010 riots in Tehran.

> If the first Gulf War had been the moment of the 24 hour news channel, the Iranian reform movement's street protests were the moment of amateur video, using a basic, open, commercial platform primarily intended for entertainment, by people in the midst of the action. Video from the BBC or CNN depended primarily on these YouTube videos; there was no one else there able to report with footage. (Benkler, 2011: 226)

The best original Internet journalism happens when an individual is on the spot of a major event with the mobile means to capture images of what is happening. This circumstance was common to the most successful citizen journalism of recent years – such as the Japanese earthquake in 2011, Hurricane Katrina in 2005 and the London bombings in 2005. These were all circumstances when professional media couldn't get access to the scene. Mobilized citizen media was the best way for those affected to get information in the first hours and days, but it was conventional journalism that provided the reliable explanation and interpretation of events. As McChesney and Nichol (2011) put it, most 'citizen journalism' still depends on mainstream media as its source, and is in no position to supplant it:

> We are enthusiastic about Wikipedia and the potential for collaborative efforts on the web; they can help democratize our media and politics. But they do not replace skilled journalists on the ground covering the events of the day and doing investigative reporting. Indeed, the Internet cannot achieve its revolutionary potential as a citizens' forum without such journalism. (McChesney and Nichol, 2011: 104)

JOURNALISM AS TECHNICAL MASTERY

Splichal and Sparks' second definition of journalists is underpinned by the notion of technical mastery separating journalists from those who are merely published. By this definition, one is only a journalist if accepted as such by the occupational group, usually (but not always) after a period of initiation in workplace practices. The Code of Ethics of the Society of Professional Journalists (Figure 2.1) clearly distinguishes between advocacy and reporting, and emphasizes professional integrity in the public interest. The Australian Journalists' Association, a division of the industrial union the Media, Entertainment and Arts Alliance (MEAA), is responsible for the ethical code guiding Australian journalists. In its preamble, the Code of Ethics describes the professional journalist as employed in private enterprise, but with public responsibilities:

Journalists describe society to itself. They seek truth. They convey information, ideas and opinions, a privileged role. They search, disclose, record, question, entertain, suggest and remember. They inform citizens and animate democracy. They give a practical form to freedom of expression. Many journalists work for private enterprise, but all these have public responsibilities. MEAA members engaged in journalism commit themselves to honesty, fairness, independence and respect for the rights of others. (MEAA, 1997: 15)

The inclusion of 'public responsibilities' is a feature of the revised code, introduced in 1998. According to the MEAA, it carries a warning that with power must come accountability:

As accountability engenders public trust, it is essential to the fulfillment of journalism's public responsibilities. ... Journalists have a special obligation to be accountable because it is they who claim to be one of the main methods of holding to account, on behalf of the public, others who wield power. (MEAA, 1997: 3)

The idea of journalism as a profession, self-regulated by its own industrial unions and codes of practice is under constant challenge. Many modern unions have no power to impel workers to join up and adhere to codes of ethics or practice. The strengths and weaknesses of journalism unions vary from country to country, but generally such organizations offer only guidance to members, not regulation.

Journalists are hired on an individual basis by media employers, who set their own definitions for 'adequate' preparation and training. This makes the notion of technical mastery problematic, as there are no universal standards applied to determining it. For example, an industrial award may specify certain competencies to be achieved by interns or cadet reporters, but has no control over an editor's decision to hire someone with no formal training at a senior level. Elliot (1986: 149–50) argues that technical mastery in journalism is based on such routine competencies as factual accuracy, speed in meeting deadlines, style in presentation and a shared set of news values. Meadows (1997: 93) says that this definition has fostered a set of anti-intellectual and anti-ethical social practices, not least because it means that the moral obligations of the journalist rest with the workplace and the employer, not with the individual.

Above all else, media associations often lack the power to regulate the practices of their members. It is true that an association can cancel the membership of a wayward member, but often it cannot prevent that person working as a journalist. An editor can dismiss a journalist who fails to adhere to a code of professional practice, but that person cannot be barred from journalism, as can, for example, accountants from their profession. Journalism associations influence the practice of members through encouraging a shared belief in certain professional values underpinning the exercise of media power. However, Meadows found there seems to be a tenuous connection between attitude and practice and that 'most journalists appear to care little about the state of their profession' (1997: 91). Ewart's study (1997: 101) found significant

The Code of Ethics of the Society of Professional Journalists

Journalists should:

— Test the accuracy of information from all sources and exercise care to avoid inadvertent error. Deliberate distortion is never permissible.
— Diligently seek out subjects of news stories to give them the opportunity to respond to allegations of wrongdoing.
— Identify sources whenever feasible. The public is entitled to as much information as possible on sources' reliability.
— Always question sources' motives before promising anonymity. Clarify conditions attached to any promise made in exchange for information. Keep promises.
— Make certain that headlines, news teases and promotional material, photos, video, audio, graphics, sound bites and quotations do not misrepresent. They should not oversimplify or highlight incidents out of context.
— Never distort the content of news photos or video. Image enhancement for technical clarity is always permissible. Label montages and photo illustrations.
— Avoid misleading re-enactments or staged news events. If re-enactment is necessary to tell a story, label it.
— Avoid undercover or other surreptitious methods of gathering information except when traditional open methods will not yield information vital to the public. Use of such methods should be explained as part of the story.
— Never plagiarize.
— Tell the story of the diversity and magnitude of the human experience boldly, even when it is unpopular to do so.
— Examine their own cultural values and avoid imposing those values on others.
— Avoid stereotyping by race, gender, age, religion, ethnicity, geography, sexual orientation, disability, physical appearance or social status.
— Support the open exchange of views, even views they find repugnant.
— Give voice to the voiceless; official and unofficial sources of information can be equally valid.
— Distinguish between advocacy and news reporting. Analysis and commentary should be labelled and not misrepresent fact or context.
— Distinguish news from advertising and shun hybrids that blur the lines between the two.
— Recognize a special obligation to ensure that the public's business is conducted in the open and that government records are open to inspection.

Minimize Harm
Ethical journalists treat sources, subjects and colleagues as human beings deserving of respect.

Journalists should:

— Show compassion for those who may be affected adversely by news coverage. Use special sensitivity when dealing with children and inexperienced sources or subjects.
— Be sensitive when seeking or using interviews or photographs of those affected by tragedy or grief.
— Recognize that gathering and reporting information may cause harm or discomfort. Pursuit of the news is not a license for arrogance.
— Recognize that private people have a greater right to control information about themselves than do public officials and others who seek power, influence or attention. Only an overriding public need can justify intrusion into anyone's privacy.

continued

— Show good taste. Avoid pandering to lurid curiosity.
— Be cautious about identifying juvenile suspects or victims of sex crimes.
— Be judicious about naming criminal suspects before the formal filing of charges.
— Balance a criminal suspect's fair trial rights with the public's right to be informed.

Act Independently
Journalists should be free of obligation to any interest other than the public's right to know.

Journalists should:

— Avoid conflicts of interest, real or perceived.
— Remain free of associations and activities that may compromise integrity or damage credibility.
— Refuse gifts, favours, fees, free travel and special treatment, and shun secondary employment, political involvement, public office and service in community organizations if they compromise journalistic integrity.
— Disclose unavoidable conflicts.
— Be vigilant and courageous about holding those with power accountable.
— Deny favoured treatment to advertisers and special interests and resist their pressure to influence news coverage.
— Be wary of sources offering information for favours or money; avoid bidding for news.

Be Accountable
Journalists are accountable to their readers, listeners, viewers and each other.

Journalists should:

— Clarify and explain news coverage and invite dialogue with the public over journalistic conduct.
— Encourage the public to voice grievances against the news media.
— Admit mistakes and correct them promptly.
— Expose unethical practices of journalists and the news media.
— Abide by the same high standards to which they hold others.

The SPJ Code of Ethics is voluntary. The present version of the code was adopted by the 1996 SPJ National Convention.

Figure 2.1   Society of Professional Journalists' Code of Ethics

anomalies between stated professional adherence to codes and the practices of a group of Australian journalists, which she argued was typical. She found that despite emphatically staunch support expressed for ethical codes, journalists indicated that they were often pressured into acting in ways contrary to the principles espoused. By avoiding critical reflection, the journalists she studied saw no paradox in their behaviour. On one level, they confidently asserted their performance was ethical, while at the same time acknowledging that in the workplace the 'reality' of gathering, writing and producing news justified unethical behaviour. On a third level, the respondents abdicated their ethical responsibility, blaming the editorial hierarchy.

Splichal and Sparks' study revealed that a code of ethics is generally regarded as essential to any group laying claim to the title 'profession'. Meadows noted the extent to which journalism relies on the notion of 'professionalism' and its prescribed ethical codes, 'which it is assumed, will empower journalists with the wisdom to make the right judgments on behalf of their audiences' (Meadows, 1997: 92). Further, it may be argued that the net effect of workplace training, in which shorthand is the educational priority and cadet lectures run a poor second to routine journalistic tasks, is that cadets learn that journalism is something you reflect on only when you have time for it. But you never do, because you are always on to the next story. Applying the technical mastery definition of journalism, employees of a newspaper who are recognized by other journalists as being 'one of us' are journalists. Like the first definition of a journalist, this description fails to take account of the product created by journalists, focusing instead on the conditions under which it is produced.

Other scholars see the need to broaden the definitions of journalism to account for writing produced under a much broader range of conditions. Deitz (2010) argues that the rise of the blogosphere and citizen journalism reflects the need for debate and discussion beyond the confines usually imposed by conventional news – which she describes as superficial.

> To those who say the public is more interested in celebrity than serious news, surely the rise of the blogosphere and citizen journalism reflect the need for debate and discussion beyond the confines usually imposed by conventional news. (Deitz, 2010: 10)

She says there is good reason to be passionate about reinventing news and journalism in the digital age. She cites activists groups, collaborative blogs and satirical TV shows as evidence that there are few people not participating in public debate. Deitz calls instead for recognition of a new media ecosystem instead of a single profession:

> In much the same way we need to scrutinise the efforts of new media on democracy; we need to engage with fourth estate ideals such as objectivity in terms of their potential rather than treating everything is static. Objectivity can never be truly achieved – which is not an argument for neglecting to aim for it – but such journalistic values need to be continually redefined since parameters such as 'the media' and 'the audience' to name but two are always subject to change. (Deitz, 2010: 13)

JOURNALISM AS A PROFESSION

It is only Splichal and Sparks' third definition of journalists, in which moral responsibility resides with the individual, that meets the broader definition of professionalism. For an occupation to be considered a profession, it must contain a moral dimension. As Lebacqz put it, 'to belong to a profession is traditionally to be held to a certain standard of conduct that goes beyond the norm for others' (1986: 32).

Shirky uses the analogy that one doesn't need to be professional driver to drive a car. You no longer need to be a professional publisher to publish, but there are still conditions that determine whether what you publish is professional:

> To label something a profession means to define the ways in which it is more than just a job. In the case of newspapers, professional behaviour is guided both by the commercial imperatives and by an additional set of norms about what newspapers are, how they should be staffed and run, what constitutes good journalism, and so forth. These norms are enforced not by the customers but by other professionals in the same business. The key to any profession is the relations of its members to one another. In a profession, members are only partly guided by service to the public. (Shirky, 2008: 57,58)

Scholars have both defended and rejected journalism's status as a profession. Ethicists Patterson and Wilkins (1994) argue that journalism is now a profession because of two modern responsibilities imposed on journalists: a greater responsibility than other people to tell the truth, and a greater obligation to foster political activity.

> Each of the traditional professions has laid claim to one of the central tenets of philosophy. Law, ideally, is equated with justice; medicine with the duty to render aid. Journalism too has a lofty ideal: the communication of truth. (Patterson and Wilkins, 1994: 18)

Patterson and Wilkins note that the 'truth' has never been harder to define because information comes to us quickly from all over the globe, overwhelming our ability to sort out 'the truth'. They argue that the modern problem of the shifting nature of truth is compounded by the globalization of media audiences, which means that 'facts that are apparent in face-to-face interaction become subject to different interpretations among geographically and culturally diverse viewers and readers' (Patterson and Wilkins, 1994: 22). Journalism educators tend to be more concerned with the motivation of journalists than the search for 'truth'. Schultz (1994: 37) argued that the primary values journalists should bring to reporting are impartiality, audience responsiveness and political independence – interpreted through news values of conflict, timeliness, prominence and proximity. Schultz says to abandon principles of professionalism in journalism would 'presage a return to an even less responsive journalism with reporter, editor and producers recast as harlots of the information age' (1994: 50).

Central to the use of a code of ethics to regulate professional conduct is the notion of professional integrity. Underwood describes the ideal journalist as one who resists all attempts at control:

> He observes the law, rendering unto Caesar what is Caesar's but morally he is his own man. Even his boss can't touch him. ... Freedom is preserved only if that lonely journalist is unfettered, acting on the basis of his own reason, sensitivity and commitment. (Underwood, 1993: 170)

This view of journalism as a profession identifies *integrity*, measured by a commitment to truth over personal gain, as a central characteristic of a *professional* journalist. Integrity is defined as adherence to the social obligations attached to a privileged position – the power of the media to disseminate information must be balanced with a social obligation to truth and justice. Integrity in this context is understood to mean a quality of incorruptibility that ensures journalists will place the advancement of the public good ahead of their own profit in the pursuit of truth. Philosopher Clifford Christians sees individual integrity and dedication to the public good as central to journalism:

> Justice for the powerless stands as the centerpiece of a socially responsible press. ... In this view, the socially responsible journalist must be society's mirror and critic and advocate for its weaker members. The mirror reflects what is before it. The critic reminds society of the standards it has yet to live up to. (Christians et al. 1987: 110, 147)

PRESSURES ON THE PROFESSIONAL MODEL

McManus (1994), Koch (1990) and others claim that the move over the past 10 years to a 'market-driven journalism' has fundamentally changed the daily role of journalists in making the news. The changes are characterized by a gradual and increasing lack of editorial independence within media organizations. Underwood's 1993 study supported this view:

> To fit into the newspaper's design and packaging needs, preplanning is essential. ... Editors who need to allot space in the news pages well in advance prefer stories that are predictable, come with plenty of lead time, and fit the preconceptions that have already been discussed in editorial meetings. In this system, it's easy to find the reporter reduced to a researcher, a gatherer of information, a functionary in the plan-package-and-market-the-newspaper bureaucracy. (Underwood, 1993: 163)

McManus described how market-driven journalism infiltrates the news selection process:

> From a market perspective, broadcasters and to a lesser extent newspapers are better off with more generalized stories such as consumer-oriented features and human interest pieces that arouse an emotional response, even if the result is news that fails to help consumers make sense of current events. (McManus, 1994: 89)

Gaunt (1990: 146) reminds us that profit-oriented modern media managers are nothing new. What is new, though, is that technical innovations introduced by profit-conscious media management, such as networking of resources and consolidation of mastheads, seem inevitably to be producing greater homogeneity of news content. Market-driven journalism places as much emphasis on presentation as it does on content, and predictability is favoured over flexibility to ensure advertisers get a reliable product.

McManus notes that journalism is seldom cost-effective and 'if a station seeks to maximize profit, less care may be taken with information. And just as the interesting topic may replace the merely important, the interesting source and quote may replace the informative source and quote' (McManus, 1994: 89). Or, as Silk put it:

> Corporate executives never find it easy to acknowledge that the public interest may not be identical to their company's. ... What could be more in public interest than for publishers to do everything in their power to protect their newspaper's profitability? (Silk, 1991: 45)

By this way of thinking, a high-circulation newspaper is seen to be serving its audience well. A high-rating TV news programme is seen in the same way. For most journalists, this is where the conflict arises between the journalist's role to inform society and the journalist's job, which is to increase the profits of his or her employer. It arises when the public interest is better served by telling people things they would rather not know – for example, things that make them feel uncomfortable or guilty.

McManus (1994: 203) argues that the commodification of news as a product for sale to advertisers creates a serious conflict of interest. The key stakeholders in the media company's profit-seeking endeavours are other corporations, which seek to increase their own profits by selling products to people who buy 'news'. This, he argues, weakens the editorial independence of journalists to make 'unfettered' news judgements.

> A reporter or editor in a profit-maximizing media firm who subordinates market standards to those of journalism may be tolerated about as long as a counter clerk at McDonalds who refuses to sell fried food. (Koch, 1990: 23)

McManus, Underwood and others argue that 'commodification' causes increasing reliance on market research, which has diminished the traditional role of 'professional' journalists as arbiters of which news and events are newsworthy. Underwood (1993) argued that managers tell journalists to let the public decide what becomes news, and value only those reports that are highly valued in the marketplace. Grattan also argues that the decline in news media consumption has led to anxiety among proprietors about how to maintain an advertising market. As strong views might offend potential readers, editors made sure that readers of news columns 'would remain unoffended long enough to glance at the ads' (Grattan, 1998: 4). These critics acknowledge that commercial media have long depended on advertising in order to be financially viable, but now advertisers have greater editorial influence than ever before. Underwood also concluded that commodification fundamentally changes the role of journalists. He found that they no longer look behind the appearance of things and unearth deeper truths, but collect material designed to fit into a package – often simply more of what the well-informed reader already knows or suspects (Underwood, 1993: 144). Kingsbury (1998) found that facts were not elusive, but the path to identifying the truth was incompatible with the demands of market-driven journalism because it required time to check and double-check. Paletz and Entman (1982) found that where the primary objective of a news organization was efficiency in the gathering, describing and transmitting of news, the result was reliance on official sources and homogeneity of reporting.

This reliance on professional media sources is a global phenomenon. For example, Warren (1995) reported that 80 per cent of stories were generated by publicity releases provided to media outlets. McManus offers a simple explanation:

> It is less costly to rely on other news providers such as wire services and on press agents to learn of community events and issues than to hire adequate staff to infiltrate the community. Such passive discovery, however, creates potential for manipulation of the public agenda by sources powerful enough to hire press agents and 'manufacture' events. (McManus, 1994: 88)

Providing 'news' for media outlets is big business. Professional news sources such as public relations personnel understand the nature and rhetoric of news. They know that if a news item is presented to the journalist in a way that is completely compatible with the news organization's usual style, it is likely be used unchanged. The modern journalist is also expected to produce much more daily copy than colleagues 20 or even 10 years ago, when editors insisted that media releases were rewritten. Under this sort of time pressure, it is easy to apply an 'if it isn't broken, don't fix it' approach to editing, or even verifying copy.

Those who provide media releases to news organizations have much to gain in this scenario. Preparing a media release as an alternative to submitting to an interview offers both the publicity-seeker and subject of media scrutiny some control over the information published about them and the images used. While the editor retains some journalistic control over what is published, the media release provider is in a more certain position than he or she would be if waiting to see the published account of an interview with a journalist. In addition, these media personnel also know how to angle information in a way that will be attractive to a certain media outlet. This increases the chances of the media outlet adopting the angle chosen by the media user. Or a media user might stage an event that will attract media and then use their attendance for a different purpose.

Reliance on news sources – and this extends to broadcast media in the form of radio 'grabs' and video news releases – can also be manipulated to affect the news agenda. Newsroom influences, such as deadlines, space and staffing, place heavy con-straints on those journalists responsible for news selection. As a result, journalists tend to take the line of least resistance and select those news items that are the easiest to find and edit. The items are those provided by public relations companies, corpo-rate communications departments and political image-makers. In an age of 'media events', photo opportunities and video news releases, the temptation to use an already attractive and well-targeted package is a strong one, especially when economies in production mean that fewer journalists are expected to produce more.

Underwood proposed that modern management of media inevitably creates 'the tension between representing reality as accurately as humans can, and misrepresenting it in favour of those who control the production process' (1993: 3).

Following the path of least resistance can also land journalists in serious trouble. In what became known as the 'News of the World Scandal', a highly successful English newspaper closed after 120 years when it was revealed that illicit practices were used to obtain stories.

Journalists do retain some control in all of this. Their activities are influenced but not determined by hegemonic influences. In fact, the 'reality' of journalists' working lives is most likely to be shaped by the values held by the individual and the organizations for which they work. On an individual level, the role and image of the journalist is affected by the details of his or her own experience – their training, the size, type and culture of the organization(s) worked for, editorial pressures and personal idiosyncrasies. Good journalism still appears despite the pressures, and journalists are not always what Epstein (1974) described as 'agents for others'. However, consideration of the context in which modern journalism is practised reveals the inadequacy of professionalism as a model for journalism, as proposed by Henningham (1998), Breen (1999) and others. Put simply, the occupational group does not have a mandate to make autonomous decisions about what is best for the media consumer. At the same time, the practice of journalism is comprised of constant independent decisions. O'Donnell (1999) argues that the combination of power without control means professionalism no longer works as a framework for what journalists do. This may also explain declining public confidence in traditional journalism and the rise of amateur publics more willing to accept the word of a virtual friend than a newspaper.

Modern journalism, as a set of practices, cannot be defined simply as 'employed by a newspaper or magazine' because there are many journalists who do not match this description. Nor can journalists rely on professional codes created by industrial unions for regulation of practices because many journalists lack the power or the inclination to adhere to the rules. Further, the codes in themselves cannot provide journalists with the ability to make the most appropriate choices on behalf of their audiences in an environment where 'every decision is at once a professional decision, a commercial decision and an ethical decision' (Sheridan Burns, 1996a: 92).

CRITICAL REFLECTION AS A MODEL FOR JOURNALISM

Schön (1983) argues that the traditional view of professionals as exclusive keepers of an expert body of knowledge is outdated and inappropriate as a model for understanding professional practice. He writes that professionals do not simply retrieve stored knowledge to inform their practice; rather, they engage with their practice through actions underpinned by intrinsic intellectual processes. They do not apply remembered rules and practices to the solution of problems; they create solutions appropriate to the context in which the problem arises by reflecting on the lessons of experience and speculating on the appropriateness of potential strategies.

This, according to Schön, is why experienced practitioners cannot easily convey the art of their practice to a novice merely by describing their procedures, rules and theories, nor can they enable a novice to think like a seasoned practitioner merely by describing or even demonstrating their ways of thinking.

> Often we cannot say what it is that we know. When we try to describe it we find ourselves at a loss, or we produce descriptions that are obviously inappropriate. Our knowing is ordinarily tacit, implicit in our patterns of action and in our feel for the stuff with which we are dealing. ... Our knowing is in our action. (Schön, 1983: 49)

Schön's model is ideal for journalism because reflective practice is also a hallmark of good journalism, however 'good' and 'journalism' are defined in the modern world (Sheridan Burns, 1999b: 4). The term describes the capacity to identify, sort and prioritize contextual elements surrounding practice. Journalists are constantly evaluating information in terms of their own experience, perceptions about accuracy, the perceived audience and its interests, and the aspirations of their employer, to name a few. Returning to the scenario at the start of this chapter, the YouTube video is not unlike the media release of the twentieth century – it purports to be something it is not. But that does not mean that it is not a prompt for some journalism. That it was the most viewed item suggests that a lot of people would like to get rid of anxiety in their lives. Reporting on this would be to the public good, but it requires the journalist to conduct independent research and conduct primary interviews to transform advertising to journalism. In fact, the YouTube video may only be news in the sense that it had a lot of 'hits'. The writer is a journalist only if he or she interrogates the information provided rather than merely rewording it. By reflecting on the message in the context of the public interest, and through the filters described above, the YouTube video is transformed from advocacy to journalism.

CONCLUSION

The reality of journalism at the beginning of the twenty-first century is that it can no longer be described simply in terms of employment status. Nor can its definition be limited to describing an individual who has completed a period of initiation into the practice of a workplace. Such descriptions attach no social responsibilities to the power that individual journalists possess in framing the world for audiences. These definitions also fail to account for the plethora of media forms to emerge during the twentieth century. This chapter has proposed that what distinguishes journalism from other media activities is the notion of *service to the public interest*. Journalists work to that end by truth-telling, even when the truth is unpalatable and unwelcome.

The most appropriate framework in which to view journalism is to see it as the result of the systematic consideration of information with regard to broad news values refined by the context in which it is collected and disseminated. This focus on the process, on the factors that guide the myriad of decisions journalists make, is explored further in Chapter 3.

FURTHER ACTION

1   Consider the stories published in a daily newspaper of your choice. How many of the reports meet the definition of news as 'what someone, somewhere wants concealed, everything else is advertising'?

2   Choose an article. What thought processes help you to decide if you believe what you read?

3   Watch a TV news bulletin. Is the news the same or similar to the print news? Do you have greater or less faith in this medium? Why?

4   Go online and seek out an alternative news medium, i.e. one not posted by a major news organization. Who owns the publication? Is this publication more or less trustworthy than a mainstream publication? Why?

FURTHER READING

Deitz, M.L. (2010) *Watch This Space: The Future of Australian Journalism*. Melbourne: Cambridge University Press.

McChesney, R.W. and Pickard, V. (eds) (2011) *Will the Last Reporter Please Turn Out the Lights: The Collapse of Journalism and What Can be Done to Fix It*. New York: The New Press.

Shirky, C. (2008) *Here Comes Everybody: The Power of Organising without Organisations*. New York: Penguin.

Tapsall, S. and Varley, C. (2001) *Journalism: Theory in Practice*. Melbourne: Oxford University Press.

3

JOURNALISM AS DECISION MAKING

A friend sends you a retweet with the hashtag #massacre. It reads:

OMG. STANDING ACROSS FROM HIGH COURT. GUY TRIED TO STOP SOME OTHER GUY BEATING GIRL AND HE JUST SHOT HIM. COPS EVERYWHERE. GUNMAN RAN AWAY. I CAN'T BELIEVE WHAT I SAW!!

Why is it news? Where will you begin?

Learning by doing may be a common approach, but doing alone does not guarantee learning (Sheridan Burns, 1997: 59). To think of journalists as professionals who routinely apply an expert body of knowledge to new circumstances is just as inappropriate. Journalists habitually modify and adapt their strategies. They accomplish this through consideration of principles or 'rules' in the light of their own professional experiences and values. These factors combine in the individual to create professional processes informed by, but not restricted to, information learned in formal education or training. In this sense, every journalist also uniquely interprets the knowledge he or she acquires about journalism. This is reflected in each journalist's intellectual and professional processes and the values brought to the work.

Journalism is about making decisions, whether they are on matters of news judgement or ethics. To make decisions reliably and effectively, we need principles, or shared beliefs, to use as a basis for those decisions (King, 1997: 22). However, one of the problems with the notion of an expert body of knowledge underpinning media practice is the acknowledgement that modern workplaces do not fit comfortably into any single 'job-ready' paradigm. As Pearson noted: 'There are many journalisms: community journalism, corporate journalism, agency journalism, niche publishing and broadcasting, social research and government journalism, which is itself undergoing rapid change' (Pearson, 1994: 105). In all these fields, journalists demonstrate their skills through their actions, which are informed by critical reflection on prior experience. Kolb argued that critical reflection 'is the process whereby knowledge is created through the transformation of experience' (1984: 38). This chapter considers how professionals 'think *by* doing', and provides a theoretical rationale for reflective practice over approaches favouring the application of an expert body of knowledge.

FROM 'KNOWING HOW' TO 'BEING ABLE'

Gilbert Ryle (1960) wrote about knowledge as developing in three stages. The first, which may be described as *knowing what*, refers to the ability to identify something; for example, to recognize the product of journalism. Applied to journalism, the second stage, *knowing how*, refers to an ability to repeat procedures, practices or skills associated with the production of journalism. The third stage, which Ryle views as evidence of knowledge, may be described as *being able to do*. In journalism, this refers to the crucial intellectual processes required for journalism, including an ability to identify 'news', and to gather and evaluate information. The journalist filters these decisions through an individual understanding of the audience to whom the writing is addressed, the priorities of the publisher and his or her own beliefs about the role of journalism in society. Most significantly, the journalist uses these processes to negotiate a professional practice characterized by exposure to new experiences.

Industry critics of formal approaches to journalism education reinforce the idea that journalism cannot be taught, only learned by experience. This view is underpinned by the notion 'there are no hard and fast rules for journalism, it all depends on the circumstances'. Certainly, *doing* journalism is always contained in its context. This usually includes the journalist's own values and experiences, the style of the publication, the perceived audience, the editor's own values and experiences, and the extent of time and resource limitations. Depending on the context, other social, political and economic pressures may also apply. However, this view of journalism suggests that the way individual journalists think is so intrinsic as to defy explanation. Journalists themselves find it hard to describe what they do, to the point of describing their knowledge *as* action. They may even argue that they 'just know what to do without thinking'. This is because their thinking processes, once internalized, are used almost without conscious thought.

Schön's books (1983, 1986) considered the ways various professional groups exercised their professional knowledge. He called this process 'thinking in action', later describing it as 'the conversations we have with ourselves'.

It may equally be described as a process of critical reflection, however subconscious. It is what people mean when they talk about 'thinking on their feet' and 'learning by doing'. Adam (1993) is one who argues that in the reporting on ideas and events as they occur, journalism involves criticism, or the conferring of judgement on the shape of things. The application of the values used by journalists is reflected in the selection of subjects and in the judgements inferred by them in their reporting about the state of the world which they reveal.

Schön (1986) says that it is common for professionals to find it impossible to articulate explicitly what is implicit in their practice. In journalism, the conscious use of critical reflection provides a structure by which decision-making skills are learned along with, and as part of, writing and research skills. Journalism requires active learning and critical and creative thinking. Journalists gather information of significance to the task at hand, assessing its credibility and its validity. In writing a story that is at once ethical, accurate and attractive to the audience, journalists are held to high standards of thinking. Reflection is the bridge between journalism theory and professional practice. It is through critical self-reflection that journalists develop self-reliance, confidence, problem-solving abilities, cooperation and adaptability while simultaneously gaining knowledge. Reflection is also the process by which journalists learn to recognize their own assumptions and understand their place in the wider social context (Sheridan Burns, 1996: 95). Critical reflection is not necessarily a negative activity. When journalists engage in 'shop talk' about a colleague's great story they are critically reflecting on what makes that story so admirable. As King argues, 'by thinking about what we do, we can make better decisions as journalists and provide the basis for a philosophy of journalism. Furthermore, such analysis does not need to lead us too far from the newsroom' (King, 1997: 22).

JOURNALISM AS DECISION MAKING

Bernard Cohen (1963) observed that the media's greatest power was not in telling people what to think, but what to think about: '. . . the world will look different to different people, depending on the map that is drawn for them by writers, editors and publishers of the paper they read' (Cohen, 1963: 13).

It is in the daily drawing and re-drawing of the map described by Cohen that the actions of journalism are revealed. For all the rhetoric about objectivity, the product of journalism can never be separated from the intellectual processes in the mind of the individual journalist. In media workplaces around the world, individual journalists from a myriad of societies make the same kind of decisions every day about how to balance their professional, commercial and ethical priorities. The answers reached by these journalists will vary widely across cultures, but all will engage in the subjective process of decision making.

REFLECTIVE PRACTICE

The rhetoric used by journalists to describe what they do may be built around a notion of intrinsic behaviours, but it also values critical reflection, although perhaps not in so many words. In the vernacular of journalism, being able to 'think on your feet' and 'keep your wits about you' are highly valued as intellectual abilities. Both these phrases also describe critical reflection in practice, suggesting that we *can* think about what we are doing while we are doing it. O'Donnell (1999) found that reflective practitioners constantly test their theoretical knowledge against practical experience, and then develop individualized action strategies appropriate for the context. Boud and Feletti (1991) suggest that critical reflection has three stages. The first occurs in the preparation stage, and focuses on what the journalist knows, assumes and needs to know. The second stage occurs during the activity, in the form of noticing and intervening in an action while there is still an opportunity to affect the outcome. The final stage of reflection occurs after the event, when the individual re-evaluates the experience with hindsight.

The notion of reflection should not be confused with inaction. Reflecting does not necessarily mean taking time out from a task to stop and think about potential strategies and ramifications. Schön defined reflection in action as occurring when 'our thinking serves to reshape what we are doing while we are doing it' (1986: 36). He argues that it is wrong to seek to separate thinking from doing, seeing thought only as a preparation for action and action only as an implementation of thought. Schön argues that through critical reflection, doing and thinking are complementary, because 'doing' extends thinking in experimental action, and 'thinking' feeds the doing and its results. All inquiry, in this sense, is a continual interaction of thinking and doing:

> When someone learns a practice, he is initiated into the traditions of a community of practitioners and the practice world they inhabit. He learns their conventions, constraints, languages and appreciative systems, their repertoire of exemplars, systematic knowledge and patterns of knowing in action. ... Through reflection, a practitioner can surface and criticize the tacit understandings that have grown up around the repetitive experiences of specialized practice and can make new sense of situations of uncertainty or uniqueness. (Schön, 1983: 61)

Thomas defines self-reflection as 'the act of processing the output of monitoring through evaluation, abstraction and attribution and encompasses self efficacy' (1999b: 3). She argues that self-efficacy, a sense of self-worth drawn from feelings of competence, plays a central role in people's beliefs about whether they are capable of exercising control over their own level of functioning and over events that affect their lives. She found that self-efficacy, which is not to be confused with self-esteem, influences the choices journalists make, their aspirations, how much effort they put into any given endeavour, and how they persevere in the face of difficulties or setbacks. She concluded that the more capable journalists judge themselves to be, the higher the goals they set for themselves and the more firmly committed they remain to them. The more self-efficacious journalists are, the more able they are to make reliable decisions about public interest.

REFLECTION IN ACTION

For mainstream media, the production process begins when executive staff first consider each new edition and it continues through to the moment of publication. Then it starts again. The exact process varies from workplace to workplace but the objectives are the same: planning the coverage.

The production process for every individual story usually involves several people who encounter the story at different stages of its production. The reporter, who gathers the information and writes the story plays a relatively small and limited role in this process. A senior staff member with sectional responsibilities, such as sport or features, usually assigns stories to reporters. They each begin by scrutinizing the stories and potential stories available to them from a variety of sources. Decisions to be made as part of this process include:

- judgements about the strengths and weaknesses of individual reporters;
- the time frame likely to be required; and
- the potential to achieve satisfactory results.

At the editorial conference used to plan each edition, the section editors articulate the strengths of the various items in a way that compels the editor to use the copy in that edition. To prepare for this, the section editor considers all the potential information with regard to several factors. These include the news value of the piece, which is measured in terms of timeliness, proximity, consequence, relativity, and other factors relating to perceived public interest.

In commercial media, the editorial team considers the potential display of the story – how it might be structured, illustrated, the angles that might be used and how the story fits with the overall style of the publication. These journalists must also consider each potential story in the light of other recent publications – whether a story is too similar to another recently published piece. In assigning priority to individual articles, the section editor also seeks to create a balance between the pieces that add up to a 'satisfying' reading experience. For example, an editor is likely to resist having too many 'dark' or serious pieces together, so may give an important story less priority than a 'light' story on a given day.

There is no model the editor can use to be certain which ideas will be popular with consumers. An editor may look at data from market research to provide insight into the audience's interests, but such data cannot give rise to certainty. For example, market research has identified that certain news values (proximity, relevance and conflict) rate highly with news consumers. However, market research cannot provide definitive answers about which of these values are most important because their relative importance changes from day to day and story to story. As a result, the choices made in these editorial meetings are ultimately subjective decisions based on professional experience and underlying personal values. This process is not the application of expert knowledge but rather a critical reflection on previous experience of professional practice. Hence the wedding of one minor TV personality may be given widespread coverage on a certain day, but an equally popular personality's wedding may be largely ignored on another day.

In subjectively deciding what is important to the audience and what is not, the editorial conference uses similar processes to those used by the section editors in their pre-conference deliberations. They discuss the strengths of relative news values as the section editors have, but their discussion focuses on the story's contribution to the publication as a whole. They predict the audience reaction to the news they are considering. They discuss whether the audience is tiring of a topic and how and if their interest can be regained. Above all, they decide what is *interesting*, which can only be defined through their own interests, values and experiences. Patterson and Wilkins (1994) posit that news reflects certain cultural values and professional norms. They say the claim that journalists have a 'nose for news' means they have a common definition of news that has developed out of their professional training and experience (Patterson and Wilkins, 1994: 4).

There is a professional perception that people are attracted to news that entertains even when it does not usefully inform. For example, in early 2000, a story about an English policeman who was bitten on the genitals by a ferret received worldwide exposure on radio and TV news as well as in print media. The reason that journalists professionally value this type of story is based on a perception that people who get pleasure from consuming a product will be drawn to consuming it regularly. That is important to them because journalists measure their professional success by the popularity of their product, and the commercial success of their product is the measure by which journalists' performance is judged by their employer.

The editorial conference does not always assign priority to every item that will be published, especially in the case of newspapers, but the conference does decide the order of importance of the stories to be presented, thus 'telling the audience what to think about'. The editor may even suggest preliminary headlines at this point, to guide the group's visualization of the total product. At the end of the meeting, the section editors are dispatched to realize the vision that has been generally defined at the editorial conference.

The news editor or chief of staff will first allocate stories to individual reporters within the staff. This process, which may take only a few minutes, can have a significant effect on the way the story develops. On one level, this journalist is 'choosing the best person for the job', but in practice this means subjective decisions about how the interview is likely to unfold and about the style of report the particular reporter is likely to write. In briefing the reporter about the story, the Editor is selective and subjective in the information provided. That is how he or she can 'paint a picture' for the reporter about the way the story is envisaged to go. The Editor is seeking to impart the news values that the editorial conference has given priority. This part of the process is a clear reinforcement of the professional understanding implicit in journalism that there are many ways to tell a single story, all equally accurate if not true.

The briefing directs the reporter's research, whether it is followed exactly or used as a guide. Even a reporter who decides to take an entirely different angle knows he or she will be required to defend the decision against the briefing. Despite this, the reporter has a lot of control over what happens next. No matter how objective reporters set out to be, every action, every word that follows will be dictated by an internal process that remains unrecognized by many journalists. The second part of this book explores in detail the professional decisions that guide reporters in their practice. This subjective process directs all aspects of the reporters' craft – how they identify news, do primary and secondary research, evaluate sources, construct and edit news. The way the reporter resolves the many questions faced in pursuit of the story is a reflection of the interaction of the reporter's professional, commercial and ethical values.

The reporter assigned the job attends the scene with an iPhone. As well as conducting interviews for a print story, they reporter will also use the iPhone to capture audio, still and moving images for use on the website. This audio-visual material is edited back at the office by multimedia producers. Before returning to the office, the reporter will send the first two sentences, images and sound back to the office. Photographers attending jobs will also shoot moving and still images. This information will be edited at a centralized editing facility by multimedia producers, who are a modern form of sub-editor. These will be used on the website to flag stories. With breaking news, the first report may be a splash in print, followed by online reports and links on the website. The reporter returns to the newsroom to write the story for online and print and other text-based formats.

Back in the newsroom, the results of the reporters' deliberations are subjected to fresh scrutiny. The news editor is the first to evaluate whether the story has come up to expectation. If it has not, this person may require the reporter to change it, rewrite it or even do more interviews. When the news editor is satisfied, the story will then be passed on to the page editor. This journalist will have been provided with a layout and the task of fitting certain stories on the page with certain priorities. The page editor will make creative decisions about the organization of the text on the page, which will have direct impact on the size and language of the headline that goes with the text. The headline will be written by a sub-editor whose priority is to write a compelling headline within the constraints of the layout. This journalist may also have to cut the text to fit the layout and make judgements about the copy without reference to the reporter who wrote it. It is here that crucial changes to copy can inadvertently occur. The final person to potentially affect a story may be a production sub-editor, who sees only the edited copy that makes it onto the production floor. As well as seeking to make the copy shorter if required, this editor endeavours to make the changes in the most time-effective way.

USER-GENERATED NEWS SITES

Much has been written in recent years about the potential of citizen journalists, user-generated news sites and blogs to revolutionize access to information for global citizens. Underpinning the enthusiasm is a perception that mainstream media, driven as it is by commercial imperatives, filters the information citizens receive to fulfil a corporate agenda. Lehmann (2011) argues that the rhetoric about Internet journalism is plausible only because it conflates several distinct categories of material that are widely available online and didn't use to be:

> One is pure opinion, especially political opinion, which the Internet has made infinitely easy to purvey. Another is information originally published in other media – everything from Chilean newspaper stories and entries in German encyclopedias to papers presented at Micronesian conferences on accounting methods – which one can find instantly on search and aggregation sites. Lately,

grand journalistic claims have been made on behalf of material produced specifically for Web sites by people who don't have jobs with news organizations. (Lehmann, 2006)

User-generated content in all its forms is seen by some as a forum to reveal what doesn't make it into the mainstream news agenda. The 2006 Pew study, found that 4 million American bloggers consider themselves to be journalists. Extrapolate that figure out to global scale and that is an astonishing number of people considering the question: What is news?

Then there are other social media platforms for discussion, including Twitter and Facebook. Twitter has become an invaluable tool for journalists when it comes to finding sources and sharing stories. TweetDeck's dashboard allows users to follow groups, track topics in real-time by keyword, organize Tweets, @replies and direct messages (DMs). You can also feed Twitter's search results (based on your keywords or hashtags) into an RSS URL, then using an RSS reader to create a Twitter result to limit your Tweets to just what you're following right now. Then there's Twitterfall, which allows users to track Twitter's trending topics and hashtags or create custom search results, even by geography. The most recent Tweets drop down from the top of the page into the feed. Users can control the speed, theme and location from where the Tweets are coming. Journalists can get email updates from Twitter to their inbox with TweetBeep. Alerts can be set up based on hashtags, direct messages, and @ replies. (Betancourt, 2009). Now the microblogging site has released a guide that shows reporters how to best use the tool in their daily travails. That Twitter has launched an official guide for journalists is indicative of the impact of social media on the news.

Facebook recently undertook a similar initiative, launching a page as a resource for journalists seeking to include social media in their reporting, networking and storytelling. Hacker and Seshagiri (2011) argue that Facebook and Twitter have very different audiences:

> Facebook is organized across 'the social graph,' which means most people follow people they've met. In contrast, Twitter is organized across 'the interest graph,' which means people follow accounts that provide valuable information, whether they've met or not. So while Facebook is used by more people, Twitter has wider reach because it can (theoretically) be accessed worldwide. Twitter's key function is as an news and information amplifier, which is why news spreads so much more quickly on Twitter than on Facebook. Because of this amplification effect, Twitter has an immediacy that Facebook doesn't have. Many big news stories have broken first on Twitter. For events and crises, nothing can top Twitter's real-time effectiveness.

Twitter has an additional advantage over Facebook as a tool for news journalism. It is likely to be the fastest way to get links to your site's content into Google and other search engines. Because search engines 'license' the Twitter stream for their real-time results, links posted via Twitter show up on Google seconds later. For all its advantages, Twitter also carries risks for journalists, especially when they mix private and professional statements. Many journalists have suffered consequences for Tweeting personal comments about people in the news. Mindy McAdams (2011) prepared a series of guidelines for journalists using Twitter that emphasizes that journalists are very rarely 'private' citizens (see Figure 3.1).

1. Check the ground rules: talk to your editor about the company's position on Twitter.
2. Start as a reader: Twitter can be used in the same way journalists used wire services as a source of ideas and to access remote news.
3. Ask 'Who cares?' before you post: a Tweet is a microblog and should have some news value.
4. Get engaged: post a picture of yourself, read and respond to replies to your posts.
5. Don't bicker: if a Twitter exchange develops into an argument, take it offline.
6. Remember you are always a journalist: think twice before commenting on your colleagues. Verify and confirm before you retweet information.

(McAdams, 2011)

Figure 3.1   Guidelines for using Twitter as a journalist

DECISION MAKING IN ACTION

Consider the scenario at the start of this chapter. On one level it is a straightforward news story where the role of the journalist is simply to collect and record the facts. The public interest in these events may be assumed to be high, based on news values of proximity, relevance, consequence, timeliness and novelty, to the extent that such killings are still relatively unusual. On another level, answering the questions 'who?', 'what?', 'where?', 'when?', 'why?' and 'how?' with certainty is a complex task, capable of being interpreted in more than one way.

In the scenario described, the first thing you must do is **establish if the Tweet is true**. You need to establish if the incident actually happened, and if the account you have been given is accurate and not exaggerated, because once it is published the story will take on a credibility it did not have before. Just because a topic is trending on Twitter, it doesn't mean that the information being retweeted is true. For example, on March 13, 2010, during the The Bigg Digg Shindigg festival in the USA, the crowd was asked to participate in the world's largest Twitter hoax. The idea of the hoax was to trick people into thinking TV host Conan O'Brien had joined an Internet television company. Some 525 Tweets containing the hashtag '#omgconan' were sent in the next three hours, making it a trending topic on Twitter. Thousands of other Tweets followed (www.recordsetter.com).

So the next thing you must do is **establish as fact the information you think you already know**. You could grab your coat and race to the scene, but your honest impressions of the scene are hardly 'facts'. You could pick up the phone, ring stores in the street in question and ask them if they heard anything. But to meet your obligation to the public interest you must provide the audience with reliable answers to the questions 'who?', 'what?', 'where?' and 'when?' You need to attribute what you assert to be true to an authoritative voice – in this case, preferably the police. Without having picked up the telephone to dial the police, you are already engaging in critical reflection as you consider the context of the interview you are about to undertake, including the strengths and weaknesses of your human source of information. For example, on the one hand, a police officer can provide facts drawn from police records and is an authoritative source. On the other hand, the police officer is an individual whose personal opinions may not be insightful at all, regardless of the certainty with which they are expressed. Hence even an 'authoritative' source of information can be completely reliable in one context and completely unreliable in another. It is only by critical reflection in the context of the moment that a reporter can make these judgements.

The reporter must also decide **what to ask the interviewee as a means of establishing the facts**. Of all the powers exercised by journalists, their decisions about what to include and what to omit from reporting have the greatest influence on the messages received by audiences. For example, is it important to the story to report the identities of the people who have been killed? What would be achieved by reporting this? If you publish the names of the dead so soon after the event, you run the risk of informing the relatives before the police do, which could cause great individual harm. At the same time, it could be argued that publishing the names of the dead serves the purpose of reassuring others that their loved ones were not involved.

During the course of the interview, the reporter is constantly reflecting on the information being collected, in the light of the reporter's own perceptions about the honesty of the interviewee and the potential presence of other agendas in the interview. How will the journalist distinguish between speculation and informed comment? As part of that process, the journalist in this scenario must also **consider if other sources are available to verify the information already collected**. Is there any information that you have gathered that you cannot verify? For example, would you include a second-hand account of shouting said to have been heard during the incident? If you decided it was too important to the story to leave out, you would probably be valuing the dramatic narrative of the incident over any legal action that might follow the crime. All the same, the journalist must consider the question 'Could you defend your choice in court?' Some facts can be independently verified by seeking out physical evidence. Are some sources, such as other media, databases, websites and books, intrinsically more credible than others? Why? This scenario illustrates the importance of self-efficacy in journalism because in practice so much depends on the journalist's competence in critical reflection. Once the interview is completed, the reporter must again consider the question **'What are the relevant facts?'** This decision is made in light of his or her own professional understanding of the role of journalism, the public interest and the interests and priorities of the audience. Before writing, the journalist must also consider 'What contextual conditions limit my ambitions and expectations?'

As we have seen, Schön (1986) very aptly described the way that professionals reflect in action as 'the conversations we have with ourselves'. The internal conversation undertaken by the journalist during the act of writing is critical reflection in action. In the scenario given, the reporter has initial control over **how the events are described**. This task is informed by the closest thing to an 'expert body of knowledge' a journalist has – a broadly accepted set of 'news values' used to prioritize information. News values are explored in greater detail in Chapter 4. In the scenario, the predominant news values are likely to be proximity, because a violent event has occurred in the local area, and relevance, because readers could be directly affected and are affected by law-and-order issues generally. The reporter's reflective judgements about the relative importance of these and other news values will drive all decisions about what to include and what to omit from the story. This will be most evident in the introduction to the story, which will establish the 'angle' taken in the story. In this scenario, the reporting is likely to be structured around the allegedly random nature of the attack, the killing of a bystander trying to help and the number of people around the crime scene.

There is a strong temptation for journalists in a situation like this to seek to answer the question 'why?' as early as possible in the reporting, because this question is the most likely reaction of readers to the news. In the case of a breaking crime story, it is easy to represent speculation as something more substantial, which may even prejudice future legal action. In choosing one angle for the story, you are dismissing others. This choice is a direct reflection of your perceptions about the audience.

> Texts do not take shape because the writer wants to say something or has something to accomplish. Writers do not merely act on readers. The shape and direction of the discourse are configured by the communicative needs of writers to balance their own purpose and intentions with the expectations and needs of their readers. (Thomas, 1999b: 26)

The third distinct phase of critical reflection occurs when the reporter **reviews the finished article** before submitting it for publication. In the scenario outlined above, the reporter evaluates the completed story against the 'conventions, constraints, languages, exemplars and appreciative systems' (Schön, 1986: 36) of professional practice. This reflection centres on the effectiveness of the writing in disseminating the information the writer set out to impart. Figure 3.2 illustrates some of the decisions based on self-observation and critical reflection that might be used in responding to this particular scenario.

The internal questions the journalist asks must include an assessment of the veracity of his or her own work. As described in Chapter 2, a journalist must be guided by public interest. Before a journalist can be confident that his or her own work is in the public interest, he or she must be satisfied that assertions can be substantiated and no questions are left unanswered. He or she must also be consciously satisfied that the reporting is fair and that any harm caused to any person by the reporting can be justified as being for the greater good. Thomas (1999b: 24) describes the use of critical reflection as being fundamental to practise because it allows journalists to reflect on, assess and understand the nature and meaning of words and the hidden meanings contained within the words and news writing as a whole.

A friend sends you a retweet with the hashtag #massacre. It reads:
OMG. STANDING ACROSS FROM HIGH COURT. GUY TRIED TO STOP SOME OTHER GUY BEATING GIRL AND HE JUST SHOT HIM. COPS EVERYWHERE. GUNMAN RAN AWAY. I CAN'T BELIEVE WHAT I SAW!!
Why is it news? Where will you begin?
You decide what to include in the story and what to omit?

↓

Is it true?
Is there anything you already know? How do you know it? How will you verify what you already know? What facts do you need to tell the story with confidence? How will you establish the facts?

↓

Who can tell you what you need to know?
Can they provide verifiable facts? Do they provide an authoritative perspective? What questions do you need to ask? Are there any official sources available to you? Are there online sources you can use?

↓

What information do you expect to get from interviews?
What are the facts as each interviewee sees them? Is the information specific or generalized? Is it information that can be verified and how? Do the interviewees seem credible? Why? Can any interviewees have an undeclared motive?

↓

What are the facts?
Is there any information that you've collected that you can't verify? Is it so important to the story you can't leave it out? Why leave it in? Are you satisfied your sources are credible? Are some sources intrinsically more credible than others? Why? Could you defend your choices in court?

continued

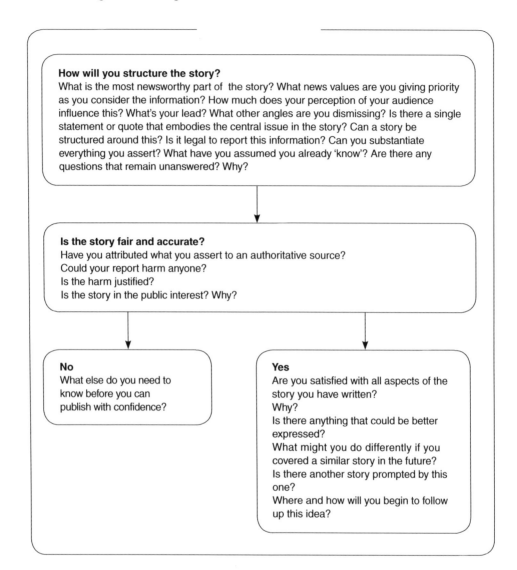

How will you structure the story?
What is the most newsworthy part of the story? What news values are you giving priority as you consider the information? How much does your perception of your audience influence this? What's your lead? What other angles are you dismissing? Is there a single statement or quote that embodies the central issue in the story? Can a story be structured around this? Is it legal to report this information? Can you substantiate everything you assert? What have you assumed you already 'know'? Are there any questions that remain unanswered? Why?

Is the story fair and accurate?
Have you attributed what you assert to an authoritative source?
Could your report harm anyone?
Is the harm justified?
Is the story in the public interest? Why?

No
What else do you need to know before you can publish with confidence?

Yes
Are you satisfied with all aspects of the story you have written?
Why?
Is there anything that could be better expressed?
What might you do differently if you covered a similar story in the future?
Is there another story prompted by this one?
Where and how will you begin to follow up this idea?

Figure 3.2   Decision making in action

CONCLUSION

Critical reflection, as part of the practice of journalism, should never be confused with the personal navel-gazing journalists sometimes indulge in at a bar at the end of a long week. It is not about indulging in guilt or defensiveness about action already taken. It is an active commitment in journalists to scrutinize their own actions, exposing the processes and underlying values in their work *while* they are doing it. Langer (1989) described how 'process orientation' not only enables more reliable professional decisions, but adds a dimension of self-efficacy:

> Awareness of the process of making real choices along the way makes it less likely that we will feel guilty in retrospect. ... On occasion, after learning the consequences of a choice, we may wish we had chosen differently, but we still tend not to be quite as hard on ourselves when we know why we did what we did. True process orientation also means being aware that every outcome is preceded by a process. (Langer, 1989: 75)

The second part of the book, 'Journalism in Action', explores the process inherent in activities performed by journalists every day in finding, choosing, sourcing, gathering and evaluating, writing and editing news.

FURTHER ACTION

1   Look at news reports in a newspaper. What sources are used in the story?

2   Watch a TV news report about a crime. What part do pictures play?

3   Choose a front page story. Do you believe it? Why?

4   Try posting a Tweet with an unusual string, then go immediately to Google and search for that same string. After the results appear, click on *More*, then *Real-Time* in the left margin.

FURTHER READING

Adam, S.G. (1993) *Notes Towards a Definition of Journalism: Understanding an Old Craft as an Art Form*. St Petersburg, FL: The Poynter Institute for Media Studies.

Betancourt, L. (2009) *The Journalist's Guide to Twitter*, www.mashable.com/2009/05/14/twitter-journalism.

McAdams, M. (2011) *Social Media Guidelines for Journalists*. http://mindymcadams.com/tojou/2011/social-media-guidelines-for-journalists (May 16 2011).

PART TWO

Journalism in Action

4

FINDING NEWS

You are waiting at the local railway station and you overhear two people talking about a commotion the evening before at a local park. The gist of their conversation is that a youth group that meets in the community hall adjoining the park is out of control, and that the group spills noisily into the park where there is drinking and other illicit activities. The conversationalists agree that decent people are afraid to go to the park at night and the police don't seem to be doing much about it. Is there a story here?

For most inexperienced journalists, the idea of 'finding' news is the most daunting part of the job. Their uncertainty about where to begin is not helped by the language still used by journalists to describe 'news'. They talk about having a 'nose' for news, and 'seeing' the story they later write. When they are pleased with the results, journalists describe copy just as colourfully. An introduction one lauded as 'punchy' might later be described as 'sexy', but a good story always needs 'legs' and sometimes has 'balls'. Few journalists, when pressed, can find a standardized definition of news, but all would say they know a good story when they see it. This chapter explores the nature of news and the factors influencing the exercise of news judgement, particularly the role of the intended audience. It provides a methodology for identifying news, and critically reflects on the processes through consideration of the scenario described above.

DEFINING NEWS

The word 'news' to describe the things journalists write about has been in use for at least 500 years, well before news*papers* were around. News, both the important and the frivolous, can be used to bind people together in a sense of community and get them talking to one another. It also provides information that people need to exercise judgement about what is happening in the world around them. People use the news to help them make up their minds so they can function as informed citizens. It also helps them organize their daily lives by advising them about predicted weather, transport problems, or the upcoming tour of a popular act.

The problem with defining news arises because such a definition requires the consideration of four questions:

- To what use do people put news?

- What are the functions of the particular news medium?

- What are the characteristics of news?

- What makes an event or opinion newsworthy?

There is no reliable rule about exactly what constitutes news because there are too many variables to predict. 'What people talk about' can be just about anything, and is usually something a little out of the ordinary. Even the weather can be important news if it is unpredictable or relentless enough. Cyclones, big thunderstorms, prolonged periods of heat, wet, dry or fog and lightning strikes are always news where they occur, because they are uncommon. Reporting on uncommon events is a major part of the journalist's repertoire, as is reporting predicted or 'expected' news.

'Expected news' is a term that may be used to describe the everyday events that journalists cover. News editors become aware of these stories through media releases, invitations and other forms of advance notice. 'Unexpected news' can be used to describe the news that is collected as a result of a regular call to the local law enforcement agency. It also covers the news that reporters become aware of through observation, a 'tip-off' from the public or from a 'contact'. Successful journalists are often known for their wide range of 'contacts' – people who provide them with news ideas or interviews. Journalists create 'contacts' by staying on good terms with the people they come into contact with, and recording the contact details of everyone who is useful to them in covering a story.

The definition of a 'good story' is one that is interesting to the target audience. All journalists, wherever they work and whatever they write, write for an audience. They exist for the people who consume the message they send. In this sense, all journalism is news journalism, whether it is a news story published in traditional news media or a monologue self-posted on the Internet. Both media are aiming to attract and move their audience in some way. Feature writers in magazines also share the news they have discovered with their readers. Finding 'news', when defined as 'what interests a news consumer', is a complex and subjective task. Looking at the range of journalism that does get published, it is apparent that journalism can be used to get bad laws changed and expose crime. It can also create useless fashions and provide a level of fame for some people that is totally out of proportion with their usefulness to society.

NEWS VALUES

In deciding what will be interesting to people, you need to consider another journalists' term: 'news values'. 'News values' are described as 'themes' that have been shown to strike a chord with media audiences. For example, audiences globally are usually considered to be most interested in things that affect them directly. That is why the deaths of five people in a local community are more newsworthy to that community than the death of 500 people in a remote foreign country. Similarly, strong value is attached to information that could affect audiences directly in the future, and information about things that could potentially cause them harm.

The basic news values are:

- impact
- timeliness
- proximity
- conflict
- currency
- novelty
- relativity.

Impact refers to the relevance a story has to the audience's lives. Stories of relevance can be about everyday things, such as freak weather that takes off scores of roofs in a residential area. It might be a price rise that affects a lot of people. It might be changed arrangements for a sporting event, or a proposed change in the law.

Timeliness refers to information that helps people organize their lives. It might be a bus strike that people need to know about before they leave for work, a hailstorm predicted for Thursday night, or a tax that comes into effect in four weeks' time.

Proximity refers to how 'close to home' a story is. That is, how a car crash that kills four people in the community where you live comes to be seen as more important than 4,000 dead in Somalia. For example, there were 96 wars on at the same time as the 1991 Gulf War, but only one got widespread international coverage.

Conflict is the news value most people associate with media, and is often seen as the most important news value in today's media. There has to be more than one side to a story of conflict and the stronger the contrast between the points of view, the greater the conflict. Conflict is also present in news that 'afflicts the comfortable' by making them anxious or guilty. It is also what is meant by the tabloid dictum to 'anchor every story to its emotional base'.

Currency is the term used to describe how 'hot' an issue is at any one time. Environmental issues have a currency at the moment that has never existed before. The women's movement had currency in the 1970s and lost it again in the 1990s. A single event can also create currency for a topic. For example, a politician making racist remarks in Parliament can give race relations' issues currency.

Novelty is given a high news value. There is an adage about journalism – 'It's not news if a dog bites a man, but if a man bites a dog then it is news'. Of course, like most generalizations, it falls apart if, for example, the biting dog is in a pack of 10 roaming a suburban street. The unusual can also be found in serious stories. For example, a politician sticking to the party line is not news, but a politician changing sides *is* news.

Relativity is the most complex and subjective news value. Sometimes, even when a story meets all the tests of news, it does not get published. The phenomenon puzzles people outside the industry. Why, for example, is the review of one amateur drama production published prominently and the next show ignored? Why is the wedding of one TV personality front-page news while another's goes unreported?

Relative news value is also affected by the medium the journalist is using. Some events, such as fireworks displays, are considered more important as 'TV stories' because the visual medium displays the spectacle of fireworks to best effect. Television prioritizes vision, or interesting pictures, which explains why TV stations around the world will broadcast images of a tall chimney stack being demolished by explosives. Or as a TV news producer once quipped, 'Fraud doesn't give you vision'. Colour photographs can also record the images, but they lack the sound of the fireworks exploding or the gasps from the spectators. Stories best suited to radio are those that are unfolding and changeable. During the 1999 conflict in East Timor, many foreigners were trapped in their consulates without communications. Radio journalists, calling mobile telephone numbers, were able to record actuality, or live information, at a time when journalists could not get in or out of the area.

Relative news values are stronger for print than for broadcast media when it comes to disseminating complex information. Print media can present in-depth information, including tables and charts, in a form that readers can digest at their own pace.

News values all come down to the professional judgement of journalists. Their decisions depend on how much news there is to choose from; how much is positive and how much is negative; and understanding the target audience. For most people starting out in journalism, news is whatever the editor says it is. Journalists hear lots of points of view, but you will have to reach your own conclusions.

NEWS SENSE

'News sense' is recognizing the potential news value in facts that might by themselves seem unimportant, and selecting the parts that will interest people. It is finding ways to bring the audience into the story. It is making connections between facts and events and predicting the way an audience will react. News sense is relatively easy to develop, if you ask yourself the right questions. Before you can do that, you must identify your own position, or point of view. Hall (1992) argues that journalists never deliver a single meaning but many meanings, in which one is preferred and offered, over others, as the 'most appropriate'.

In such a scenario, individual journalists, and their editors, play a crucial role in whether a dock strike is represented in the media as a defence of workers' rights or a minority group holding the public to ransom. The position from which the journalist observes the 'facts' as they unfold determines the presentation of the 'truth'. Patterson and Wilkins (1994: 26) conclude that news reflects certain cultural values and professional norms. They argue that the journalists' 'nose for news' is a definition of news that has developed out of their professional training and experience. Gurevitch (1990: 282) found that adherence to professional definitions of news values may also act as a powerful force for conformity, that is, for arriving at a common answer, across an otherwise diverse set of news outlets, to the question 'What is the most significant news today?'

FINDING NEWS IN ACTION

The scenario set out at the beginning of this chapter is a common experience for journalists. Journalists become accustomed to almost subconsciously assessing the news value of ideas as they arise. Many good ideas have come to mind when a journalist was doing something else. It might be something observed on the way to work, a conversation at a party, or it might be something read in other media that triggers a memory or idea. In the case of the people congregating in the park, you must decide whether the idea warrants further investigation. This is the internal process of professional decision making – Schön's 'conversations we have with ourselves'. The most important question to be answered is '**Would people be interested to know about this?**' To answer this question, you must answer several more related ones. In this case, you must identify the stakeholders in the story and decide if they would want the story told. In this case, the people most affected by the subject of the potential story are the residents living near the park, the people who go there and the general public, who may, if the complainants are right, be inhibited from going to the park because of the alleged activity.

Next, you must identify the 'news values' or factors that make a story interesting and important to audiences by asking yourself: '**What are the news values attached to these conclusions?**' In the case of this scenario, the answers might include *proximity*, because people are interested in the things that affect them directly; *relevance*, because parents need to know if their children are at risk; *timeliness*, because if there is danger, people should be aware of it; and *public interest*, because people have a right to know if there is anything to worry about. Are there other important values to consider?

In resolving these questions, the journalist is ultimately deciding if telling the story is 'in the public interest'. The 'public interest' is not the same as 'what the public is interested in'. The public interest or 'public good' is served by telling an audience things they need, or have a right, to know. As part of deciding whether something is in the public interest, you must decide if telling the story could harm anyone, and if this harm is justified. Before proceeding, you must decide if using information overheard in a private conversation is justified. First, consult your conscience. How do you *feel* about what you are considering? Will the conversationalists be identified? Could they be harmed by your appropriation of their information? How would you feel if you were in their position?

Secondly, ask yourself: 'Is there another way to achieve my objective without using the information?' In this case, the information is an idea, or tip-off. Could you tell this story without the element of conflict you have overheard? Is all conflict newsworthy? Why? Should you identify yourself to the conversationalists at the station and tell them you have overheard their conversation? Should you ask their permission to follow up the idea? What will you do if they say no? If you do not follow it up, are you then meeting your obligations to your audience and to your employer?

Finally, conduct conversations in your head with all the parties involved, asking 'How will my decision affect others?' Your boss would probably say: 'If there's trouble in a public place, people have a right to know'. The local residents would stand to benefit if the alleged noise problems stopped. You might assume that the people complained about would deny the allegations, and if the conversationalists were wrong, then the people gathering in the park would likely want to be vindicated.

Before you finally decide whether the story is in the public interest, you need to consider the social context in which the alleged activity was happening. Some societies and communities take an uncompromising stand against breaches of public order, while in others there is a high level of tolerance for public conduct. Depending on the prevailing social attitudes and laws, your conclusions about public interest might include the notion that residents have a democratic and legal right to privacy and to not be disturbed at night. You might conclude that there are laws against excessive noise and if illegal activities are taking place, they should be stopped. You might also conclude that if potentially dangerous activities go unchecked, someone may be harmed, and the park is a public place where all citizens have a legal right to feel safe. You might decide that this is a local story affecting local people who are part of the target audience; and if people are already talking about the allegations, the audience would be reassured to know if the rumours are unfounded.

PURSUING THE STORY

Based on your conclusions reached from the discussion above, you may decide that the story is worth pursuing. This decision creates a whole new series of questions that must be answered and it is here that the reporter first exercises the media's power to define 'the taken-for-granted world'. Each individual journalist has the responsibility of knowing something, of deciding what questions are raised, getting answers, and selectively putting it together to tell a real story about real people. The individual reporter has so much power because it is the journalist who makes sense of information, who tells people what to think about. That is why reporters need to know *what* they understand and *why* before they can identify the right questions to ask others.

First, you must ask **'What do I already know?'** There are three kinds of knowledge: what you know; what you don't know; and what you *don't know* that you don't know. For reporters, this means facts you can substantiate; questions you want answered; and factors you have yet to consider. To establish what is *known*, you must first establish *how* it is known. The first step is to identify if any of the 'facts' are actually assumptions. You must establish the veracity of information – whether it can be independently proved or is an unsubstantiated opinion. In this scenario, the 'tip-off' is an opinion shared by two strangers who are overheard at a railway station. How can their opinion be verified and by whom? You might opt to seek the points of view of other groups likely to be affected by the alleged incidents before making a decision.

This leads to the second important question in this part of the process. '**How do I choose interviewees?**' It is an important question because the sources you choose and those you prioritize will direct what you eventually write.

All the potential interviewees must be evaluated for their strengths and weaknesses as sources of information. In this scenario, the *local residents* may provide first-hand experience of the alleged problems and be a source of colourful quotes about their experiences that enhance the audience's understanding of the facts. These same residents may also feel very strongly about the issue and may even be prone to exaggeration, so information provided by them that is outside their personal experience would need to be substantiated in an authoritative way.

The police should be able to provide facts about any incidents reported to them or official action taken, but are unlikely to offer opinions. Police officers might also be expected to focus their information in accordance with the official perspective on whether there is a law-and-order issue surrounding the complaints. The *local government authority* or *park owner* can provide substantiated facts about whether any damage has been found at the park or any other evidence of large public gatherings. This body should also be able to substantiate if residents have complained under any noise pollution laws.

The *youth group organizers*, whose activities have been criticized, should have an opportunity to answer the allegations before you publish them. Apart from a right of reply, this group offers another perspective on the youth club activities and may offer other insights into the source of the complaints. Individual *youth group members*, like the local residents, may offer colourful quotes to assist in bringing the story to life for the audience. If they deny their gatherings are rowdy and out of control, information from these sources can help the reporter and the public to decide if the criticism is warranted.

Once you have identified the informants necessary to substantiate the idea, you must decide '**Who do I speak to first?**' This is an important decision because as you collect information, it is tested against the information gained before. The order in which you conduct any interviews can profoundly affect the direction of the story.

For example, speaking to *local residents* first might seem a good place to start, to establish if the story is worth pursuing. This group offers a human and emotional perspective on the issue in everyday language accessible to the media audience. This group is also usually less expert than statutory bodies in dealing with media interviews and may be ignorant of the legal implications of strongly held views. To speak to this group first will define the conflict element of the story in human terms, but may assign untested credibility to this perspective in the preparation of future interview questions. On the other hand, if your first stop is the *police*, the perspective you get on this story will be in relation to the potential law-and-order issue and the authority's general desire positively to reinforce community perceptions of police responsiveness. This group is usually experienced in providing information to the media and may be sceptical about media interest. The police often take a minimalist approach to providing information to the media to decrease the likelihood of the story being taken further. You also need to be aware that individual police officers are sometimes more expansive than official policy allows and offer personal opinions mixed with official information.

If you go to the *local government authority* first, you might reasonably expect its perspective to focus on the effects on council property and issues about where jurisdiction lies in responsibility for the ratepayers' concerns. You might expect that the authority's perceptions will be coloured by a general desire to be seen in a good light. If you go to the *youth group organizers* first, you might expect their answers to focus on ensuring the continuation of the youth group. Because this group has been the subject of complaint, do you assume they will be hostile to your approach? Will this affect your questions and the way you ask them? If you speak to this group before the residents, what effect will it have on your questions to the latter group? Do you need to establish the exact nature of the allegations before you talk to the group organizers? Is this group more credible than the individual young people who are members of it? If you go first to individual *youth group members*, you face the same problems as faced in interviewing residents – they can offer opinions rather than facts. You must also consider whether you have assumed what they are going to say and how this has affected the preparation of your questions.

Because the reporter will be the one conducting the interviews, it is important that you have considered the relative strengths and weaknesses of the various groups used as sources. So, before and after the interviews, you must ask: '**What information do I reasonably expect to get from them?**'

For example, it is very important not to ask people for answers they are not able or qualified to provide. In the case of the *local residents* you can expect to be told 'the facts' as the interviewees see them. But is the information specific or generalized? Is it information that can be verified and how? Do the interviewees seem credible? Why? Could the interviewees have an undeclared motive for wanting the youth group meetings stopped? All these factors could significantly affect the amount of credibility you assign to this source.

In interviewing the *police*, you are primarily seeking to establish verifiable 'facts', such as recorded information about whether anyone has been charged with a crime. Do the police facts support the story you set out to pursue? What is the official police position on the allegations? Interviews with individual police officers can be a source of quotes, including the more general social issue of public behaviour. The *other statutory authority* can also substantiate if any reports of damage to the park or the hall have been recorded. Officials might be able to verify if the authority is aware of complaints about noise or other disturbances. This body can also provide facts about any regulations or restrictions covering the hire of the hall.

When it comes to the *youth group organizers* and *youth group members*, you find yourself asking similar questions to those asked about local residents. Is their information specific or generalized? Is it information that can be verified and how? Do the interviewees seem credible? Why? Could the interviewees have a motive for denying the allegations? As the accused, are they less credible than are the local residents? Are there additional considerations involved in interviewing young people? The processes used in gathering news are explored in detail in Chapter 7.

After you have completed preliminary interviews, you are in a position to make the crucial decision about whether the emerging story should be offered for publication. One little understood feature of news gathering is that journalists' preliminary enquiries often lead to nothing. Before you decide whether to offer the story, you must be able confidently to answer the question: '**What are the facts?**' To find this answer, many more questions must be asked. You must decide if any of the information collected cannot be verified. If that is the case, is it so important to the story it cannot be left out? If the decision is yes, what news values are you assigning priority to in using unverified information?

The journalist must also decide if sources are credible. They will certainly appear to be credible once the media is a forum for their views. Are some sources, for example 'official' ones, intrinsically more credible than others? You must be satisfied that you can substantiate everything that is asserted and that your decision can be defended, in court if necessary. As part of this, you must once again ask yourself if any information is assumed to be 'known', without substantiation.

Before taking the decision to write, ask yourself if there is a single statement or quote that embodies the central issue in the story. Can a story be structured around this? What news values are given priority as you consider the information? Why? Have you assigned 'hero' or 'villain' status to any party? Have you been fair to all parties? How you evaluate your information and construct the story is explored further in Chapters 5 and 6.

Finally, you reach the point of deciding: '**Is there a story worth telling here?**' How that question is answered is a reflection of the sum of the decisions already made about the relative values associated with this story. Throughout, you have been making decisions based on your understanding of the audience and the public interest. In the workplace, you also consider the news values given priority by your news organization. News organizations usually have a particular audience in mind when they prioritize news values. Demographic profiles prepared by market research organizations are used to direct news content by providing a profile of news consumers' interests. This is achieved by conducting surveys on the lifestyle of the target market. News providers buy the results so they can provide evidence for advertisers that their message is likely to reach the right consumers. Editors can also use the findings of such surveys to establish a profile of their readers' interests, which provides insight into whether their product reflects the perspective on the world shared by the consumers. Many editors are sceptical, however, about such research, relying on their own understanding of what the audience wants.

In the case of the people in the park, the demographics of the community and media audience are significant. If the park is an area of the city that is always busy late into the night, and most residents are young and/or transient, then the news value attached to public disturbances is less than if the area is residential and populated by elderly home owners. If the audience is known to be an older demographic, then it might be assumed that issues about public disturbances would be more important to them than to a younger community. If you are writing for a youth-oriented radio station, the angle you take on the complaints might be quite different. Similarly, if the news organization publishes only to a local audience, the activity in a local park is more relevant than it would be to an audience that includes a whole metropolitan city. A news organization that publishes to this group would likely require a wider news value, such as indications of a bigger problem, before publishing to its audience.

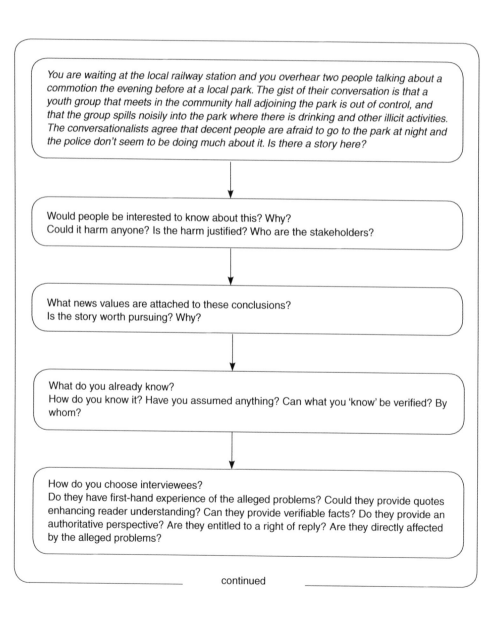

You are waiting at the local railway station and you overhear two people talking about a commotion the evening before at a local park. The gist of their conversation is that a youth group that meets in the community hall adjoining the park is out of control, and that the group spills noisily into the park where there is drinking and other illicit activities. The conversationalists agree that decent people are afraid to go to the park at night and the police don't seem to be doing much about it. Is there a story here?

Would people be interested to know about this? Why?
Could it harm anyone? Is the harm justified? Who are the stakeholders?

What news values are attached to these conclusions?
Is the story worth pursuing? Why?

What do you already know?
How do you know it? Have you assumed anything? Can what you 'know' be verified? By whom?

How do you choose interviewees?
Do they have first-hand experience of the alleged problems? Could they provide quotes enhancing reader understanding? Can they provide verifiable facts? Do they provide an authoritative perspective? Are they entitled to a right of reply? Are they directly affected by the alleged problems?

continued

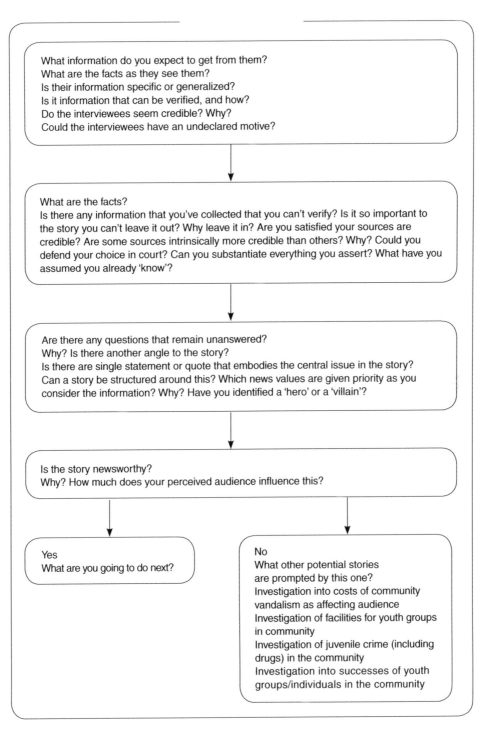

What information do you expect to get from them?
What are the facts as they see them?
Is their information specific or generalized?
Is it information that can be verified, and how?
Do the interviewees seem credible? Why?
Could the interviewees have an undeclared motive?

What are the facts?
Is there any information that you've collected that you can't verify? Is it so important to the story you can't leave it out? Why leave it in? Are you satisfied your sources are credible? Are some sources intrinsically more credible than others? Why? Could you defend your choice in court? Can you substantiate everything you assert? What have you assumed you already 'know'?

Are there any questions that remain unanswered?
Why? Is there another angle to the story?
Is there are single statement or quote that embodies the central issue in the story?
Can a story be structured around this? Which news values are given priority as you consider the information? Why? Have you identified a 'hero' or a 'villain'?

Is the story newsworthy?
Why? How much does your perceived audience influence this?

Yes
What are you going to do next?

No
What other potential stories
are prompted by this one?
Investigation into costs of community
vandalism as affecting audience
Investigation of facilities for youth groups
in community
Investigation of juvenile crime (including
drugs) in the community
Investigation into successes of youth
groups/individuals in the community

Figure 4.1   Finding news in action

To reach a reliable decision to proceed, you must again consider all you know in the light of public interest and the public's right to know. In this case, the decision is achieved by revisiting the questions asked in your first internal conversation about the story. Will the story harm anyone? Can the story be told without harming anyone or their interests? Does the good done by publishing this information outweigh any harm that might be done? Why?

Finally, you can decide whether your idea is 'news'. Whatever the decision, there is one more thing to think about. Consider the sum of the 'facts' and ask: **'Are other potential stories prompted by this one?'** Even if you decide to proceed with the park story, part of your job is to consider ways in which the story that exists might lead to other potential stories. For example, the park scenario could prompt an investigation into the cost to the community caused by vandalism. How would a reporter pursue this idea? Where would be the best place to start? The same scenario could also generate an idea about the range of facilities for youth groups in the community. Whose perspective is the most authoritative on this? A follow-up story on the park might be an investigation of juvenile crime or drug use in the community. If so, what facts need to be established first and where would the information be found?

CONCLUSION

This chapter has revealed the process used by journalists to identify and evaluate potential news stories. It has revealed it as a series of decisions that may be applied to every idea a journalist encounters. The 'right' answers in every case are a direct reflection of other aspects of the context in which the decisions are being made. These factors include the role of the news publication in the community; the community's pre-existing attitudes to the topic; the demographic profile of the target audience; individual values and your view about the media's role in serving the public interest. How you might organize and express the 'facts' as news involves a whole new series of decisions, which are explored in Chapter 8.

FURTHER ACTION

1   Take a walk in your local area, looking for potential stories. Or take a bus and observe your fellow passengers, again thinking about story ideas.

2   Choose a news story in print, on TV or online. Try to describe the target reader by considering the language, angle and style of the piece.

3   Conduct an audit of magazines, first identifying the range available. Concentrate on a particular publication. Reflect on its news values and stylistic qualities.

4   Find a report of a local police matter. What other, related, stories are prompted by the events?

FURTHER READING

Hedges, C. (2011) 'The disease of objectivity', in R.W. McChesney and V. Pickard (eds), *Will the Last Reporter Please Turn Out the Lights: The Collapse of Journalism and What Can be Done to Fix It*. New York: The New Press.

Hirst, M. (2010) *News 2.0: Will Journalism Survive the Internet?* Sydney: Allen & Unwin.

Layton, R. (2011) *Editing and News Design: How to Shape the News in Print and Online Journalism*. Melbourne: Palgrave Macmillan.

Patterson, P. and Wilkins, L. (1994) *Media Ethics: Issues and Cases* (3rd edn). Dubuque, IA: McGraw-Hill.

5

CHOOSING NEWS

You are reporting cases at the local court. Company policy is that court reports are published without fear or favour. You are surprised to see a very prominent politician there and discover that the politician's 21-year-old son has been charged with common assault and assaulting a police officer. You attend the hearing and learn that police were called when the politician's son became extremely agitated at a railway station when asked for his ticket. When police arrived, a scuffle broke out and a police officer suffered a broken nose. The court is told the 21 year-old is receiving treatment for a psychotic illness and was frightened and deluded when approach by police. The court finds the offence is proven but no conviction is recorded. Will you report the story? If so, how? Are there limits on the public role of a public figure?

Perhaps the greatest power wielded by journalists is in choosing, from a myriad of happenings, the information that will be presented to the audience as news. Every decision to report is accompanied by decisions to ignore other happenings as less important or interesting. The audience, too, is aware that news media provide edited highlights of a day's events, rather than comprehensive coverage. So when something is selected for publication, its prominence in the public sphere is inevitably increased.

Journalists are traditionally urged to be 'objective' in their selections of news, thus mediating their power with social responsibility. The trouble is that objectivity is a value-free concept, whereas journalists' decisions are always a prioritizing of values. True objectivity dictates that every story is published, no matter how interesting it is perceived to be. When a professional value system is applied to choosing news, it should be assessed on its importance to society, but 'good' photographs still get boring stories published at the expense of important ones. It is imperative to present news in an attractive package because news providers are in commercial competition with one another. This leads to a focus on 'scoops' that argues that for your package to be desirable, it must be different, new, first. News stories usually seek to provoke a response in the reader, be it revelation, illumination or something more emotional, such as anger. This can lead to a form of narrative built around conflict or drama.

As journalism is tailored to serve markets, critics argue that instead of providing a clearer picture of the world, the media provides one that satisfies and reassures the dominant group in society. The effect is to create a climate where journalists cease to challenge or confront audiences, unless it is over an issue where the public's position is clear. Some journalists still aim to disturb the complacency of their audience, but by-and-large mainstream journalism supports the status quo and 'mirrors' the society. Minorities, or any people that challenge the universality of the status quo, do not have news value. Or, as a metropolitan daily editor announced at a news conference after the publication of a series of articles about homelessness, 'I don't want any more stories about losers. Our readers aren't losers.'

Another way that journalists exercise enormous power is in their capacity to bring private citizens to public attention. It may be argued that the media creates public figures by giving them repeated prominence. Certainly, the media sometimes directly assigns celebrity or public status to private individuals. Consider the case of Monica Lewinsky, who became internationally notorious when her affair with US President Bill Clinton became public in 1998. The objective news value of that story was that the US President was accused of acting with impropriety and lying about it, so the actual identity of the person with whom he had consorted was irrelevant, unless there was something illegal in their association. More than 15 years later the activities of Miss Lewinsky are still attributed with sufficient news value to justify reports about her being published in international media as recently as this year. She has her own Wikipedia entry and an Internet search for her name returns more than 4,000,000 hits, despite the fact most people under the age of 30 don't recognize her name. In this sense, it may be argued that she has become a public figure, although she did not seek public attention, nor did she hold a public office. Whether an individual is a public or private figure is significant in the relative values applied to choosing news. In some countries, such as the USA, a public figure has fewer legal rights to privacy than a person without a public profile.

The ethical values that journalists bring to these decisions about choosing news are often called into question these days. Janet Malcolm began a controversial article published in *The New Yorker* with the words:

> Every journalist who is not too stupid or too full of himself to notice what's going on knows that what he does is morally indefensible. He is a kind of confidence man, preying on people's vanity, ignorance or loneliness, gaining their trust and betraying them without remorse. (Malcolm, 1989: 38)

The real sting in Ms Malcolm's article and later book, *The Journalist and the Murderer* (1990), is not its powerful language, but in its essential truth. Most journalists at some point know the triumph of interviewing, for example, a petty bureaucrat who inadvertently reveals his disdain for the people he is supposed to help. The journalist gleefully records the damning comments, knowing the official will regret them when he sees them published, that he will feel used and that he will have to answer to his superiors. Yet, putting the phone down, the journalist does not *feel* unethical. It is 'Yes! Got him.' Journalists face such decisions every day. All professions face ethical conflicts, but journalists publish the results of theirs. The journalist's decisions about the public interest are in the open and open to wide scrutiny.

CHOOSING THE NEWS

Every day journalists take information known only to a small group of people and publish it to a wide audience, invoking professional decisions about public interest, veracity of sources and invasion of privacy. Journalists constantly find a balance between the way they want to write the story, the way to write the story to get the biggest audience, and the way to write the story while doing the least harm to the fewest number of people. Often there are dilemmas to resolve because the things that journalists write about are real. The people and places are real and so are the consequences of published journalism. While the scale of the dilemmas encountered in deciding what should be published varies, the potential for harm is undiminished. The decision whether to publish details of a crime for fear of prompting copy-cat attacks may be, in practice, no more crucial than the decision whether to publish the name of a person arrested for indecent exposure whose elderly mother has just had a stroke. Somebody could die. Somebody's family could be permanently ruptured.

Journalists make ethical decisions constantly in ways that profoundly affect their work. Even not thinking about the impact of what you write is an ethical decision of sorts. The evidence of these decisions is found in the way you portray the man you just interviewed, whether you publish that a bank manager was booked for urinating in the gutter. If you do make this public and he is humiliated or he loses his job, the effect of your ethical decision will be as devastating for him as any legislative changes to the right to fair trial.

Making an ethical decision is never easy and the only way to be able to do it with confidence is to practise. Deciding what to do is seldom as simple as consulting your conscience and deciding what is 'right', because a decision requires weighing numerous, often competing, factors. In everyday journalism, values are multiple. There is the desire to get to the truth, and to write the best story you can in a compelling way. There is the desire to please the employer, by meeting the editor's definition of a good story. There are also social or ethical values to consider, such as acting in the public interest and maintaining the individual's right to privacy.

Of all the journalist's 'internal conversations', the most crucial surrounds the balance between the public interest – what the public is interested in – and the potential harm publication could do. All the decisions that follow – how to research, evaluate sources, construct the story and write it – are dependent on the subject position adopted by the journalist at this point.

An ethical dilemma occurs when competing moral values collide. A moral value is a tenet or rule of conduct, such as 'lying is bad' or 'thou shalt not kill'. But what if there is someone at your door who wants you to reveal the whereabouts of a third person so that person may be murdered? Lying is bad; killing is bad; you must choose. Perhaps you will opt to say nothing, avoiding the lie while not telling the truth, but in doing so you are choosing to distance yourself from whether a third person dies. Every decision has consequences. In journalism, the dilemma might revolve around choosing to publish something that will cause someone to be embarrassed. Making a decision is a no-win situation because some important value, such as the individual's right to privacy, is going to be devalued. How comfortable journalists feel with the implications of their choices depends on the ethical value-system they bring to their deliberations.

NON-NEWS VALUES IN CHOOSING NEWS

Predominant ethical value-systems have shifted over time and this chapter does not provide an overview of this development. Rather, it considers several positions in relation to journalism.

Virtue ethics, as defined by Aristotle, separated ethics from actions by emphasizing the influence of the individual's character. From this approach, if a journalist was a morally upright person, then his or her decisions were ethical by association. Later, a reliance on professional codes of practice, or codes of ethics for journalists, shifted the focus to conduct – *acts* were ethical or not. Ethical people could do otherwise unethical things if the circumstances were appropriate. Then came the view that one did not require a moral *character* to be capable of moral *conduct*, only to be motivated by *duty*. From this perspective, the moral worth of an action did not depend on its consequences. Using the categorical imperative, journalists have rationalized lying and using secret means to obtain the story on the grounds that *duty* justifies such conduct. For example, the journalist criticized by Janet Malcolm was attacked for lying to his source (who was in prison) about his motives for writing a book about the prisoner. His defence was that a journalist's duty to the 'truth' overrode all other ethical obligations.

Another approach values *consequence* in considering an ethical dilemma. It was argued that if the *result* of an action is for the greater good, it is ethically justified. The advantages for investigative journalism are quickly apparent. Using this approach requires consideration of the potential for 'pleasure' against the potential for 'pain'. It may be argued that this approach justifies any action, if no one gets hurt. For example, it would be ethically OK for a TV crew to set up a disreputable businessman, however dishonestly they obtained their information. Journalists aligning with this ethical position often find themselves accused of 'playing God' with people's lives.

Modern philosophers focus on ethical decision making as a balancing of competing values. Patterson and Wilkins argue that the core is a process for decision making:

> Thinking about ethics is a skill anyone can acquire. It first requires some background study of ethics. ... While each facet of mass communication has its own ethical quandaries, thinking about ethics is the same, whether you make your living writing advertising copy or obituaries. ...

> Thinking about ethics won't make those choices easier, but, with practice, ethical decision making can be more consistent. Ethics will then become not something you have, but something you do. (Patterson and Wilkins, 1994: 3, 4)

Consider a situation where a person you are interviewing says something they later regret and tells you so. Your problem arises because you know that what was said is timely, relevant and would be very interesting to your audience. You know your editor would want the information included and you know that the interviewee will be hurt if you do include it. You can do the 'right' thing by either your boss or your source, but either way you may feel uncomfortable with the consequences of your decision. The reason you will feel guilty is that loyalty is the strongest of all moral motivators. The work of a journalist is almost defined by conflicting loyalties. There are your loyalties as a person – to treat people with dignity and respect, to be truthful and open and not cause harm to them. There are professional loyalties – to write good journalism, to give your audience what they want, to become a better journalist, to stand up for the little guy, to make the world a better place. Then there are loyalties to the employer – to meet deadlines, to produce useable copy and to meet employer expectations. Finally, you consider loyalties to the media and its obligations to promote free speech, to uphold truth, to be a voice and mirror for society. The one constant, inescapable aspect of every ethical decision faced by a journalist is that there is never the opportunity to consign it to the 'too-hard' basket. When it comes to making a decision, the exits, as it were, are blocked. Even a decision to do nothing has consequences. Some journalists argue that their editors make the decisions, not them, so the individual's ethics are irrelevant.

> Yes, the editor wants you to do it. Yes, you're in a weak power position. Yes, there are others perfectly willing to do it if you don't. Yes, the adrenaline is pumping and yes, it's a great story. But an approach focused on the decision asks: How do you rise above the pressures? How do you do the ethical thing and minimize damage to your career? If you can't ethically write the story the editor wants, what story can you write? OK you'd be human to be weak in making the right choices, but that doesn't make faltering acceptable. (Sheridan Burns, 1996a: 95–6)

CHOOSING NEWS IN ACTION

While journalists are not always alone in making decisions about what will and will not reach the public eye, they always have a measure of control over the information they provide. Consider the scenario at the start of this chapter. As court reporter, you cover the court sessions as a matter of course. If you do not tell your editor about a case, the chances are that the story will not be published, unless other media are present. That is a lot of power, so you do need a system for making fair and reliable decisions. Bok (1978) argues that professional ethical decision making always revolves around two questions: 'What duties do I have, and to whom do I owe them?' and 'What values are reflected by the duties I've assumed?'

Consider the rest of the scenario. You cover the weekly sitting of the local court, and court reports are published in the paper. Company policy is that names are published without fear or favour. Internal policies like this are not unusual, especially in regional media where such everyday goings-on are a staple part of the content. Court reports are often popular with readers as they satisfy a desire to know what is going on in local people's private lives. The editor may contend that publishing court reports is always in the public interest. He might argue that the public needs to know if a schoolteacher drinks too much, because it could affect professional performance or behaviour. Information that a local mechanic has been charged with beating his wife is relevant news, because potential customers may need to know if he has a violent nature.

As a court reporter, you make decisions about what will and will not be reported dozens of times a day when court is in session. When you see a very prominent politician in court, your interest is piqued because reporting misconduct by a public official is in the public interest. When you make enquiries, you discover that the politician's 21-year-old son has been charged with common assault and assaulting a police officer. Again, you consider the public interest. You attend the hearing and learn that police were called when the politician's son became extremely agitated at a railway station when asked for his ticket. When police arrived, a scuffle broke out and a police officer suffered a broken nose. The court is told the 21 year-old is receiving treatment for a mental illness and his psychiatrist gives evidence that he was suffering a psychotic episode. The defendant appears to be calm and relaxed in the dock. The magistrate finds the offences proved but records no conviction and the son is released into the custody of his mother and psychiatrist.

DEFINING PUBLIC INTEREST

Sometimes helping a large number of people effectively means damaging other people. Will you choose to record what happens in the case before the magistrate? Is the reporting of this case warranted? Is it anyone's business to know he was arrested? Is your decision affected by the fact he was in a public place? Are people entitled to more privacy at home than in public? You might take the view that the politician's son gave up his right to privacy when he broke the policeman's nose. Consider how many others in court that day were charged with common assault. Are some people more entitled to privacy than others? To evaluate this, you need to consider the relative impact of publication. Is it more embarrassing for the politician's son to be in court than it is for any other citizen? Why? Does the politician's reputation in the community entitle her son to special consideration? Or is revealing mental illness in the politician's family in the public interest? Is it more interesting because the politician is a woman?

Would you consider omitting the story if you were satisfied if the son had a 'good' reason? Do you need to be satisfied that the son really is mentally ill? How much do you need to know about mental illness, if anything? On the one hand, no conviction has been recorded against the man, but on the other, this approach would seem to go against your professional responsibility to follow company policy. Can you absolve yourself of responsibility for harm caused by taking refuge in company policy and leaving it to others to decide? On what basis would you decide a reason is 'good' enough to make an exception? Would all cases be reviewed in that way or is the need to do so balanced against the scale of potential harm?

Is it in the public interest for the story to be published? You might certainly think that others would be as curious as you to know the circumstances of his arrest. You might consider that people are already gossiping about the issue and the 'truth' should be told. Is a *desire* to know the same as a *right* or *need* to know? What public interest might be served by reporting the incident? *Does* the public need to know? Will knowing this help them in the performance of their duty as citizens? What purpose is served by publishing the story? Depending on the priorities you assign to your loyalties, you may decide that this family's crisis is nobody's business and censor it, or you may decide that the public has a right to know anything that happens in the public domain. A third consideration is that responsible reporting of mental illness can be in the public interest because it aids community understanding and reduces stigma against people living with mental illness.

Before you can decide you must establish the extent to which the politician's public role is a news value in your deliberations. Is the son, by extension, also a public figure? The legal definition of a public figure varies around the world. In some countries, a person must earn a salary in a public role to be deemed a public figure. In other societies, anyone who occupies a position of privilege and whose activities are reported by the media is considered a public figure. By this definition, successful professional athletes are public figures because they are admired by a section of the community.

In assessing public interest in this case you would need to consider that the community might take a different view of the politician politically if they had a lower opinion of her personally. Is it fair to expose the politician to this harm over something her son has done? Is there a limit beyond which the politician may not be scrutinized? In a landmark Australian invasion of privacy case (*Ettinghausen v. HQ Magazine* 1995), a prominent footballer was awarded a record compensation payment after a magazine published a photograph of the player showering after a game. The footballer claimed that his privacy was invaded because his genitals were partly visible in a photograph taken without his knowledge. The magazine argued that the image was taken by a photographer who was authorized to be there, that the shot was not pornographic, and, significantly, that the footballer was also a male model who was often photographed wearing very little. What was important about the court's decision was that it found that the footballer retained control over how much of his body was private; in other words, that there is always a limit on a person's public role.

As part of the conversation you are having with yourself about reporting on the politician's son, ask: 'What would I do if the man charged was unknown?' If you answer that a crime such as assaulting police by an 'ordinary person' would not be news, then you have decided that the story's currency turns on the public prominence of the defendant's mother. If you are tempted not to publish because of the distress the story will cause to the politician's son, you must consider the extent to which you have considered mitigating factors for all the other people whose cases you will report.

MAKING ETHICAL DECISIONS

Bok proposes a three-step model for making the decision (see Figure 5.1). How do you *feel* about what you are considering doing? How would you feel if you were the son? You might feel sympathy for the man, or none at all, depending on any previous experience of him and what you know about mental illness. You might find yourself reflecting on all the people who asked for their names to be withheld and were refused in the past. Perhaps you have no opinion of the defendant, but you see the politician as fair game because of her position. Once the story has come to your attention, why should you treat her differently from all the other mothers of those in the dock?

Next you must ask yourself 'Is there another way to achieve my objective (publishing a report) without doing the contentious act (causing harm)?' In this particular scenario, this could mean publishing the story but not the names. Would this show favouritism towards a powerful person in the community? Would you not publish anything? What of the individual's right to privacy? You have the power to decide if the politician's son is an exception to the employer's policy because if you do not write the story it cannot be published. If you give priority to privacy, are you then meeting your obligations to your audience? How would you justify missing out on the story if confronted by an angry editor? Could any harm be done by *not* publishing the story? Perhaps other media were represented at the court that day. Will the decisions of the other journalists affect your decision? Could your publication be accused of favouritism if you do not run the story?

The final conversation you have with yourself begins 'How will my decision affect others?' In this case, your boss would probably say 'Politician's psycho son in rampage' is news and they may even want to move the court report from its usual page 21 to page 3. Readers might find some relief from the humdrum of their daily lives by speculating on parenting in high places. The politician may be thinking of her career and the damage it may do. She may feel very strongly that publicity would be unfair, when her son's conduct has nothing to do with her job. She may also feel protective towards her son and the attention her position brings.

1. Consult your conscience. How do you *feel* about the proposed act?
2. Is there another way to achieve your objective without doing the contentious act?
3. Conduct a discussion in your head with all parties, asking 'How will my decision affect others?'

Figure 5.1   Bok's model for decision making

The son presumably does not want his humiliation made public, but then probably neither do the other people in court that day. Will you exercise your power as a journalist to keep the news quiet? How will you decide who is 'good' enough to be protected? On the other hand, most people have heard about the incident anyway. It is a relatively small town so anyone who is interested knows already, so what harm would it do? The audience might accuse you of a cover-up if nothing appears, given the company policy, so as a professional can you take that risk?

As you consider the public interest, you must ask yourself, if reporting the case will achieve a greater understanding of mental illness by those who read it. Will it reduce or perpetuate stigma? Does it suggest the politician's son is violent? Is this justified?

Black et al. (1997: 61) propose 10 questions to guide the journalist through the decision-making process. Using this model (Figure 5.2) you would first ask yourself what you knew and needed to know. In this case, you know that matters discussed in a court of law are on public record and may be legally reported. Next, you consider your journalistic purpose. At one level, you have an obligation to truth-telling and to acting independently of influence. You also have an obligation to minimize harm and to be accountable for what you do. The potential for humiliating a fragile and vulnerable person and the possibility of public scorn being directed at him or his mother are real. There is also potential harm to the credibility of the paper if readers blame the journalists for highlighting his problems. Does the potential good done by truthfully telling this story outweigh the harm that might be caused?

So you consider the principles provided in the Journalists' Code of Ethics that applies to you (see Figure 2.1, pages 21–2). What guidance does it offer about intrusion,

1. What do I know? What do I need to know?
2. What is my journalistic purpose?
3. What are my ethical concerns?
4. What organizational policies and professional guidelines should I consider?
5. How can I include other people, with different perspectives and diverse ideas, in the decision-making process?
6. Who are the stakeholders – those affected by my decision? What are their motivations? Which are legitimate?
7. What if the roles were reversed? How would I feel if I were in the shoes of one of the stakeholders?
8. What are the possible consequences of my action? Short term? Long term?
9. What are my alternatives to maximize my truth-telling responsibility and minimize harm?
10. Can I clearly and fully justify my thinking and my decision? To my colleagues? To the stakeholders? To the public?

Figure 5.2   Black et al.'s (1997) 10 questions

reporting of mental illness and dealing with vulnerable people? What is your employer's policy on these matters? In this case, the paper usually offers a broad coverage of the matters to go before the court.

Next, seek other perspectives on the decision. Do you think there is a case to be argued for making this woman an exception? How would you make that case to your editor? Who else could you consult before approaching him?

Black et al. (1997) would suggest you then consider stakeholders' motivations. In this case there is the defendant and his mother the politician, the readers, the court, and the newspaper you work for. You might assume that the politician and her son wish the incident had never happened and fear negative publicity. The readers may have a demonstrably strong appetite for court reports but is this motivated by the desire to be a better-informed citizen? The newspaper may value consistency in its approach to reporting court cases but does this value justify causing harm? Ask yourself how you would feel if you were one of the stakeholders. If it was *your* illness or that of a close associate that came before the courts, you may not want people to know. You might feel very protective. Thinking as a reader, would you feel deprived of the juicy gossip? Would you feel angry at the paper if you felt sympathy for the son?

Consider the consequences. In the short term, your action will highlight the illness affecting the son and draw public attention to his condition. In the longer term, you might see a benefit in educating the public about the pervasiveness of mental illness in the community. However, the credibility of the paper may suffer if readers blame the newspaper for making the story public. What are your alternatives? Is there another way to tell the story truthfully that also minimizes harm? You might consider running the story without the name, but would it have the same news value? In this case, you might form the view that reporting the case sympathetically, including all the mitigating evidence, would minimize the chances of readers scorning the politician or her son. Finally, you must ask 'How can I justify my decision to the stakeholders?' If you use ethical principles as a guide and can articulate values in your decision-making process, you can ethically justify a decision even when others object.

Another model for ethical decision making applicable to journalism is The Potter Box (see Figure 5.3), named after the theologian who developed it. It uses values and principles defined by philosophers such as Aristotle, Kant and John Stuart Mill. According to The Potter Box, you must begin by deciding 'What are the facts?' In the case of the scenario described at the beginning of the chapter, the facts are that you are a journalist and it is your professional duty to report the local courts. Your employer values interesting stories, defined as those likely to attract readers. You know people would be interested in this case. There was no malice in your pursuit of this story and, in addition, fair and accurate reports of court proceedings are protected at law. Further, the charges are a matter of public record, but will you publish it to a wider audience?

Ask yourself: 'What values am I giving priority here?' Do you value telling the truth over any individual's privacy? Is the concept of justice more important than the rules? Is it professionally more important to be consistent or compassionate? Are the audience's interests always more important than those of the subject of a story? Do you

1. What are the facts?
2. What are the values given priority in your thinking?
3. Consider your principles.
4. Articulate the loyalties you are valuing.

Figure 5.3   The Potter Box

You are reporting cases at the local court. Company policy is that court reports are published without fear or favour. You are surprised to see a very prominent politician there and discover that the politician's 21-year-old son has been charged with common assault and assaulting a police officer. You attend the hearing and learn that police were called when the politician's son became extremely agitated at a railway station when asked for his ticket. When police arrived, a scuffle broke out and a police officer suffered a broken nose. The court is told the 21 year-old is receiving treatment for a psychotic illness and was frightened and deluded when approached by police. The court finds the offence is proven but no conviction is recorded. Will you report the story? If so, how? Are there limits on the public role of a public figure?

Would people be interested to know about this?
Why? Do people need to know about this? Do people have a legal right to know? Do people have a moral right to know? Who are the key stakeholders in this story?

No

Yes

Who are the characters in this story?
Are they private or public figures? Does their status make a difference to their right to privacy?

Why treat them differently?   Yes   No

What are the likely consequences of telling this story?
Consider each stakeholder, including the audience, and how each is affected by your decision? Is it positive or negative?

Yes

What duties do I have and to whom?
Which loyalties are most compelling?

No

continued

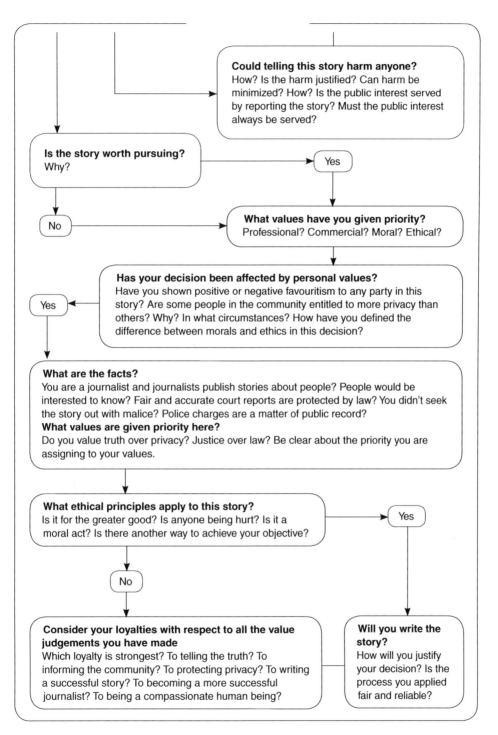

Figure 5.4 Choosing news in action

value writing a professional story over social obligations? In this case, you might decide that while you value truth-telling, you value justice more so the public interest is not served by truth-telling in this instance.

Now consider the ethical principles underpinning your practice. What purpose is served by publishing? Is anyone being hurt? Is telling this story for the greater good? What good does it do? How is the good achieved greater than the harm done? What is your primary motivation? Is it to advance your career as a journalist? Is it to raise an issue of community significance? Is it to treat all potential news subjects equally? If you decide that your ethical motivation is to treat everyone the same, it is a moral act to publish the story. You could argue that the politician's son is responsible for the consequences of his actions and you are simply fulfilling a professional duty to report. To make a decision, you must prioritize your loyalties with respect to all the value judgements you have made up to now. In this case you need to weigh up your loyalty to telling the truth, to informing the community, to protecting privacy, to writing a great story, to becoming a more successful journalist and to being a compassionate human being, for a start. Would you write the story of the politician's son?

One thing is certain: you cannot avoid making a decision. Some journalists consign such dilemmas to the 'too-hard' basket and try to shift the responsibility onto others. Such a journalist writes the story and leaves it to someone else to decide whether to publish. But even that journalist, who sees him or herself as 'just a cog in the wheel', decides on the angle the story will take, which parts of the evidence will reach the wider public and define their understanding of what has happened. There is no escaping the consequences of individual choices about news. How would you justify your decision to whichever party is unhappy with your decision? You need a process for evaluating your decisions because a process, or system, lets you apply your values, loyalties and principles to every new set of circumstances or facts. In this way, your decision making will be fair in choosing the news.

You might be thinking 'What about the editor?', but it is you who controls the words you use to tell the story, the points you emphasize, the extent to which you sensationalize. Your editor will have a great influence over what you write, but is unlikely to throw your copy back at you, claiming 'This is responsible, ethical copy. We don't print that stuff here.'

CONCLUSION

News is presented to audiences through a process that reflects the social and cultural context in which it is produced. There are certain professional processes used to choose some information as more newsworthy than other information. These are structured around public interest and the media's perceived mandate to give citizens information they need to participate in society. The choices made are not objective, but are the result of balancing competing professional, ethical and commercial values. In defining public interest, journalists seek to balance their power to set the agenda about what people talk about, and their obligation not to abuse that power for professional or commercial gain. Ethical decision-making systems, such as Bok's model and The Potter Box, offer a means for journalists to consider the social ramifications of their activities in choosing information as news.

FURTHER ACTION

1   How is a public figure defined in your society? What is the difference between a public figure and a celebrity? Do public figures have a greater or lesser right to privacy than other people?

2   What is the difference between the public interest and what the public is interested in?

3   When, if ever, is it in the public interest to censor information?

4   Is it in the public interest to publish information about everything that happens in public institutions such as Parliament and the courts?

FURTHER READING

Black, J., Steele, B. and Barney, R. (eds) (1997) *Doing Ethics in Journalism* (3rd edn). Boston, MA: Allyn & Bacon.

Malcolm, J. (1989) 'The journalist and the murderer', *The New Yorker*, March: 38–73.

Samaritans (UK) (2000) 'Guide to reporting of suicide and mental illness', www. samaritans.org.uk.

Sheridan Burns, L. (1996) 'Blocking the exits: focus on the decision in ethical decision-making', *Australian Journalism Review*, 18 (1): 87–99.

Sheridan Burns, L. and Hazell, P. (1997) *Response ... Ability: Curriculum Materials for Journalism*. National Youth Suicide Prevention Strategy, University Curriculum Project, Hunter Area Mental Health, Newcastle, www.responseability.org.au.

6

SOURCING NEWS

You're on Facebook and one of your friends reposts the news there has been a fiery crash and a young couple killed. Friends of the couple who were following in another car have now created a memorial Facebook page. You follow the link to the page and see the comments and photos of a young male sitting on the bonnet of a modified car with racing stripes and party photos of people drinking. You also read numerous posts, some commenting on the cause of the accident and some very critical of the deceased. Someone has posted a photo from the scene, showing the mangled wreck with visible bodies. How will you use this information now you have it?

For most people, the Internet is the first resort when searching for information, and journalists are no different. Web search engines offer speedy access to many traditional sources too, such as government departments, which post policy statements and archive media releases. In fact, the use of online services by journalists is becoming increasingly inevitable as more and more official documents are filed directly onto the Net. A great advantage of the Internet is that it offers fast results to specialized questions, much as the newspaper's own archives do. In this sense, the Internet gives reporters access to sources of information, both documents and human, that they would never have known existed before. Tapsall describes how journalists use the data they collect 'to add authority and weight to an existing story, or to generate new ideas and stories' (1998: 121). She also points to major problems in using electronic resources – reliable verification of information and assessing the authenticity of online sources are just two. This chapter considers the processes used by journalists to evaluate and verify sources used in reporting.

Journalists and the institutions they write for are finding Facebook to be an important resource in conducting the reporting that they do. Facebook is a means to connect to communities, to which they might not otherwise have access, to find leads and sources for their reporting. Many reporters have used their Facebook friends to help hone questions for interview subjects, to discover sources for articles which they didn't know existed, or to learn about issues or events that turn into full-blown stories. Timely topics can also bring together Facebook members on a fan page or group.

Reporters and media companies are also using Facebook to engage with their audience, connect with sources and build their brands.

The tension between the role of the traditional uninvolved reporter and the engaged social media user causes problems for journalists, social networks and news organizations alike. To be effective, the journalist needs to develop a relationship with sources whether the sources are real or virtual. It's no different as a user on a social networking site. There is an expectation that the community won't share with you the journalist unless you've shared (your experiences, your thoughts, your passions) with them. A journalist using Facebook professionally is expected not to be a detached observer, but be a participant who shares and gives back as well as taking. Because Facebook is about sharing, not broadcasting, journalists can't expect audiences to share their thoughts unless the journalists also openly share their own. Parachute social networking, in which journalists descend on a group related to a particular event (such as the Virginia Tech shootings), but to which the journalists have no previous relation, is seen by social media networks as 'parasite' behaviour.

Most news organizations realize how valuable social networking can be, both as a newsgathering tool and as a way to promote the news organization's 'brand'. But media companies must strike the difficult balance between these competing interests without stifling the exchange of ideas. Some are still uncomfortable with the personalization of the connection between journalists, sources and audiences. Some journalists too are concerned that joining a Facebook group could lead to their work being perceived as advocacy instead of journalism. For example, the *Wall Street Journal*'s policy on online activities states:

> Sharing your personal opinions, as well as expressing partisan political views, whether on Dow Jones sites or on the larger Web, could open us to criticism that we have biases and could make a reporter ineligible to cover topics in the future for Dow Jones. (Lasica, 2009)

The *Journal* also counsels its reporters not to discuss articles that haven't been published, meetings attended or planned with staff or sources, or interviews conducted. Betancourt (2009) posits that this approach reflects the misguided persistence of the notion that reporters are blank slates, which in turn is part of the reason newspapers are losing readership and relevance in the digital age.

EVALUATING NEWS SOURCES

Mencher argues that journalists have a tendency 'to venerate the printed word, no matter what its source, perhaps because the journalist spends his or her life so close to words on paper' (1991: 287). Journalists are often less rigourous in assessing physical sources than they are in assessing human ones.

To evaluate a physical source, you first need to be satisfied that it is accurate. Just because information is contained in a book or on a website, for example, does not mean it is accurate. Journalists should always consider the date of publication in assessing the currency of information. Textbooks written in the 1960s, for example, often portray a different picture of social history from those written more recently. The publication and author may be reputable, but the writer's views may have changed over time. Any other influences on sources must be identified and considered. Paletz and Entman (1982) found that where the primary objective of a media organization was efficiency in the gathering, describing and transmitting of news, the result was reliance on official sources and homogeneity of reporting. McManus (1994) offers a simple explanation for this global trend – it is cheaper to rely on other news providers, such as wire services, and on media releases to learn of community events and issues than it is to hire enough journalists to find stories on their own. Such passive journalism, McManus argues, creates the potential for the public agenda to be set by those in the community powerful enough to hire press agents and manufacture events:

> Reliance on news sources – and this extends to broadcast media in the form of radio 'grabs' and video news releases – can also be manipulated to affect the news agenda in a way journalists seem unable, or unwilling to resist. (McManus, 1994: 88)

Electronic news sources, such as the Internet, databases and news groups are very attractive to journalists due to the speed with which information can be accessed and disseminated. Online 'databases' place an enormous amount of specific information at the command of the reporter or writer. The information on these databases would take months to search manually, but a computer search program that allows a search to be specifically refined can cover the accumulated literature in almost any field in minutes. Koch argues new technologies, which he defines as online or electronic databases, will:

> force a re-evaluation of the relation between 'official' expert and passive reporter or publicist while breaking down within news or public information agencies those bailiwicks of individual expertise – 'beats' – that have traditionally defined and limited the topical responsibilities of individual writers. (Koch, 1990: xxiv)

Koch takes a positive view of the role of online technologies in the future of journalism. He argues that with the Internet and other technology for storing information, the context of newsroom is broader than ever before:

> They are empowered to examine, discuss, or focus a story through intelligent questioning based on a large background of objective information. Writers, in short, have the opportunity, if not independently to set the general agenda, then at least to modify it, and in the process to become the gatekeepers of their own stories – wherever they may lead. The electronically generated, informational background allows the newsperson, advocate, public relations writer, or interested citizen to access a context greater than that ordained by a partisan but necessary source or subject. (Koch, 1990: 312)

Koch describes a bright future for journalists newly empowered by the freedom to engage with as many sources as they choose. He hopes that these journalists will ask more challenging questions because they will have more background information at their disposal. He argues that this will improve the quality of journalism and the self-esteem of those who practise it. He also acknowledges that there is some resistance among journalists and editors, who see archival research as too time-consuming to be worthwhile.

Online sources such as the Internet are also often fraught with risks. The same freedom of access that means anyone can post information on the Net means that those who do are not subject to regulation about the accuracy of their information. In a recent case, the National Rifle Association (NRA) of the USA posted information on its website stating there had been a 30 per cent increase in gun-related crime in Australia since the introduction of tough gun laws. These statistics, which are stated as fact, are not supported by the data collected by the Australian Bureau of Crime Research and Statistics. A journalist who accepted the NRA figures over those of the statutory body would be hard pressed to verify the information even if the NRA was a credible source. White says this difficulty in verifying information is a real danger. She cautions: 'You still have to ask yourself what is the authority of this information, how up to date is it, and to what extent can I take it at face value?' (White, 1992: 17)

Lack of regulation on the Internet also means that authors do not go through the same legal scrutiny as those working for commercial or government media organizations. The website *The Drudge Report* broke the story of US President Clinton's affair with Monica Lewinsky, after which it was in the public domain. Information published on the Net may also be actionable, wherever in the world it is accessed. Something posted on a US website may be legal in that country, but defamatory if accessed in another country:

> The Internet provides a virtual community in which people can develop a reputation that others can damage. This is in addition to the real community in which they live and work. ... With publication on the Internet, people throughout the world see, read or hear material, which means defamation action could arise in each jurisdiction where information is posted or accessed. (Breit, 1998: 132)

Koch (1990) and others have argued these new technologies provide an opportunity for journalists to create a context in which relatively 'objective' journalism becomes the norm. This potential will not, however, change the forces of media management in corporate and government sectors, which will probably continue to influence the public agenda, and proprietors may still seek to put profit over public interest.

USING SOCIAL MEDIA SOURCES

Social media sites such as Facebook and Twitter allow individuals to share their thoughts and experiences with others in a virtual community where information is easily downloaded and/or shared. While this information is openly available, it is not usually intended for media scrutiny. The extra ethical dilemma is that it allows a journalist to collect first-person information from a source without the source's knowledge. Martin Hirst (2010) provides a 2010 example:

> An Auckland-based newspaper provided a good example of this issue and a remarkably frank account of how it staff had access to a woman's Facebook page through first contacting one of her online friends and then used posted photos and comments made online to track down her physical address. Then, using Google maps, the paper was able to direct a reporter and photographer to her home. The paper claimed that by cross-referencing online sources it had 'put our people on the woman's doorstep'. What's missing here is any indication that the paper's reporters and editors had considered any ethical implications of what they were doing. That Facebook's privacy settings allow users to leapfrog through one person to another is claimed as a justification rather than a problem. There is no reflexive consideration that the paper itself is breaching someone's privacy and trust in pursuit of the story just to claim that the paper had done it before. (Hirst, 2010: 140)

Many social media commentators and users describe this practice as journalists being 'vultures'. Outspoken critic Laurel Papworth argues that while social media users expect their posts to be discussed within their networks, they don't expect to see them in the context of mainstream media. She warns that journalists can't hide behind the anonymity of their organizations any more:

> If journalists take our content and broadcast our stories beyond our usual personal audience, we will take actions that they won't see as being ethical, without even realising it. Namely, naming, shaming, discussing, dissecting, offering up gossipy tidbits, dredging up the past, suggesting mutual contacts of the journalist. After all, if our private information, discussed in our social network (with no thought for the Invisible Audience) ends up on the front page of the *Sydney Morning Herald*, then why should the journalist remain safe from prying eyes? (Papworth, 2009)

In an online social sphere, where it can be unclear whether the profile online is truly that person, identity is key. If a journalist does decide to access social media sites for information, it is important to verify those sources are who they say they are. Fact-checking information from social networking sites is also critical. Facebook can a great source for story ideas, but no news story should be solely sourced through social media. Journalists should be upfront that they are members of the media, provide their real name and real affiliation – and the fact that they are gathering news for publication. It is not enough to assume that the people they are dealing with recognize this, especially if the source is a young person or someone not accustomed to dealing with the media. If at all possible, interview the person either by phone or face-to-face.

It is so easy to lie on the Internet, and to misrepresent oneself. No journalist wants to spread falsehoods or be taken in by a hoax. So if you are thinking of using an online source, you still must verify facts and satisfy yourself that the source is genuine. As with all other sources, you must be as certain as you can be that the information you are providing is truthful and accurate, and make the source very clear. You should always disclose that Facebook was used as a source.

McAdams (2011) cautions that you should always bear in mind that what you reveal about yourself on Facebook can be accessed and used by others. There is no way to truly separate your opinions from your role as a journalist and what you say as an individual may be seen as evidence of bias in your work. If you 'friend' an unnamed source on Facebook, you are breaking confidentiality. Be very careful about using images and content from sites such as Facebook and don't jump to conclusions about what you see and read. If you can't verify it, you run the risk of spreading lies.

> Here's an example of something you might think would never happen in a top-class newsroom: *New York Times* Executive Editor Bill Keller wanted to keep his staff in the loop about planning for a pay wall. At a meeting, though, several reporters tweeted what he said. They spilled the beans, which were quickly picked up by a myriad of blogs and other news organizations. What he said became a story, and then a subsequent chiding of the staff for tweeting led to more stories. Now the ground rules are clear at meetings. Reporters are expected not to tweet private deliberations. (McAdams, 2011: 16)

Twitter is also free to use, unfiltered, and offers access to many different voices and perspectives. It can democratize news selection because the followers determine the trending topics, albeit usually generated in mainstream media. It can be a great source of eyewitness accounts and to source other information on a topic. Because it is unfiltered, using Twitter as a source carries inherent risks. Verification is the most significant as Twitter can easily be used to spread gossip and rumours, especially at times of breaking news. Because people use pseudonyms, there are issues of verifying identity and associated questions around fake accounts and accountability.

Journalists use Twitter to engage with their audience, connect with sources and continue building their personal brands (Betancourt, 2009). Some journalists use Twitter to develop a personal brand that enhances their professional reputation and to source stories by 'crowd sourcing' ideas. Crowd sourcing occurs when a journalist puts a question to followers and uses the feedback to develop a story.

Journalists need to be familiar with Twitter and Facebook because they are important tools, but should always be aware that they represent more than a personal opinion. Anything a journalist Tweets may be taken directions not intended by the writer and a journalist is vulnerable to to criticism for swapping objectivity for advocacy. Employers will hold journalists accountable for what they say on Twitter and some impose conditions on its use by staff. The American Society of News Editors released a set of guidelines for working with social media (see Figure 6.1). *The Washington Post* created its own social media policy after they were asked about it. When it comes to Twittering for *The Post*, reporters are required to inform senior editors beforehand if they plan to use Twitter or otherwise live-blog something.

> *The Post* insists that reporters don't use Twitter to pursue arguments with rivals or advance personal agendas. While there are lots of tools for doing journalism with Twitter, remember to keep perspective in the Twitterverse. Just because a news story is big on the microblogging site, doesn't always necessarily mean it is offline. Nor does it replace one-on-one engagement with sources. Like email and the telephone before it, social media is the latest change in how people are connecting and communicating. But the change is purely tactical; the standards and values of journalism don't change. (Betancourt, 2009)

USING NEWS SOURCES IN ACTION

In the scenario given at the start of this chapter, you must first decide if the facts 'stack up' to suggest a bigger story. As explored in Chapter 4, you decide the news value of the story idea. Is reporting the story in the public interest? Here you might consider the public's right to know about dangers on the road. Could anyone be harmed if the story is true and you do not write about it? Could anyone be harmed if you do write the story? Is preventing road deaths among young people worth the pain it might cause the families and friends of the dead.

If you decide to continue, you need next to establish your facts and how you know them. For this, you need evidence such whether speed was a factor. You also need to get some background on what has already been reported about the issue and verify any of this information you choose to use.

When you consult the social sources available to you, you find a range of comments about the two people killed. On the memorial page, there are many photographs of the couple, including many of the dead man sitting on the hood of a car with racing stripes. The man is shirtless and has numerous tattoos and sits with his arms folded. There are also smiling images of the couple together and candid photos from parties where people are seen to be drinking. You can easily save these images to your own computer. Will you use these images for publication? If so, how will you choose which ones to use? Will you use the image of the wreck? Should you ask those who posted the images for permission? What will be the impact of the images you choose on the interpretation of the events?

It is natural for people to seek an explanation following an unexpected death and the media can serve an important public function in this regard. In this instance, the community may have a strong interest in and perceived entitlement to information about the death. On the other hand, can a news report provide the answers the community is looking for? Can the comments of bystanders provide real insight into the dead man's state of mind? What harm could be done by reporting speculation?

Based on comments on the Facebook memorial page, the journalist may be tempted to speculate that the deaths were caused by drag-racing. Can this inference be justified? How do you know speed was a factor? Although journalists may be keen to explain to people why a needless death has occurred, they should consider if such speculation is in the public interest. For example, community attitudes towards death caused by speeding range from 'the ultimate selfish act' to 'a tragedy of circumstances''. Such opinions and attitudes would be circulating via social media in response to the death and it may be tempting for the journalist to tap into this 'community tide'.

The information that is available via social media should be considered carefully. While this information is available publicly, the sources via Twitter and other social media platforms are anonymous, with their contributions character-limited and highly subjective. How might character limits on communication impact the information that is received? How might anonymity shape the way information is communicated? People gathering at the site may not be emotionally touched by the death so much as by the hype and likely media frenzy associated with it, and may wish to appear to know more about the events than they really do.

The difficulty for the journalist is that the status of the 'observer' and their proximity to the event is difficult to determine via social media. What steps should the journalist take to establish the credibility of sources and verify the information received? While publicly available, consent for publication or use of the content has not been obtained. In all, you have a wire report (Figure 6.2), comments posted on Facebook (Figures 6.3 and 6.4) and two media releases (Figures 6.5 and 6.6).

To evaluate this material you ask a series of questions of each separate piece of information. Tapsall (1998) calls this 'interviewing' the information. The first question is: **'What's the angle of this story?'** The stories in your file have very different angles. For example, the Facebook comments (Figures 6.3 and 6.4) focus on the emotional distress of the situation. This is in contrast to the report quoting police (Figure 6.2), which appear to provide facts. Is emotionally-based information less reliable? Why? Next consider how the angle has been developed. Is it in the 'facts' or is it in the way the journalist has organized the facts? Is the emotional strength of the copy in the quotes selected or is it in the words used by the journalist? Whose perspective is the story told from? What news values underpin this story? Relative news values are explored in Chapters 4 and 5. Will you track down and speak with the people who posted the comments and photos? In this way you evaluate the information as if you got it in an interview. Can you use the information without speaking to the source because it is in the public domain? The Facebook site clearly identifies the name and other personal details about the dead couple. Do you need to check this information before you use it? Can the people who posted the comments expect to control how they are used?

How will you check that the Facebook users are who they say they are? Have you noted any errors of fact in the published reports? Consider if relevant information is missing from any of the accounts. Are the Facebook allegations substantiated? Is the Facebook group a credible source of facts in the matter? Figures 6.3 and 6.4 provide plenty of opinion but scant 'fact'. Is there a way you can check the comments for accuracy, for example the one suggesting he had been charged with driving offences?

1. Traditional ethics rules still apply online.
2. Assume everything you write online will become public.
3. Use social media to engage with readers, but professionally.
4. Break news on your website, not on Twitter.
5. Beware of perceptions.
6. Independently authenticate anything found on a social networking site.
7. Always identify yourself as a journalist.
8. Social networks are tools, not toys.
9. Be transparent and admit when you're wrong online.
10. Keep internal deliberations confidential.

Figure 6.1   Using social media as a source (American Society of News Editors (ASNE), 2011)

CAPITAL CITY: Two people have been killed when their car went over an embankment and plunged into the Georges River early this morning.

The couple, who have not been identified, were out with friends who were following in another vehicle and raised the alarm.

Police said investigations were continuing as to how the couple's car left the road at the popular drag-racing spot.

Police spokesman Greg Good said it was tragic when young people's lives were lost through recklessness.

Figure 6.2   dragdeaths/blame/smith 22/6

OMG. You were one of the greats, Speedy. Race on.

Speedy UR a legend, mate.

I heard he cracked 160 and the car flew over 50 metres before they hit the water!

Speedy and Rachel – together forever flying the freeway.

RIP Speedy and Rach – live fast, die young.

Speedy was an idiot and now he's killed Rachel. I'm glad he's dead.

Get a life. Roll on Speedy – they'll never take your licence now!

Figure 6.3   Selected comments on Facebook

Name: Speedy

Age: 19

Sex: As much as I can get …

Status: 'Get your motor running, head out on the highway. Looking for adventure and whatever comes my way …like a true nature's child I was born, born to wild' (Steppenwolf)

I Like:

https://www.streetracing.org

https://www.youtube.com/watch?v=1ylQKgx4Ls

Figure 6.4   Facebook profile page

Ban performance cars, says MP

The Federal Member for the West, Mr John Silver, has called for performance cars to banned for young drivers after a couple died last week.

'People under 40 don't need access to powerful cars and banning them will save lives', he said.

'The previous government failed utterly to stop the roads being taken over by hooligans with cars. It is time we stepped in.'

Mr Silver said he blamed poor infrastructure in the West and high unemployment on the rise in driving offences being recorded against young people in his electorate.

Figure 6.5   Media release

Performance Cars 'not dangerous'

Performance cars are a great hobby, that bring fathers and sons together for quality time, according to the president of the Capital City Performance Car Club.

'Our club, which has lost a valuable member, would never condone drag racing,' he said.

'There's nothing we can do about young idiots giving performance cars a bad name. The girls are as crazy as the boys these days.'

'We urge all drivers of performance cars to obey the speed limit at all times. There is no proof the young man killed was speeding.'

Figure 6.6   Media release

Next you must consider the source of this article and whether one may be an agenda at work. In the case of Figures 6.5 and 6.6, you might note that the media releases are written in the style of news stories, complete with an angle. Given that journalists need an angle for everything they write, there is a strong temptation for them to repeat an angle provided by a public relations department if it has a relevant news value. Media releases are always written in the hope that the journalist will simply repeat the information contained within. The journalist must resist this temptation because a media release may, in its wording, make an apparently plausible argument for two plus two to equal five. What might motivate the Federal Minister to contact the media (Figure 6.5)? As a politician, his general political priorities are served by casting the government in a good light. He has a personal professional motive as well, in that his public profile is raised when he is quoted in the media. On the other hand, he is an elected official, charged with a mandate to comment on issues of public interest. What of the media release from the car club (Figure 6.6)? Is this an unbiased source of information because it is removed from the actual events? Does the fact that the source appears to be remote from the local story lessen the likelihood of another agenda?

CRITICAL REFLECTION

Before you can resolve the dilemma posed at the start of this chapter, you must evaluate what you do and do not know. Is there a *prima facie* case for a story about the dangers of speeding? Where did the information originate? Is it possible to track the sources of these stories? In the case of the media releases, the source is apparent, but what of the information published in social media? Consider the information you have. Is there any information you must discard? Why? Is there any relevant information missing? If so, do you need to find the missing information before you can make an informed decision about whether there is a story? How will you do that? Consider if all the information is relevant to your story. The politician's view of the government may be dramatic (see Figure 6.5) but does it add to the understanding of the issue? To answer this question, consider your research as a whole. What central issue emerges? Can you substantiate it? Are you sure of your facts? Before you go any further, ask yourself if you have identified a hero or a villain. Could the story harm anyone? Is the potential for harm justified by the public interest?

> *You're on Facebook and one of your friends reposts the news there has been a fiery crash and a young couple killed. Friends of the couple who were following in another car have now created a memorial Facebook page. You follow the link to the page and see the comments and photos of a young male sitting on the bonnet of a modified car with racing stripes and party photos of people drinking. You also read numerous posts, some commenting on the cause of the accident and some very critical of the deceased. Someone has posted a photo from the scene, showing the mangled wreck with visible bodies. How will you use this information now you have it?*

continued

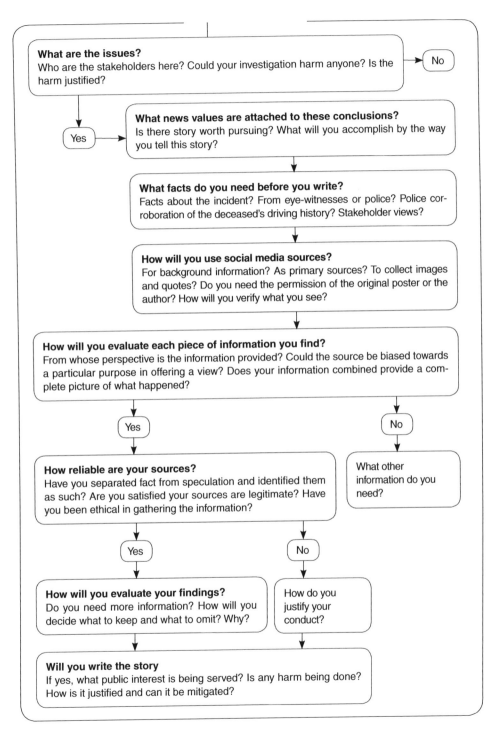

Figure 6.7   Evaluating sources in action

CONCLUSION

Physical news sources must be interrogated in the same way journalists scrutinize information provided by people. It is easier to fall into accepting published material as fact, even when journalists well know that constructing journalism is a subjective process. Technological changes mean that journalists are exposed to more sources of news than ever before, which creates a great potential for freedom of information but the freedom is constrained by other sources. With changes in information technology have come information managers, whose job is to manipulate the way journalists access their sources and evaluate information. The information selection process used in writing news is explored further in Chapter 8.

FURTHER ACTION

1   Read your local newspaper and consider which stories have come from media releases. Is there a product or service advertised in the story?

2   Take a published news story and use Internet search engines to substantiate the facts in the story.

3   Take a tour of Facebook pages you can access. Is there material publicly available that the owner may not wish to see in the media? How many pages have adequate privacy settings?

4   Consider your own Facebook page. Is its content a source of facts or speculation? How would a reader know?

5   Find published reports that quote politicians. Can you determine whether the politician instigated the contact with the media?

FURTHER READING

Tapsall, S. (1998) 'Spreadsheets and databases', in S. Quinn (ed.), *Newsgathering on the Net*. Winchelsea, Vic.: Precision Press.

Tapsall, S. and Varley, C. (2001) *Journalism: Theory in Practice*. Sydney: Oxford University Press.

Underwood, D. (1993) *When MBAs Rule the Newsroom: How Markets and Managers are Shaping Today's Media*. New York: Columbia University Press.

7

GATHERING NEWS

You receive a tip that a prominent Indigenous footballer has been found hanged at the city's Dreamtime Cultural Centre and that suicide is suspected. Interviews are conducted at the scene and the outside the home of the grieving family. What are the boundaries in reporting about death and grief? When is it in the public interest to report on suicide?

When a journalist sets out to 'cover' a story, the aim is to gather the information required to write an accurate and meaningful story. Sources of information available to a journalist are *primary* first-hand information gathered by the journalist, and *secondary* information gathered from archival research. Archival research refers to library research, searches on the Internet, searches of media archives and the use of other information in the public record. Secondary sources are explored in detail in Chapter 5. This chapter focuses on interviews, although journalists sometimes conduct primary research by recording their own observations. Through considering the scenario set out above, a methodology is revealed for evaluating primary research and critically reflecting on the inclusion and omission of information.

INTERVIEWS AS A PRIMARY SOURCE

The interview allows a journalist quickly to obtain answers to specific questions on a topic previously unknown to him or her. For example, if the government issues a 400-page report on an issue, a news journalist realistically is unlikely to have the time to read and digest that report and meet a deadline in two hours. Unless the journalist has some expertise in that area, they are not the best person to comment on the meaning of the report, because it would be a personal interpretation and lack authority. So the journalist calls a person who has some authority to speak in that area and asks them specific questions deemed to be of interest to the intended audience. Interviews allow you to gather information quickly and directly from primary sources.

You can also ask questions of an interviewee you cannot ask a document. Even on the phone, you can draw inferences from non-verbal clues, like the person's demeanour. Face-to-face, their body language helps your understanding of what they are really saying to you. In an interview, you can press your subject for more information on specific points and find, through previous answers, new areas of discussion.

The interview is also preferred by news organizations as a primary source of information because it is considered to be the most up to date. Interviews are also considered a livelier approach than the restating of information found in a document. In broadcast journalism, a variety of voices is considered essential to an interesting news bulletin, and the use of interviews reinforces the idea among news consumers that the information received is 'the facts'. Credibility is assigned to the person doing the talking, rather than the journalist. Twenty-five years ago, when media consumers were less sophisticated in their understanding of news gathering, stories routinely appeared without attribution for the information within and also without an acknowledgment of the fact that it was written by a journalist. In those days, it was considered that these were 'facts', so no attribution was required. Today the expression 'it was in the paper so it must be true' is more likely to be a cynical reflection on the accuracy of media reports.

The questions that a journalist asks in an interview are a reflection of his or her objective in conducting the interview. For example, the questions asked by a journalist doing an *informational* interview would include 'What happened?', 'How did it happen?', 'Who was involved?', 'Where did it happen?' and 'When did it happen?' An *investigative* interview seeks to find out more than *what* happened. These questions might revolve around 'Why was this permitted?', 'Who is responsible?', 'What will be done now?', 'What does this mean for the future?' and 'When was it realized that this had happened?' If a journalist is seeking *background information*, the questions would include 'What usually happens?', 'Why is that?' and 'What is the effect?' Similarly, if the journalist is seeking to *interpret information* received, then the questions will likely include 'What will this mean?', 'Who is affected?' and 'How will things change?' Finally, there are *personal* interviews, in which a journalist seeks to obtain anecdotes or opinions from an interviewee to illustrate their character.

Brady (1977: 68) says journalists' interviews seek only two things – trust and information – and the first is sought only to gain the second. Journalists need the trust of the people they interview so the interviewee will be comfortable answering the questions asked and respond honestly. The journalist then decides whether to believe what he or she has been told. Although journalists use interviews to gain first-hand information, there are limitations on the interview as a reliable source of 'facts'. Mencher reminds journalists that they can never be sure if the information they collect from people is accurate:

> The reporter must keep in mind that he or she is relying on someone else, and that fact alone makes the story vulnerable. No reporter can ever feel certain that another person's observations are as accurate as his own or that the person lacks bias or self-interest. (Mencher, 1991: 285)

In other words, a journalist never knows what the interviewee *thinks*, only what the interviewee *says*. So interviews can be a potentially misleading source of 'facts' if it is assumed that the person providing information is being completely truthful.

Interviewees can have their own agendas. The interviewee may want to put the best, or worst, face on the 'facts', or may hope to steer the line of enquiry away from its current direction. For this reason, a journalist collecting information through an interview should always employ a degree of scepticism. This means you should listen closely for things that do not gel with what you already 'understand', and then question those things. The interview is an exchange between people, each filtering what they hear and understand through their own perceptions and experience. Everybody has their own truth, and when we exchange information with one another, we inevitably make assumptions about things that are already 'known'. An interview subject may provide inaccurate information without malicious intent. The same applies to the pre-existing perceptions of journalists, which affect what they think, see, hear and understand. Mencher (1991) describes a famous experiment in which journalism students were found to make more errors when they wrote stories about a report that was contrary to their own biases and predispositions than they did when the report supported their pre-existing feelings.

The interview is also often maligned by its subjects, who routinely accuse journalists of misquoting them, of distorting the information provided and of 'getting it wrong'. This can happen without any malice on the part of the journalist, not least because when you ask a person to tell you the 'facts' about something, you are really asking them to make a subjective assessment of the truth in the light of your own assessment. You then assess what you have been told and what you think it means. It is relatively easy for the reporter and source to unwittingly combine to distort the truth. Time is often the problem because journalists are always working to a rigid, specified deadline. You could go to the editor and say 'I can't get everything I need straight away, so I'll need more time to do this story justice', but more often than not the response will be 'Then give me what you've got'. Yesterday's news is yesterday's news and if the story is hot now, the pressure will be on to report on it *now*, whatever the complications. So the journalists compromise and reason that if they get two interviews, one from each 'side', and throw in a bit of background they have a story. This common approach is flawed because we all listen and retain information selectively: one plus one can equal three. It is easy, especially when you have already decided, as an experienced journalist does, what your story will cover before you do your interviews. Interviews are not a case of 'Tell me all about it, I'll consider it all and then write something'. It is 'Here's my story, now can I get some quotes?' The more people you speak to, the more perspectives you seek on an issue, the less likely you are to be misled or simply get it wrong.

Use of too few sources is another common complaint levelled against the interview as a news source. An issue may be quite complex and yet, in the telling, the issue is polarized. Attributed quotes are used to articulate those two positions only. Sometimes the story raises an issue and only seeks one perspective, which supports the assertion expressed by the journalist in the opening sentence. Some news organizations actually embrace this approach, with the view that 'We'll put this point of view today and when there's a huge uproar from the other side, we'll get another story out of this issue for tomorrow'.

There are other forms of distortion of information. The greatest of these is silence, the things the interviewee *didn't* say, the questions the reporter *didn't* ask. Leaving part of the story uncovered by the interview gets journalists into trouble all the time, particularly when the reporter falls back on assumptions. Distortions can also be caused by pressing a person for information they do not have, or cannot adequately articulate, or by seeking elaboration of information the subject has told you they cannot clearly recall.

You can also distort the information gained from an interview by asking leading questions. The way questions are phrased is likely to direct the answer received. In an episode of his 1985 TV comedy series *Yes Prime Minister*, writer John Mortimer neatly illustrates the problem with leading questions. In the story, the government decides to implement a survey to establish whether the general public would support the reintroduction of a period of compulsory Army service for young people. A bureaucrat demonstrates for the politician the way questions may be manipulated to achieve different results. The first group of questions goes like this:

1   'Are you worried about the number of young people without jobs?'

2   'Are you worried about the rise in crime among teenagers?'

3   'Do you think young people welcome some discipline and direction in their lives?'

4   'Do you think they respond to a challenge?'

5   'Would you be in favour of reintroducing conscription?'

The second group of questions takes a different perspective:

1   'Are you worried about the danger of war?'

2   'Are you worried about the growth of arms?'

3   'Do you think it is wrong to force people to take up arms against their will?'

4   'Do you think there is a danger in giving young unemployed people guns and teaching them how to kill?'

5   'Would you oppose the reintroduction of conscription?'

Mencher (1991) found that people are often less reliable than physical sources. It has been empirically proven that people often respond to questions by looking for clues within that point to the 'right' answer. It has also been demonstrated that some people pretend to know an answer, rather than admit ignorance. Lastly, some people's answers are distorted by vested interests.

You can control the questions you ask, but how can you tell if you are being misled? That is where the use of healthy cynicism comes in. Ask yourself: 'Could this person have an ulterior motive?', 'Could this person be telling me what they *think* I want to hear?', 'Is there a reason why this person might distort this information?' and 'Does this person know what he is talking about?' It is not necessary to openly challenge everything you are told, but as a journalist you are legally liable for everything you write. To claim that 'A policeman told me it was true' is no defence at law for publishing something that is untrue. As a journalist, all sorts of people will tell you all sorts of things, but ultimately you will control how much credibility is assigned to their information and whether it should be published to a wider audience.

The final thing to consider is the context in which the interview takes place. Protocols for seeking information differ across cultures. Journalists have no right to impose themselves on interviewees and should treat them with respect. After all, the interviewee is helping the journalist with information he or she could just as easily keep to him or herself. Consider the state of mind of the person you are interviewing, especially if he or she is upset or grieving. People in an emotional state of mind may express views that do not reflect what they think when they are clear-headed, as can people who are affected by alcohol or drugs.

Once you have collected the information you need to test it for fact. A source may tell you that something happened in 1999, when in fact it happened in 1998. That person is not lying to you, simply mistaken, but that will not help you to explain how you came to publish something that is clearly incorrect. You should seek to verify the information provided by primary sources as 'fact'.

GATHERING NEWS IN ACTION

Given that prominence and human interest are important news values, it is fairly certain that your audience would want to know what has happened in the scenario outlined at the beginning of the chapter. Still, you need to have an internal conversation about how much the public has a 'right' to know. You need to evaluate your information, particularly with respect to interviewees' credibility. As you consider this, you should also consider the impact of highlighting drama, violence or sensationalism in the reporting of death or grief, particularly after a suicide. Before you write the story, you need to decide if some facts should never be reported.

The first questions you ask yourself are: **'Would people be interested to know this?'** and **'What news values are attached to this conclusion?'** In reaching a decision, you would consider that the event occurred in the local community and the deceased is known to the audience and his misfortune is likely to attract public attention. You would reflect on the background information that the dead man's family has lost other members to suicide, adding a tragic element to the family's story. Finally, you might take the view that the suicide of a young person with seemingly every advantage is a question of public interest that may enlighten people about the problem of youth suicide.

Interviews are the most active research a journalist can do, whether the interview happens on the phone or face-to-face. Because it is an exchange between two or more people, the reporter's individual response to the interviewee affects the credibility he or she assigns to information gained from the interview. The first related question to ask of the scenario at the start of this chapter is **'How do I choose interviewees?'**

Consider whether the potential interviewees have first-hand experience. Could the interviewees provide quotes that will enhance the reader's understanding? You must also be satisfied that the interviewees can provide an authoritative perspective, because publishing their comments will make them appear credible. Next, consider the question '**What do I expect to get from the interviewees?**' In this case, the reporter might reasonably expect the police at the scene to provide verified facts about the discovery of the body. The boys at the scene might be able to provide first-hand information about the circumstances of the discovery, and the reporter might seek to interview the boy's parents or friends to see if they can provide any insight into the dead youth's state of mind. Before starting the interviews, you must also decide '**What facts do I need to tell the story?**' Consider the story in terms of *who*, *what*, *when*, *where*, *why* and *how*. Do you need answers to all of these questions for your story to be complete and meaningful? Do you need to find out *why* it happened? Is it possible for you to do that with confidence?

In this case, the reporter first speaks to police at the scene where the body was found. The policeman is affable and cooperative. He confirms the identity of the dead man and the time the body was discovered. He also tells you that he smelt alcohol on the dead man. He tells you that several other members of the large family have committed suicide. Off the record, he tells you the family is dysfunctional and the footballer was the only one to 'make good'.

You and your colleague also attempt to speak to an Indigenous official at the scene but are refused entry. Outside, you see two young men hanging around waiting to be interviewed by police. The boys tell you they found the body, but do not seem to be upset. They are happy to answer questions and ask if their names will be in the paper. They seem to be enjoying the attention.

You go to the deceased's home to speak to the parents. You are met in the driveway by a man who tells you the man's mother is too upset to be interviewed. You can hear weeping coming from inside the house. The man agrees to give you a short statement, after which you ask some questions. Because the deceased is a well-known footballer, you also seek out his coach for comment. The notes from the interviews are given in Figures 7.1–7.5.

Before you write a single word in this story, you must first evaluate the information collected by asking '**How reliable are my sources?**' The information from the interviews ranges from factual statements about the time and place of death to personal opinions about the motivation of the dead man. The process for assessing the reliability of your sources calls for a new series of questions, starting with '**Did all the interviewees seem competent to answer?**' The answer to this question is particularly significant when reporting on grief. Could you be causing unnecessary harm by publishing something said under duress? People in the first throes of grief are often prescribed drugs to help them cope, which affect a person's perceptions. A person may be confused in his or her thinking but still able to answer questions. People might like to know, for curiosity's sake, how the dead man's mother is feeling, but do they *need* to know, and is the harm you could potentially do justified? In attempting to get information, you encounter hostility from Indigenous officials. Is the rudeness you experience part of the story? Why? What is the significance, if any, of this encounter?

At approximately 3pm today, the body of a man was found in the stairwell of the Dreamtime Cultural Centre. The body has since been identified as Andamooka Gunjitmurra, 30, who plays in the Titans, current football premiers. The family have been now been notified and have asked for privacy. Investigations are continuing but there appear to be no suspicious circumstances.

Figure 7.1   Interview 1: Constable John Smith

Hey, hey you! Come back here now – you can't go in there.

I don't care if you are a journalist, go away now before I make you!

Lady, I don't care who you are with, you're a woman and women aren't allowed here. There's a ceremony on.

@#*&! And don't come back.

Figure 7.2   Interview 2: Official, Dreamtime Cultural Centre

This is a sad day for our whole community. We have known someone who was a good person and a hard-working Gurruna man. That fella was always happy. His mum, his brothers and sisters, his cousins, his aunties and uncles are all gutted. Now you mob leave us alone so we can concentrate on being together.

I don't care what you heard about drugs. His mother always does her best for her kids and she's had enough heartache already without you mob making trouble.

Figure 7.3   Interview 3: Uncle Ben, Gunjitmurra family home

Rocky was a good man and a great footballer. Like a lot of his kind, he could run faster than most other big blokes.

It's a real tragedy that he ended up the way he did. We all thought that he was the one kid in that family that would make it. He had everything to live for.

Aborigines have lost a real role model on how civilised people behave.

Figure 7.4   Interview 4: Jock Black, Coach, the Titans

Kelly:	We're the ones what found him.
Murphy:	Yeah, he was our auntie's cousin eh. We found him hanging in the stairwell out the back, all stiff, man.
Kelly:	I reckon it would take lots of guts to jump, no matter how off your face you are.
Murphy:	Family curse, man. Live hard, die young eh.

Figure 7.5   Interview 5: Jai Murphy, 15, and Trent Kelly, 16, outside Dreamtime Cultural Centre

EVALUATING THE SOURCES

Asking questions is only part of the skill of interviewing. How a journalist listens and deals with what they hear is the other part. Mencher (1991: 284) offers three questions to guide your evaluation of an interviewee's information:

1 Was the person an observer of the incident, or did he or she hear about it from someone else?

2 Is the person a competent observer?

3 Can the source provide precise details that have a ring of truth and seem consistent with the facts?

Consider the quotes and other information provided by the interviewees. There is a lot of speculation about the reasons for the suicide. You may argue that 'Why?' is a natural reaction to a tragic and unexpected incident, and that the media serves an important public function in seeking to explain it. On the other hand, is there a real likelihood of you being able to explain meaningfully the death in a 300-word news story? Are you satisfied that the interviewees are competent to provide real insight into the dead man's state of mind?

The next question is whether any of the information collected should be discounted as unreliable or inappropriate for publication. There are numerous published guidelines about ethical reporting of suicide (Sheridan Burns and Hazell, 1997). Using these guidelines, you may decide to reject some information even though it is accurately recorded and 'colourful' copy. For example, what public interest is served by publishing graphic details about the corpse or its location? If you provide details about the exact site, it may attract voyeurs to the scene. You need to decide if people would benefit from knowing that the corpse was hanging in a particular spot and what that looked like. Similarly, you must decide if public good is served by drawing attention to the method of suicide.

You may be keen to explain to people 'why' a needless death has occurred, but you must decide whether to include or omit speculation about the dead man's motivation. For example, if you include the quote from his coach, 'He was a great example to his people on and off the field, especially with what he had to put up with. Aborigines have lost a real role model on how to behave', you would be inferring that the dead man's family had a negative effect on his state of mind. Other speculation, such as whether the death of the other family members is significant, is also problematic. Can you justify inferring this in the way the story goes together?

It may be considered respectful to 'not speak ill of the dead' but if you construct your story from quotes that emphasize the deceased's positive characteristics without acknowledging that he had problems, you create the impression that people without problems suddenly decide to attempt suicide. This in turn infers to the reader that suicidal people cannot be identified or helped. References to the death as inexplicable could erroneously suggest that the youth killed himself for 'no reason'. If you use such quotes, you are assuming the death was suicide when this is not yet a decided fact.

Sometimes the people closest to a story are not the best source of factual information. In this case, people might be very interested to know what the family is feeling after the death. But grieving people do not often present themselves in the best way. Does the fact that you accurately recorded what it said mean that you should automatically use the material? Other people, such as the coach is this scenario, may know a lot about once aspect of a person, but not be qualified to comment broadly. The diversity of Aboriginal and Torres Strait Islander communities is often lost or ignored in reporting, with generalizations made across communities and comments sought about all Aboriginal and Torres Strait Islander people.

In evaluating the accuracy and reliability of your information, you also need to be aware of the dangers in reporting hearsay. For example, the policeman at the scene tells you that he suspects the dead man was affected by alcohol. This is not yet a fact because only an autopsy will reveal the deceased's blood alcohol content. You should not report hearsay as if it were fact, including information provided by the police. The coach may have honestly held views about the dead man's childhood, but these may not be accurate as he wasn't there. The boys who found the body are not emotionally touched by the death so much as by their new celebrity, and may wish to appear to know more about the events than they really do. Add to all this, the fact that you are an employee in a newsroom, where particular news values prevail.

CRITICAL REFLECTION

Once you have considered all the information, you need to decide what the 'facts' mean. As the journalist writing the story, you will decide how much information the public is told. What you choose to include and omit will directly affect what the audience understands about the story. This directly affects what the audience understands about the general issue of youth suicide and how it might affect them directly. You may feel pressure in the newsroom to highlight the sensational aspects of the story, but you can only be part of the solution or part of the problem. More importantly, you can meet the objectives of a 'good' news story without doing unnecessary harm.

Next, you decide 'What facts must be included in the story?' To resolve this, you must answer several related questions, including 'Are who, what, where, when, why and how always appropriate information to include in a story?' In this scenario, the man's identity is important to the story as his high public profile would increase public interest in the news. If you decide to use the name, does this mean that public curiosity is a more important value than a family's individual rights? There is a need for greater cultural sensitivity concerning the content of media reports and how they are reported. In particular, reporting of suicide should respect both the community's right to grieve, and cultural protocols about not naming or showing footage of a deceased person. In many Aboriginal and Torres Strait Islander communities, the depiction or mention of a person who has passed away can cause great distress to people, as can showing their image through visual media. Even using the same name as the deceased person, or a similar sound, can cause distress for a period of time.

When it comes to describing 'how' the death occurred, you have a lot of information at your disposal. In evaluating this, you need to consider the implications of including details about the method of suicide. Research into reporting suicides (for example, Sheridan Burns and Hazell, 1999) has demonstrated that detailed reporting of methods tends to be followed by 'copy-cat' suicides using the same methods. You might conclude that the general public would be very interested to know exactly how the suicide was achieved, but you would need to be satisfied that the public interest would be served by repeating it. The reporting of suicide should be handled sensitively. Identification with the person and method in the story is seen as a risk factor for copy-cat suicide, particularly among young Aboriginal and Torres Strait Islander males.

You need to think about what you expect to achieve by reporting the story. On the one hand, you can be fairly certain that human nature dictates your audience will speculate about the reasons for the death. On the other hand, is it your job to encourage that speculation by providing unsubstantiated opinions about cause? It is desirable to have positive and helpful stories about mental illness and suicide; however, careful consideration is required about how this is done. In particular, more information on mental health promotion and the prevention of suicide would be beneficial, with an emphasis on warning signs, risk factors and where people can go to access culturally appropriate assistance. As you reflect on the choices that you have made so far, you must again consider the public interest in terms of what you set out to achieve.

'**Does my story meet the ethical objective of increasing understanding about suicide?**' A story with the elements described in this scenario creates the temptation to portray the events as a tragic narrative, built around the grieving mother doomed by fate to be robbed of her children 'despite' their success. The news value satisfied by this approach is the desire to tell a 'good story', one that moves the audience. You must beware of reinforcing the inaccurate notion that such incidents are either 'acts of fate' or the result of unspecified failures of parents. Journalists wishing to report on Aboriginal or Torres Strait Islander suicide and mental illness should be Aboriginal or Torres Strait Islander themselves, or at least be educated about Aboriginal and Torres Strait Islander cultural issues.

Finally, because in writing this simple news story you are either part of the solution or part of the problem about reporting on suicides, you must ask, '**Is my report consistent with ethical guidelines provided for writing news stories about suicide?**' While there may be no clear answers as to why the man died by suicide, the story could be framed around the major risk factors and warning signs for suicide, and the help that is available to people experiencing problems. Having an understanding of these factors may assist people in the community to identify when a friend, family member or colleague may be in need of some additional support and professional assistance. Sometimes the demands of the newsroom seem to be at odds with a journalist's priorities in the private exchange between reporter and interviewee. If you need to negotiate with an editor who favours sensationalism, ensure you are armed with the facts about the damage such reporting may do. Even if your editor insists, you still control the extent to which you emphasize the sensational aspects of the story.

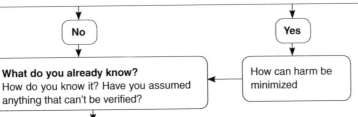

At approximately 3pm today, the body of a man was found in the stairwell of the Dreamtime Cultural Centre. The body has since been identified as Andamooka Gunjitmurra, 30, who plays in the Titans, current football premiers. The family have been now been notified and have asked for privacy. Investigations are continuing but there appear to be no suspicious circumstances.

Would people be interested to know about this?
What news values are you prioritizing in this decision? Does the notion of celebrity affect your decision? Who are the stakeholders? Could publishing the story do harm?

No   **Yes**

What do you already know?   How can harm be
How do you know it? Have you assumed   minimized
anything that can't be verified?

How will you choose your interviewees?
Do they have first-hand experience? Can they provide quotes that add depth and understanding to what you write? Do they speak from authority?

What information do you expect to get from your various interviewees?
Can the interviewees provide first-hand information? Is their information specific or generalized? Is it information that can be verified and, if so, how? Do the interviewees seem credible? Why?

Are your sources reliable?
Did any interviewees express opinion as fact? Did any provide information that was hearsay? Did the interviewees appear competent to answer truthfully? Did they have enough knowledge to answer accurately? Is there any information you have collected that you can't verify? Why leave it in?

What facts do you need to tell the story?
Who has died? What happened? Where? When?

Do you need to find out why?   **Yes**

                                   Is it possible to do so?

How will you choose your facts?
What must be included in the story? Are there quotes you must discard? Why? What would the audience be most interested in? How would someone feel when they finished reading the story?

How will you write the story?
Does your story meet the ethical guidelines for reporting suicide? Have you identified a 'hero' or 'villain'? What is your angle? How much does your perceived audience influence this decision?

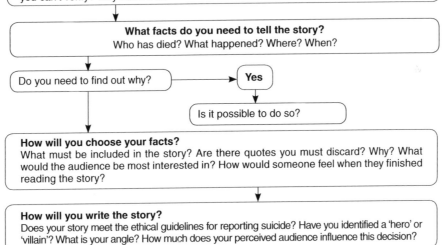

Figure 7.6   Gathering news in action

CONCLUSION

Journalism would look very different if reporters did not use interviews as research. For a start, it would take much longer to gather information and make sense of it. Journalism would be less direct and interesting too, if journalists relied on 'dry' facts and ignored the input of the people involved and those with an expert knowledge. For example, if people wanted to know about something that had happened in Parliament on a particular day, they could wait for publication of the full transcript of that day's parliamentary discussions. However, the information would be expressed in parliamentary language and the reader would have to wade through volumes of material to find the information that was interesting to him or her. Even then, the reader may be no wiser as to the individual effect the information might have. Journalists have some control over what people tell them, usually exercised through the questions they choose to ask. However, the journalist always has control of decisions about information that is useful and should be included, and the information that should, or could, be omitted from the story. This control is explored further in the next chapter, which focuses on the writing processes used in turning research into journalism.

FURTHER ACTION

1   Read a published profile of a prominent person you don't know much about. Do you like the person after reading the profile? Why? Describe the person's general character based on what you have read, and then look for the clues in the text that are the basis of your opinion.

2   Read an account of an interview and ask yourself what other questions might have been asked of the interviewee. Where did the ideas for the extra questions come from? Was it your own prior knowledge or a question raised by something published in the article?

3   Ask someone to interview you about a controversial topic and then consider their version of your opinions. Being an interviewee is a good way to understand the limitations of an interview.

4   Investigate the cultural protocols required when interviewing Indigenous people.

FURTHER READING

Hunter Institute of Mental Health (2008) *Response Ability*. Resources for Journalism Education, www.responseability.org.au. Newcastle, NSW: HIMH.

Samaritans (UK) (2000) 'Guide to reporting of suicide and mental illness', www.samaritans.org.uk.

Sheridan Burns, L. and Hazell, P. (1999) 'Youth suicide and the media's response ... ability', *Asia Pacific Media Educator*, 6: 57–71.

Sheridan Burns, L. and McKee, A. (1999) 'Reporting Indigenous issues: some practical suggestions for journalists', *Australian Journalism Review*, 21 (2): 103–16.

8

WRITING NEWS

Civil unrest has broken out in a country with a military government. The government acts to quickly shut down television and radio stations and block access to the Internet. However, mobile communications are still active and soon Twitter is abuzz with first-hand accounts and commentary. As the story unfolds, you must file for online, radio and print news.

News journalism is a diverse but very specific writing genre. It is bound by numerous conventions and contributing factors, the most significant of these being a defined audience and time frame. At its worst, journalistic writing can be reduced to a formula, but at its best it can be compelling. This chapter explores the processes used in transforming research into journalism targeted at an identified audience. This is followed by a systematic critique of the decision-making processes used, alternatives and implications. 'Constructing' news is not the same as making things up. The word 'construction' here refers to the processes journalists use in deciding what to omit and what to include from their research material. Construction in this sense is more like the process a builder uses to build a house from raw materials. There are many ways that the builder can put the parts together to make a house, and how he does that is a reflection of the budget or resources available, and also the style of house his customer wants. In the very useful book, *How to Write a Sentence and How to Read One*, Stanley Fish describes the power exercised by choosing words:

> It is often said that the job of language is to report or reflect or mirror reality but the power of language is greater and more dangerous than that; it shapes reality, not of course in a little sense – but in the sense that the order imposed on a piece of the world by a sentence is only one among innumerable possible orders. (Fish, 2011: 37)

RELATIVE NEWS VALUES

Today's journalist needs to be able to construct a story in multiple ways to suit cross-platform delivery. All media, commercial and non-commercial, are targeted to specific demographic groups within the community. Editors may use the findings of market research to establish a profile of their audience's interests, so that their newspaper can reflect the 'right' perspective on the world. More often though, the editors rely on their own feelings about what readers want. This often comes down to a professional judgement based on 'My reader is like me, therefore what I like, my reader likes'. The problematic part of this approach is that it tends to focus only on voices from the mainstream – the dominant ideology – and ignores alternative points of view. This can create a distorted view of society: one that does not acknowledge the perspectives of those on social welfare, or those in a cultural minority. One reason is that these groups are perceived by advertisers as being too poor, or too small, to be a viable advertising target.

Perceived audience affects the angle or perspective that you take, and the language reinforces the angle. What is most interesting about the Ford motor company closing down one of its operations will be different for readers of the financial press than it is for those directly affected by the closure. Knowing your audience allows you to refine the assumptions you inevitably make about what is already 'known'. As a journalist, it is important you are aware of these assumptions. You will also need to resist the culture of rationalization that says 'our readers are all in one social group, so we'll ignore everybody else', if you are to make a useful contribution. McManus (1994) and others argue that the effect of audience on the modern media is a tendency only to tell readers what they already know or suspect. Given that the proprietor is most interested in making a profit and pleasing advertisers, no one is going to be putting pressure on you to find alternative points of view. A colleague recalled how, when asked to prepare a list of where the country's most influential thinkers had gone to school, he had worked hard to ensure that women, disadvantaged people, artists and those who had had non-traditional educations were included in his list. He was dismayed to find that when the article was published, it had been sub-edited down to a list of men with similar exclusive private school educations. The features editor had taken the view that the readers came from the same group, and were not interested in the histories of the others in the reporter's original story.

Most news comes down to reporting an event, speculating on the repercussions of an event, or predicting the likely outcome of one of the first two. Most, but not all, journalism audiences demand that news can be absorbed quickly. It is an abbreviated medium, in some instances more than others. Feature journalism can be intended to be consumed slowly and thoughtfully, but your average radio news item consists of about 50–100 words and perhaps one or two questions and answers. A three-minute TV news item is a feature. This has a major impact on what you can say because each message you send must be meaningful. Writing must be clear and self-explanatory, the 'newest' news, so a report always starts with the most recent information. The basic structure of news writing is that information is organized in order of 'newsworthiness'. Newsworthiness, discussed in Chapter 4, is based on a subjective assessment of 'what interests people?' Sometimes a fact is deemed newsworthy because it is important or significant, sometimes because it is interesting or unusual.

WRITING NEWS

Fish (2011) reminds us that a sentence is a structure of logical relationships; the relationships are finite and learnable; the contents that can find expression in the structures formed by the relationships are infinite and incapable of being catalogued. So it follows that the skill of writing well-formed, clear and tightly organized sentences will be acquired by focusing on forms of sentences. While there are some basic rules, the range of sentence types at the disposal of a journalist is very broad. A sentence can be short or long, formal or colloquial. A sentence can surprise, disturb or reassure. It can shout at you or whisper. The impact of a sentence is achieved by carefully choosing every word for its maximum impact.

> Know what makes a sentence more than a random list, practice constructing sentences and explaining what you have done, and you will know how to make sentences forever and you will know too when what you are writing doesn't make the grade because it has degenerated into a mere pile of discrete items. (Fish, 2011: 33)

One of the most legendary twentieth-century journalistic writers was Ernest Hemingway, who was lauded for his spare, highly evocative journalism and later novels. Hemingway's views on writing stemmed mainly from his early career as a journalist. Hence his famous advice to writers: use short sentences, write clearly, use simple words, don't overwrite, avoid adjectives and leave yourself out of it. The result was a style that has been described as realistic, hard-boiled, spare, minimalist and lapidary. A lapidary style is polished and cut to the point of transparency. It doesn't seem to be doing much. It does not demand that attention is paid to it. It allows the objects to shine through as a master stonecutter allows the beauty of the stone to shine through by paring away layers of it. Simple sentence structures and transparent paragraph structure lead the reader to continue reading, and so form the basis of news writing. Gibson (1989) offers two central pieces of advice – get rid of comma clauses and use verbs instead of nouns:

> You can keep a lot of your sentences down to a reasonable length with some careful trimming, and a little thought. Practice helps. You need to get the habit of eliminating excess baggage in your prose. If you learn to delete it when you see it, soon you will learn to avoid it as you write. (Gibson, 1989: 15)

News writing always starts with the most important fact. When you report on a football game, you do not start with the kick-off, you begin with the final score. So it is with news. If someone were to blow up the building across the street from where you work today, when you got home you would not start the story by saying, 'Today seemed like an ordinary sort of day, little did I know how it would turn out'. You would say, 'Someone blew up the building across the street!' In other forms of journalism it is fine for your story to have a beginning, a middle and an end. News stories, in contrast, blurt out something and then explain themselves by attributing each assertion to the evidence of a source with authority to speak on the subject. For example, a story might begin:

> A bystander was shot dead in broad daylight after he went to the aid of a woman outside the High Court today [assertion]. Police [attribution] said when the man approached a woman being assaulted he was shot by her assailant.

You should also establish the context:

> The gunman escaped on foot, sparking a police shutdown of the CBD of Capital City.

Fish (2011: 99) says first sentences have 'an angle of lean'. They lean forward, inclining in the direction of the elaborations they anticipate. Once you have indicated, with the first two sentences, what the main point of the story is, you add additional or supporting information linked in a logical sequence. But the news story expands rather than continuing along a line. You do not build up to the interesting bits or start at the beginning. If there are three major points, news writing does not deal with each in detail consecutively. One goes in the introduction, the other two go in the second sentence, the introduction is substantiated and linked to the second sentence in the third, some colour added and then the two secondary points are substantiated in turn.

In constructing a news story, it is not possible for journalists to include everything. A speech might contain 800 words, but the reporter has a limit of 300 words for the news story about it. The reporter has to decide what to leave out, and in the process is defining what the story will say. So before you start writing you need to be clear on your theme. That is the core of the story, the one-line description:

> A building was destroyed by fire today.

> A new tax will make life harder for families.

That sentence may be your introduction, or it may not appear in so many words anywhere in your story. Your news writing will be constructed of concrete, specific facts but your theme will emerge. The message is disseminated through the selection and arrangement of those specific, concrete details. How the information is arranged, or constructed into news, is a result of professional decision making in the newsroom, which is discussed in Chapter 3.

> Of course the press is biased. How indeed could it not be? The gathering, editing and publishing of news involves decisions by people who inevitably bring their own background, values and prejudices to bear in deciding what to select, emphasize and color as news. The issue is not if the press is biased but the nature and extent of that bias. (Barr, 1977: 5)

Barr reminds journalists that it is shortsighted to deny the existence of bias or to think of themselves as arbiters of objective truth. Rather than ignore the context, or pretend it has no effect, he argues that you must declare it and let the context be part of the message. The fact that you cannot escape your own preconceptions is not a mandate for writing carelessly, nor is the absence of objectivity. Fairness is the gauge by which journalism is judged. At law, as in life, that which is fair is acceptable, even if it is unpalatable to some. To be fair means providing as much information about the context as possible in the circumstances. For example, if you report the fact of a strike, and the inconvenience it will cause, fairness dictates that you should also include the reasons or justification for the strike and the events leading up to it. Let the reader, the audience, decide if the strike is justified. Being fair does not, however, extend to writing about someone as you would have them write about you. That reporting would likely be unbalanced, overly sympathetic and probably not very accurate! Much better to follow the advice of a great Australian newspaper editor of the early twentieth century, Sid Deamer, who wrote:

> There is no such thing as a good objective journalist. If you are not sensitive enough to feel for your subject, to have a point of view, to suffer joy or agony or sympathy about a story you are covering, you will never be a good journalist. Don't strive to be objective, strive to be fair. (cited in Whitington, 1978: 3)

The objective of news writing (see Figure 8.1) is to convey the salient facts about a set of circumstances in a way that is easily comprehended. News writing must be as competent at telling the story in 25 words as it is capable of telling it in 250 or 2000 words. In constructing a news story, you must always consider six elements:

- *who* (the subjects in the story)
- *what* (the action that prompted the story)
- *where* (the physical context)
- *when* (the time context)
- *how* (substantiates *what*)
- *why* (authoritative comment).

For example, Figure 8.2 shows how the questions above fit into the structure of assertion, substantiation and attribution. These elements are necessary to establish the facts and it is a formula of sorts, but that should not mean that all reports are the same. Notice that the sentences are comprised of plain speech, the language is direct and the verbs are active. As in most journalism, there is an assertion, i.e. that a man was shot, and the reason why. In Figure 8.2, each assertion is substantiated by providing the context in which the assertion occurred. To explain or to emphasize what has already been reported, quotes are added. Quotes, and in this sense that includes

1. Write simply. Simple words in the right combination can be powerfully evocative.
2. First things first. News writing starts with a bang and then explains itself.
3. Always attribute what you say to an identified source.
4. A good introduction is everything.

Figure 8.1   News writing basics

A bystander was shot dead in broad daylight after he went to the aid of a woman outside the High Court today.

(The bottom line comes first. This sentence also answers who, what, when and why.)

Police said when the man approached a woman who was being assaulted he was shot by her assailant, who escaped on foot.

(Second sentence substantiates what and why and adds how.)

The dead man, believed to an office worker returning from lunch, was shot in the head and died at the scene. The woman he helped was taken to hospital with fractures and lacerations.

(Third paragraph establishes the context.)

'Capital City police won't rest until this offender is brought to justice,' Sgt Tom Yui said.

(Quote is linked to the next assertion.)

Police have cordoned off six blocks around the High Court, where the injured woman was to have appeared on a Family Court matter.

Figure 8.2   Basic news structure

interview 'grabs' in radio and TV news, are a powerful way of getting a message across – the more authoritative the source of the quote, the more powerful the message. The quote provides the sense of immediacy in journalism, the eyewitness part. This is also known as 'colour'. The term is based on the perception that a 'fact' is black and white, and not open to interpretation. 'Colour', then, adds depth, nuances to the meaning of the fact in its specific context.

Direct speech is also lively. When you quote someone, the reader reads not only *what* was said, but the *way* it was said. In doing so, the reader picks up clues about the speaker. Quotes are also used to add variety to the message. Radio and TV use a variety of voices because it has been shown that people's attention wanes when they have to listen to one voice for an extended period. Even when a report is a verbatim reproduction of questions and answers, it is still edited to establish and substantiate a theme constructed by the journalist. Otherwise, quotes, like *cinéma-vérité*, may be the closest thing to reality, but lack meaning without a narrative to hold them together.

While quotes can add colour to a news report, the strength of the writing is found in the language used by the reporter to tell the story:

The suggestion he is dishonest has been rejected by the Senator.

The Senator has denied allegations he is corrupt.

The first sentence is passive because the subject, 'the Senator', is at the end, not the beginning of the sentence. The use of verbs and nouns is also weak because it downplays the conflict inherent in the sentence. Consider the relative strengths of 'reject' and 'deny', or 'dishonest' and 'corrupt'. The second sentence is more concise and yet conveys more of the story than the first.

When you come to put together facts, quotes and anecdotes into a story you will be seeking to organize them into a complete message. For a message to be complete you cannot, for the sake of brevity, allude to part of the story but then not explain it. In those circumstances you must leave something out. The aim is always to provide the most accurate representation you can of what it all means.

For something to be accurate it must be demonstrably correct within the clearly defined context in which it is offered. This differs from the concept of truth, which is absolute. For something to be true it must be so at every level of meaning and in every context, and in journalism that is not always possible. For instance, a journalist may write that according to police, the fire started at 10pm. The next day it may be revealed that the fire started at 6.30pm. What the journalist wrote is no longer truthful, but it is still accurate in that the police, an authoritative source, did say it on that day. That is why journalists must attribute what they assert, and lay out the justification and context for what they assert. If the journalist had written, 'The fire started at 10pm', without any attribution, the next day it would be just plain wrong.

Perception about audience affects what gets into the paper, or included in news bulletins, and it also affects the way the story is told and the language used. For example, consider these two introductions to the same story. The language in each clearly places the journalist on one side or the other and reveals much about where the audience's sympathies are presumed to lie:

1   'A group of hot-rod hooligans had to face the music today when they were in court to defend charges resulting from Monday's wild free-for-all brawl with police.'

2   'Members of a Capital City car club today told a magistrate that police had overreacted when club members became angry when told they could not have their weekly gathering at a local beach.'

You must also be aware of the potential for personal bias in your writing and ensure every claim you make is substantiated. For example, another reporter covering the story could take a different angle from that given in Figure 8.2:

Police are helpless after a mad gunman shot dead an innocent bystander outside the High Court.

The simple use of the word *helpless* positions the author as rejecting the police's management of the situation and the word *mad* presumes facts not known. Look for that sort of thing in your writing; be aware that your prejudices do show. Be fair. The worst of bad journalism makes judgements and delivers loaded messages. As Hemingway wrote in *A Moveable Feast*:

> Ezra Pound was the man who taught me to distrust adjectives as I would later learn to distrust certain people in certain situations. (cited in Phillips, 1984: 34)

CONSTRUCTING NEWS IN ACTION

Consider the scenario at the beginning of this chapter. Journalists now work in a multi-platform environment where they use a range of media platforms to disseminate their reporting. News websites bring together text, audio and vision to present news, and the same reporter may be responsible for gathering all the content in the story. In pulling together the story from several sources, you are using a process for applying relative news values to a specific audience. The task is also technically challenging because you must also look for inaccuracies, anomalies, hidden leads, time differences and other factors that affect how you evaluate the information you have. Some of the sources are not traditionally 'credible' because they are anonymous or generated by social media users remote from the action, but in a scenario such as this they are valid, if flawed.

> No doubt the existence of YouTube channels devoted to the Iran issue link to the omnipresent mobile phone culture into Iran and other centres made it harder for the regime to carry out its repression in secret. Indeed, it appeared to have effectively circumvented the clampdown on both local and foreign journalists. But at the same time, much of it was dross, which did not add to any real understanding of what was happening on the ground. (Hirst, 2010: 140)

As a dissemination platform, Twitter has the advantage of being 'real-time', instantaneous and worldwide, and allows you to link to more detailed information. It allows journalists to be linked with thousands of people at once and is a powerful tool in considering 'what people are talking about'. However, what people are talking about may not be in the public interest, and may also be inaccurate. For example, rumours can take on the appearance of facts if enough people repeat them. The brevity of the medium calls for a return to a more telegraphic form of writing, with a focus on short words and strong verbs. This requires the journalist to focus on every single word in the 140 characters to convey maximum information. But it isn't sound-bite style reporting. Sentence structure is crucial to putting information in context within 140 characters. Consider the Tweet at the start of Chapter 3.

OMG. STANDING ACROSS FROM HIGH COURT. GUY TRIED TO STOP SOME OTHER GUY BEATING GIRL AND HE JUST SHOT HIM. COPS EVERYWHERE. GUNMAN RAN AWAY. I CAN'T BELIEVE WHAT I SAW!!

This Tweet contains key pieces of information about what has happened, but it doesn't contain all the information needed to put the events in a context. The Tweet contains some unnecessary information, such as the last sentence, and is missing important information, such as the location of the event. Consider the difference in this version:

SHOOTING OUTSIDE CAPTIAL CITY SUPREME COURT. GUN MAN DRAGS WOMAN FROM CAB AND BYSTANDER WHO WENT TO HELP IS SHOT DEAD. MAN SHOOTS WOMAN, ESCAPES. GEORGE ST LOCKED DOWN.

In the process of writing the story, you will also engage the concepts of active and passive voice, the use of verbs, copy logic, sentence structure and the role of language and tone in refining media messages. Fish (2011) posits a sentence is a structure of logical relationships and the number of relationships involved is finite. In his view, there is only one rule to follow: make sure that every component of your sentences is related to the other components in a way that is clear:

> But just as you can't produce a sophisticated meal without thorough knowledge of the ingredients, seasonings, sources, temperatures, utensils, pots, pans, and much more, so you can't produce powerful content in the shape of sentences that take your readers by storm without having a command of the devices – formal devices – that are at once content's vehicles and generators. (Fish, 2011: 35)

You must also consider the assumptions you attach to the news values or interests of your audience. Before you edit the stories into one, you will need to work through a process for evaluating the information at your disposal. There are hundreds of words to choose from and, as you write a 140-character Tweet, a 100-word online story with audio links and a 300-word news story, you will omit most of them.

The first question to resolve is '**What are the main points in this story?**' To decide the news values that will drive your selection of the facts, you will consider those facts in terms of timeliness, proximity, prominence, consequence and human interest. The relative news values in this story are affected directly by your perceptions about the values of your audience. On one level, the scenario described is a human tragedy, which carries news value. At the same time, there is a *low consequence* value, because the site of the incidents is remote from to your audience. *Proximity* plays a crucial role in the news value applied by audiences, so the death of one local citizen takes on greater significance than the deaths of more people in a remote place. In the cases of Figures 8.3, 8.4, 8.5 and 8.6, the relative news value attached to the information is a direct reflection of the proximity of the audience to the source of those reports. There are always exceptions, however, depending on the circumstances.

World events in recent years have shown that Twitter can be a powerful source of information during unfolding events, especially when access to non-mobile media is disrupted. It is a direct, real-time way for people who witness events to spread the word. It is also a way for people far removed from the events to comment on them. Figure 8.3 illustrates Twitter feeds on the events in this scenario. How will you determine if the Tweets are genuinely from people in Shah? Does it matter if they are not? How will you assess the veracity of what you read? Is there a way to check the information? How will you use the Tweets? As facts? For example, some of the Tweets link to the US public broadcasting system or citizen media. Does that make them more reliable? Do you need to verify comments before using them as colour in the story? Are all the Tweets relevant? Will you use the links provided in the Twitter feed? To what purpose?

#InShah #Freedom: Thousands of protesters now marching in Shah capital. Police has responded with tear gas. Police are attacking with batons.

@shah1: Around 10 people have been arrested near Azadi square in central Shah,

#InShah Report: security forces attack silent pro-democracy protests. Jailed journalist dies after 10-day hunger strike. to.pbs.org/jginshah

RT @rantboy: Eyewitness account of #Shah silent protest: So many security forces present, Azadi Square "was like an armed camp." http://to.pbs.org/inshah

#Shah: bling ban: Now no necklaces for men. Saber hunger strike death called sign of "human catastrophe in Iran prisons." to.pbs.org/ppkPV

@faran: The 'jinn' is in the jeans... why #Shah men shouldn't wear them so tight http://to.pbs.org/k77gTV

@Khalid: 9.14pm GMT: Here is terrifying YouTube video footage of Shah riot police charging protesters. We can't verify the clip but it was forwarded by a reader in Shah.

@zoltman: Another first-hand account of yesterday's scene in the #Shah capital: "The Basra again brought out child recruits." http://to.pbs.org/inshah

#Shah @ Kooeji: Catastrophic failure by MOI to handle today's peaceful situation. Overreaction, paranoia, and mindless. Shameful.

#Shah: Many direct head injuries in protesters more than 20 people carried to hospital by ambulence including many women

@maryahawaja, head of the foreign relations office of the Shah Centre for Human Rights: Around 300 people just got attacked at human rights activists march #shah they just fired straight at our car

@oxfordgirl: OK mssg I think from Shah saying although have been clashes number of protesters growing and safe. Attacks target activists

@ onlymehi: Live: Clashes in Shah with tear gas #shah #freedom

@orlando: CrowdSource.org has good images of protesters. It is a good resource for photos, videos of protests as well as links to news stories and reports.

Figure 8.3 Twitter feeds

9.00pm GMT Security forces on motorcycles tried to run down protesters in the Shah capital.

Witnesses said demonstrators had tried to gather in small knots until the police turned up in force, at which point they would run into traffic to seek refuge with strangers who opened their car doors.

Cellular telephone service was shut off around the main squares and the Internet slowed to a crawl, activists said. Echoing tactics in Hamandi and Mousavi, sympathizers outside Shah set up the Freedom Facebook page to collect videos, eyewitness accounts and any information. Twitter feeds informed demonstrators to gather quickly at a certain intersection, then disperse rapidly.

The authorities had made no secret of their resolve to stop the demonstrators. 'The conspirators are nothing but corpses,' Hossein Mehdi, a top commander of the Revolutionary Corps, said last week in comments published by the official news agency. 'Any incitement will be dealt with

Figure 8.4   shah riots/jones

7am GMT The Sraf news agency, a semi-official service linked to the Islamic Revolutionary Corps, indirectly confirmed the Shah protests by saying an unspecified number of demonstrators had been arrested. It called participants 'hypocrites, monarchists, ruffians and seditionists' and ridiculed them for not chanting slogans about Hamandi, the nominal reason for the protests.

The authorities' tactics on Monday indicated that they were resolved to stifle unrest – starting with the refusal to issue a permit for a nationwide demonstration. Reports that did emerge suggested that security forces had tried to prevent people from gathering by blocking the access routes to main squares in major cities and closing train stations in Tehran.

Figure 8.5   add shah riots 2/allen

5.30am GMT Hundreds of riot police officers in Shah beat protesters and fired tear gas Monday to contain the most significant street protests since the end of the 2009 uprising there, as security forces around the region moved – sometimes brutally – to prevent new unrest in sympathy with the opposition victory in nearby Hamandi.

The size of the protests in Shah was unclear. Witness accounts and news reports from inside the country suggested that perhaps 20,000 to 30,000 demonstrators in several cities defied strong warnings and took to the streets.

The unrest was an acute embarrassment for Shah leaders, who had sought to portray the toppling of the secular rulers of nearby countries, Hamandi and Mousavi, as a triumph of popular support for Islam in the Arab world.

The Shah authorities have shown that they will not hesitate to crush demonstrations with deadly force. Other governments across the Middle East and the Persian Gulf also moved aggressively to stamp out protests on Monday.

Figure 8.6   add shahriots/jones

Figures 8.7, 8.8 and 8.9 offer *human-interest* angles on the larger story. Such angles can be very strong but usually only if supported by proximity. Human interest can also be generated through a combination of consequence and prominence. For example, if a community has a large Shah population, there may be direct consequences even though the audience is geographically remote. Through consideration of these questions, you will arrive at the relative news values that will direct your inclusion and omission of information.

8.30pm GMT Audio Interview with Paul Jones, ABC correspondent in Shah.

'Essanid Street looked like a war zone: smoke, dust, tear gas, screaming people, flying stones and regular attacks by the well equipped motorcycle riding guards.

A petite young girl with a small backpack was walking to my left. Just before we reached Navab Avenue the guards charged from behind, one of their clubs hit my left leg but three of them attacked the girl relentlessly. She screamed and fell to the ground, but the guards kept hitting her.

I ran towards them, grabbed the girl and pushed her north towards Azadi Square away when the guards charged towards us. This time the crowd fought back and stones of all sizes were directed back at them.

This gave me a bit of time to ask one of the restaurants to open their doors and let us in. The girl was crying uncontrollably and in pain. Her clothes were dusty, her backpack was torn and her hands were shaking. "Why?" she kept asking.'

Figure 8.7 Audio interview with ABC Shah correspondent

9am GMT:

A group of six Australians is caught up in the dangerous unrest in Shah.

Police locked several thousand fleeing protesters inside the State University campus near where they had been holding their rally. Five people were wounded in the melee, an opposition source said. The six Australians haven't been seen since.

The students, from Sydney, Melbourne and Brisbane, are part of an humanitarian student exchange in Shah. They are part of a larger group including American, Norwegian and Indian students.

Government loyalists armed with broken bottles, daggers and rocks chased down thousands of pro-reform demonstrators in Shah's capital on Monday, turning unrest increasingly violent.

Figure 8.8 Add shahriots/aussie/joness

9am GMT:

A Capital city mosque is in shock today as it comes to terms with the news that a favourite son is missing in the Shah riots.

Mohammed bin Lau, 22, son of cleric Sheik Bin Lu, travelled to Shah to study theology.

'My son is only interested in peace,' the Sheik said.

Nothing has been heard from Bin Lu, or the other missing Australians – nurses Jenny Greene, 20, and Kylie Mazzaro, 19, from Brisbane and Samir Said, 25, from Melbourne.

'Jenny and Kylie wanted an adventure and to help people,' said Jenny's distraught mum Sue in Brisbane.

Figure 8.9 Add shahriots/aussie/joness

CHOOSING THE NEWS

Now you must evaluate the sum of information you have. Some of the reports are culturally specific, targeted at a specific demographic community. You must decide when, and if, race, nationality or ethnicity are relevant. Consider the **relative news values** of all the information and discard anything you consider irrelevant or uninteresting to your audience. Now you must consider the **reliability of information** left to choose from. How will you evaluate the accuracy of the information in a context where you cannot make independent checks? Have you noticed any errors of fact or inconsistencies?

In addition to inconsistencies and errors of calculation, you must also decide whether the information you select is **substantiated**. Is it reliable to include in your report? You must also consider the harm that might be done by repeating this allegation.

Next, you need to **prioritize the elements of news writing** – who, what, where, when and how. Evaluate your findings, deciding what information should be discarded as unreliable. Is there any information you cannot verify that is too important to the story to leave out? How will you resolve this dilemma?

Next, evaluate the elements of the story that must be included. What are the relative news values applied to the information you have selected?

The priority you assign to various components reveals your assumptions about the interests of your audience. For example, does the local angle (proximity) take prominence? If so, why is the disappearance of four Australians more important to an Australian audience than the deaths of 300 Shahs? Is it newsworthy that the missing man's father is a Muslim cleric? Why? Are the missing nurses more newsworthy because they are on a humanitarian mission? And what of the other missing foreign humanitarians? Are they only newsworthy outside their own countries if they are dead?

CRITICAL REFLECTION

Review the choices you have made and reflect on the values underpinning your professional decisions. Consider the angle you have chosen. Why is it the best for your audience? Think about the other possible angles you are rejecting by adopting this one – is there a better angle? Confirm with yourself that you are sure of your facts and have attributed the things you assert. If there is anything in the story that is not attributed, ask yourself why it has not been omitted. Consider if your report could harm anyone, and if that harm can be justified in the public interest. As you come to write the report from the various pieces, you will find you are choosing your own words to link the elements, rather than just editing the pieces together. In the writing of the final report, you again put a personal stamp on what people will understand from this report. Does your report focus on the dramatic or emotional elements? Does it focus on the scale of the incident? Consider the verbs you have used. Are they active or passive? Is your report intended to provoke an emotional response in the audience?

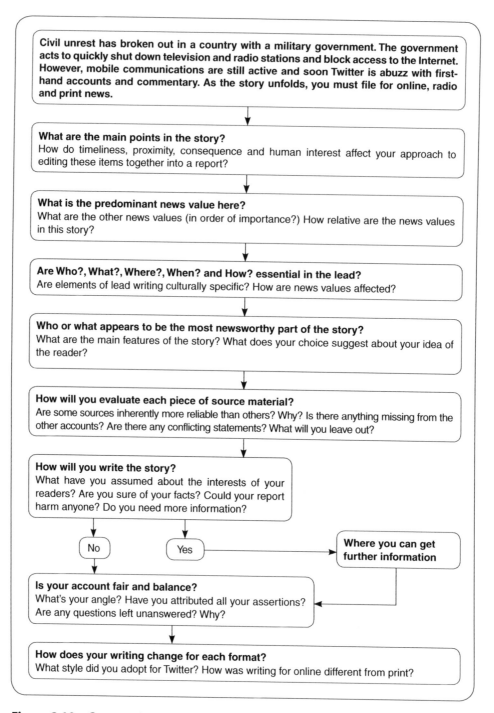

Figure 8.10   Constructing news in action

Scrutinise every part of your sentence and ask, 'What does it go with?' or 'What does it support?' or 'What information does it give about some other part?' or 'What is it referring to?' All variations of the master question, 'How does it fit into the sentence's logical structure?' (Fish, 2011: 21)

CONCLUSION

News as a written or spoken form of communication is always constructed, in the sense that journalists never reveal all the information they have on a topic. Instead, information goes through a process of professional evaluation that includes not only the reporters and their sources, but also a range of other journalists involved in the production and dissemination of the news. The process by which news is constructed is a reflection of professional judgements about the interaction of relative news values, the accuracy of information and the style and language used to impart the information.

FURTHER ACTION

1   Take a short news story published in the media. From it, make a list of the facts, then use the facts to write a 140 character Tweet. How do you decide what to keep?

2   Take a childhood nursery rhyme and rewrite it as a news story. What do you notice about the language you use?

3   Read a page of your national newspaper carefully, highlighting all the verbs. What do you notice?

4   Write a descriptive passage of 50 words without using any adjectives. What do you observe about the verbs in your sentences.

FURTHER READING

Aylsen, B., Sedorkin, G. and Oakham, M. (2011) *Reporting in a Multimedia World* (2nd edn). Sydney: Allen & Unwin.

Betancourt, L. (2009) *The Journalist's Guide to Twitter*, www.mashable.com/2009/05/14/twitter-journalism

Fish, S.E. (2011) *How to Write a Sentence and How to Read One*. New York: Harper Collins.

Layton, R. (2011) *Editing and News Design: How to Shape the News in Print and Online Journalism*. Melbourne: Palgrave Macmillan.

McAdams, M. (2011) *Social Media Guidelines for Journalists*, http://mindymcadams.com/tojou/2011/social-media-guidelines-for-journalists/

9

EDITING NEWS

You have the task of editing a single breaking story. First you will Tweet, then file 100 words plus a headline for online, followed with a 500-word news story. Where will you begin? How will you decide what to keep and what to cut out? What needs to be changed and why? Where will you use images and sound?

From the three-word advertising slogan heard often but never seen to a daily blog, eloquence remains a deciding factor in whose messages receive most attention. The writing process has expanded beyond organizing words into designing communication environments which are visually as well as textually articulate. Words still have primary importance as the means by which members of society communicate with each other. In today's media environment, where there have never been so many competing voices, writers need more than ever to understand how to organize words and sentences to maximum effect. New developments such as Twitter have forced journalists to really think about each of the 140 characters that make up a message to ensure maximum use of the medium. Blogs and wikis allow for much more expansive self-expression, but the relevance of an individual blogger is measured by his or her following, indicating that persuasive writing is the key to influence and reputation in social media environments.

A well-written news story has the facts, written in the right order and with the right emphasis, and tells those facts simply. The editing process is used to correct over-writing, clumsy sentence construction and faulty grammar. It translates jargon into plain English, and explains technical or complex ideas. This process includes deleting unnecessary words and checking the vocabulary of a story to ensure it suits the audience. Copy editors also ensure that punctuation, grammar and spelling are accurate. Most news organizations have 'style guides' that offer preferred usages and spellings. For example, newspaper style dictates that numbers from one to nine are spelled out while two-digit numbers such as 10 are expressed numerically. Readers want to comprehend immediately.

This chapter explores the editing process through consideration of several ways of writing up the same information for different media contexts. A more complex kind of editing, where a writer negotiates with a commissioning editor over a longer news feature, is explored in Chapter 10.

THE BUTCHER'S ART

Many years ago the author was required to cut an article by a senior columnist from 1500 words to 500. The task was approached with trepidation because the columnist in question was known to be very vocal in his disdain for copy editors. The next morning, he approached and held out a brown paper bag. 'This is for you,' he said with a wink. 'Credit where it's due. You've earned it.'

Inside the bag was a crisp navy blue and white striped butcher's apron.

The analogy makes a lot of sense. A professional butcher knows how to get the most meat out of a carcass, by cutting away everything that is superfluous but nothing that is useful. In the wrong hands, the same carcass can be divided in a way that wastes its potential as a source of food. Every decision about what to keep and what to discard directly affects the final product. And so it is for copy editors.

> Today's editors, technicians, and cultural gatekeepers – the experts across an array of fields – are necessary to help us to sift through what's important and what's not, what is credible from what is unreliable, and what is worth spending our time on as opposed to the white noise that can safely be ignored. (Keen, 2008: 45)

The relationship between writers and copy editors is often contentious. Copy editors complain they are made into scapegoats for lazy journalism. Writers complain that the copy editor has deleted the best parts of their work. Reporters face the wrath of the public after editing errors change the meaning of a story. Your aim is to take things out in such a seamless way that even the writer will be hard-pressed to recognize the deletions. This is done by first removing any information that is not essential to the meaning of the original story. If the story is still too long, the copy editor looks to the construction of individual sentences to find ways to reduce the number of words required to tell the story.

THE COPY EDITING PROCESS

There are some simple ground rules to guide the editing process. The first step is to understand exactly what the writer intended. A copy editor does not impose his or her own interpretation of the facts, but aims to make the writer's intention clear. A good way to begin is to read what the story is about. Once you have a clear idea, you can evaluate how successful the writer has been in getting the story across.

> Think about what you do when you revise a sentence: you add something, you delete something, you substitute one tense for another, you rearrange clauses and phrases; and with each change, the 'reality' offered to your readers changes ...

> The skill it takes to produce a sentence – the linking of events, actions, and objects in the strict logic – is also the skill of creating a world. (Fish, 2011: 37)

The next thing you do as a copy editor is to apply your news sense to the facts and evaluate the choices made by the reporter. Sometimes copy needs to be restructured or reordered to emphasize the most newsworthy aspects. Newsworthiness, as discussed in Chapter 4, is a relative value and your decision is partly based on your understanding of the audience, their interests and values.

You know a news story must contain who, what, where, when and why. If this information is in the story but not at the beginning, you need to rework it. Decide in what order those elements should be presented. Does 'who' come before 'what'? Is 'where' more important than 'who'? Sometimes 'when' is the most important fact but rarely does a story begin with 'why', although 'why' should never be left to the end of the story. Often 'why' is followed by the sixth element of news, 'how'. Sometimes a report contains answers to the five Ws but the reporter has missed the main point. Ask yourself again 'What is the most interesting part of the story?' The ideas in the story should flow logically and easily. Are the ideas in a rational order? Do they lead on naturally from one to another? If you were telling this story, where would *you* begin? If the place where you would start the story is not at the beginning of the story in front of you, then the 'lead', or most newsworthy information, is said to be 'buried' in the story. It must be 'on top' or in the first sentence.

If the order of information needs improvement, you may be able to fix it without rewriting the whole story. Try reordering the paragraphs. Once the paragraphs are in the right order, look for gaps in the way the story is told. You will probably need to reconstruct some sentences or change their direction so that the new order makes sense. You will need to write a new introduction. Some information may need to be moved from one paragraph to another, tenses may need correction, nouns and pronouns may need to be rearranged. If you attend to the structure first, you avoid wasting time correcting typographical errors in paragraphs that you cut out or change for structural reasons.

> Examine the copy again, this time looking for errors in sentences. Inexperienced writers often lack confidence in taking on sentence structure. They 'fear committing one or more of the innumerable errors that seem to lie in wait for them at every step of composition'. (Fish, 2011: 20)

Formal grammar texts, such as Hodgson (1998), insist that sentence structure is the key to good writing. All sentences must have a subject and a verb. The verb, if need's be, can be qualified by an adverb. The sentence may also have an object, as in the following example:

> The boy [subject] ran [verb] quickly [adverb] towards the ball [object].

Sentence structure and punctuation are the tools used in journalism to make copy comprehensible as well as concise in expression. Often you will recognize that something is wrong with a sentence, but be unsure of how to fix it. In this situation, rewrite the sentence to make it clear. Some of the most common problems are described below. A copy editor is responsible for ensuring that the punctuation in a story is correct and assists comprehension. This requires checking the use of tenses and verbs, nouns, pronouns and qualifying adverbs. Other basic rules must be applied regarding sentence and paragraph length, and the use of prepositions. Punctuation must also be accurate. This requires critical reflection on the use of full stops (points), semi-colons and colons, dashes, brackets and ellipsis (information left out). You must also check the use of apostrophes, hyphens and exclamation, quotation and question marks. To aid meaning, you engage with other writing conventions fundamental to journalism.

Active voice should be chosen by you

News writing convention is that the *active voice* is always preferable to the passive voice:

> I did it. *[active]*

> It was done by me. *[passive]*

The simple reason for this is that passive expression is harder to read and wastes words. In news journalism there is rarely a good reason to say 'Passive voice should be avoided wherever possible' when the alternative is 'Avoid passive voice wherever possible'. To identify the passive voice, look for phrases such as 'is to be' and the word 'by'. For example, 'will be done by' and 'should be done by' can be replaced by active language such as 'will do' and 'should do'.

Don't use no double negatives neither

Such sentences are wasteful of words, passive and harder to comprehend immediately.

Try to not ever split infinitives

This is for the same reasons. Often it is better to rewrite the sentence:

> Try not to split infinitives.

When dangling, watch your participles

A participle is said to 'dangle' when confusing the subject and object. Consider the following sentences:

> The children climbed the mountain with their teachers and their rucksacks on their backs.

> With their teachers, the children climbed the mountain with their rucksacks on their backs.

About them sentence fragments

Sentence fragments are grammatically incorrect. But in journalism sometimes the subject is implied and the sentence is followed by a fragment that does not need to be explained. For example:

> The boy ran towards the ball. Too quickly.

Verbs has to agree with their antecedents

A verb must agree with its subject. Double subjects need plural verbs:

> Boys and girls do not play the same way.

If the sentence is joined by a preposition, the verb is singular:

> A reporter, along with police, is affected by experiencing crime scenes.

'Is' can be a weak verb in journalism. Sometimes, *is* is precisely the right word for a situation. At other times – most other times – it weakens your sentence. If that happens, cut it out.

Between you and I case is important

'You and I' or 'you and me'? Check the case by removing the first part of the sentence:

> (John and) I went to see a movie.

> (John and) me went to see a movie.

But prepositions don't start sentences

It is grammatically incorrect to begin a sentence with a preposition. But in journalism, this rule may be broken if it adds comprehension or impact to a sentence:

> George Smith thought he was safe. But he was wrong, dead wrong.

Don't use commas, that aren't necessary

Commas are used to enhance meaning of complex sentences and to indicate pauses in reading. Consider the different meaning of the following two sentences: 'What is this thing called love?' and 'What is this thing called, love?' The basic rule applying to commas is that you should use neither too many nor too few. Your aim is always to increase clarity. Commas are used singly:

> Once you realize a sentence is grammatically incorrect, you must correct it.

Verbs are also used in pairs within sentences and removing only one of the pair usually causes grammatical errors:

> The diplomats were seen in Haikou yesterday buying clothes for the detainees, who are being held in pairs, and for their commander, who has been kept in isolation.

Another problem; semi-colon over-use

Another problem for writers susceptible to comma abuse is over-use of semi-colons. There are times when a semi-colon is the appropriate punctuation, but this is rare in news journalism because it prefers short, concise sentences. If you need to divide the information in a sentence, consider writing two sentences.

Don't capitalize Generic Terms

Capital letters at the beginning of words are also sometimes subject to misuse. Generally, proper nouns require initial capitals but generic names do not. For example, the programme for the following event might describe thus:

> The Annual General Meeting of the National Bank was addressed by the Chairman of the Board of Directors and Chief Executive Officer of the National Bank.

In the language of journalism, the sentence is somewhat different:

> The chairman will address the National Bank annual general meeting today.

Don't use apostrophe's to pluralize

Apostrophe abuse is rife in English language newsrooms around the globe. That is when a writer uses apostrophes to pluralize words:

> The commando's were detained by the airport security troop's.

Apostrophes are used to indicate ownership, e.g. David's car, and to indicate contraction in a phrase, e.g. *is not* becomes *isn't*.

Use direct statements

Consider the difference between the following two sentences. The first, which is indirect, contains the same information as the second, but the second sentence conveys more:

> Mr Smith said that he is very angry and will consider direct action if the problem is not resolved.

'I am very angry about this and might take matters into my own hands if the problem isn't fixed,' Mr Smith said.

Always use a short word over a long one

For example, police said the getaway car was seen (parked in the vicinity of) *near* the bank shortly before the robbery. Or, don't use *facilitate* when you can use *help* or *demonstrate* when you mean *show*.

Kill the jargon

Some words are familiar only to a specialized group – the jargon of journalism, for example, uses terms such as news sense, copy, intro, write-off and sidebar to describe aspects of its work. Journalists use the word 'kill' when they mean 'delete'. These terms may be unintelligible to people outside the group. When faced with jargon, the copy editor's first reaction should be to replace the jargon with plain speech that anyone can understand. If that is not possible, the term should be clearly explained.

Diss the slang

Don't assume that readers are familiar with the same terminology. Reported as part of a direct quote, slang can sometimes add colour and impact, but the meaning must be clear. One section of Australia's youth uses the expression 'heaps sick' to describe something wonderful, but don't assume everyone knows the definition. Words can have different meanings in different parts of the world. For example, the word 'bum' is used in the UK and Australia as a slang term for a person's buttocks, but in the USA the term describes a person of no fixed address. The US slang word for buttocks, fanny, has a very different meaning in Australia and the UK.

Correct spelling is essentail

For ordinary spelling, use a dictionary, street directory, atlas or other reference works if you think a word is spelt incorrectly. Sometimes a word may be spelled in more than one way. News organizations produce 'style' booklets that list the organization's preferred spelling of words and give advice about capitalization and other presentation requirements. Don't necessarily rely on the spelling and grammar check functions in a word processing program. You need to ensure that the dictionary loaded on the computer is the same one used your by organization and that 'house style' is added to the database.

Adjectives can be useful, interesting, colourful and over-used

Adjectives are used to add colour and nuanced meaning to sentences but colour is best inserted into a story through the careful use of verbs and active sentence structure. Adjectives should not be avoided altogether, but over-use interferes with clarity rather than enhancing it. Sometimes adjectives paired with nouns repeatedly become clichés, e.g. *gory detail, brutal assault, bouncing baby*.

Metaphors are signposts to meaning

Without metaphors and similes, our writing would be considerably barer because metaphors are full of imagery and connotations. Be appropriate. Be original. Be understandable. Don't go overboard. Don't mix metaphors.

Avoid clichés like the plague

Once-meaningful expressions are diminished by over-use. Journalists are also a source of many clichés, such as 'corpse found *in a pool of blood*' and 'guests dined on lobster, *washed down* by fine champagne'.

Over-writing is thoroughly unnecessary

Over-writing is the term used to describe sentences that contain more words than are necessary to get the message across. Gibson (1989) posits that 20–25 words is the proper length for an easily comprehensible sentence. Legendary British newspaper editor Harold Evan put it even more succinctly: One simple sentence for an intro, one idea to a sentence. Sometimes that is just not possible. Gibson points out that copy editing is not only for those employed to assess the work of others. Writers who edit their own copy before giving it over to copy editors increase the likelihood of their work being published unchanged. 'If you learn to delete it when you see it, soon you will learn to avoid it as you write' (Gibson, 1989: 15).

WRITING HEADLINES

Hodgson describes the headline writer as having two main functions, both to do with manipulating words. He describes a copy editor as 'a synthesizer, filtering the material so that its essence is refined into a simple "read-me" message' (Hodgson, 1998: 125). The second function is to accommodate the words within the character (letter) count prescribed by the layout. The size of the type and the width of the headline are deter-mined by the layout, which may not be created by the copy editor. The number of words in a headline also depends on the style of the publication. Tabloid newspapers tend to use large type across narrow widths, which means a headline may need to comprise only a few short words. Broadsheets are a larger format and can offer wider column widths for headlines, allowing the use of more words per line. Headlines attract the reader's attention, so good headlines excite curiosity. They may also engender strong emotions in the reader, such as amusement, sorrow or anger. The headline should always indicate what the reader will find in the story so readers can decide if they are interested.

> Writing a headline is one of the more difficult of sub-editing jobs. It takes a high concentration on the materials of the story – the facts and supporting quota-tions – to render them quickly into a few short words that will tempt the reader to read on (Hodgson, 1998: 125).

Today, headline writing skills are in new demand as social media such as Twitter call for the brevity of just 140 characters RSS feeds are also headlines of a sort. Online headlines are quite different from those found in print because search engines use an algorhythm to rank pages. Online headlines must take account of search engine optimization, so online headline tend to group key words.

Print headline writers sometimes amuse their readers through the deft use of humour. While these approaches are well-suited to some stories, they are seldom appropriate in news reporting. For example, a pun over-used becomes a cliché and should be avoided. Gibson (1989) warns that while good headlines are often clever, they must always be true at all levels of meaning. Headline words must have clarity (plain words that are easily understood) and impact (words with nuances used). A headline is a contracted sentence and needs an active verb, preferably early in the headline. Omitting words can inadvertently change meaning, as Gibson (1989: 30) illustrates with this unfortunate headline:

Blizzard hits 3 states; 1 missing

The copy editor looks for keywords in the text of the story and considers synonyms for those words. The headline is a direct expression of the keywords. The strength and power of a good headline can often be traced back to the verb. Verbs should be strong and colourful and the structure should be active. Headlines should never be misleading because they are subject to the same tests of proof as the rest of journalistic writing. Some words, especially the short ones favoured by copy editors, have more than one meaning so you must be careful to ensure a headline is clear. A headline should be based on the story's introduction (which should contain the most newsworthy elements of it) but not repeat the same words.

EDITING NEWS IN ACTION

Consider Figure 9.1 and ask yourself 'What's this story all about?' It is about a man who survived against the odds, but this aspect is not introduced until the sixth paragraph. What else is interesting about the story? The man had been forced to stay in an area populated by dangerous crocodiles and had to kill his own food. He also made a shelter for himself in a tree (reminiscent of the literary figure Robinson Crusoe or the movie character Crocodile Dundee). More than that, he was unconcerned about a giant tree snake which also lived in the tree. There is also news value attached to the fact that the man at the centre of the story is quite laconic in describing experiences most people would find terrifying. You might conclude these aspects are more interesting than the feelings of the people who found him. What should come first? This is a news story so the most important thing should come first – in this case that the man has been found safe and well, followed immediately by the fact he has a remarkable tale to tell. How important is the information about what the cowboys were doing before they found him? What is the most interesting part of the story? What news values are you giving priority? In this case, it is how the man survived in such an inhospitable place. Once you've answered the question 'What's this story about?', you

The four cowboys had been travelling for days in the forbidding landscape of the far north.

The trip was hot, dry and dusty but the four persevered because one of their number was fulfilling a long-held dream to visit his Aboriginal tribal homeland.

They rode cautiously because they know that in this desolate place the only inhabitants were deadly snakes, scorpions and crocodiles.

To be injured here or lose your horse means certain death.

So you can imagine their surprise when here of all places, they meet up with Kununurra buffalo catcher Rod Ansell.

The group had headed down to the Fitzmaurice River for much needed water when they encountered Mr Ansell living in a makeshift bush camp.

He told them he had left his home in the remote Western Australian township two months ago for a couple of months fishing in the Queens Channel of the Victoria River, near the border between Western Australia and the Northern Territory.

But tragedy struck on the first day of his holiday when Mr Ansell's 18-foot boat which was towing a 12-foot dinghy drifted into the tide and up the estuaries that formed the entrance to the Fitzmaurice, which also empties in the Queen's Channel.

It was sunset when Mr Ansell and the two dogs he had brought with him for company had a terrible shock.

'It was pretty quite, then something heaved up under the boat and threw me and the pups and all my stuff into the water.' He said today.

Mr Ansell said he retreived the dinghy and emptied out a tin of powdered milk from his supplies and used it to bale water out of the dinghy until he was satisfied that it was floating properly.

'I had been drifting all this time and didn't quite know where I was. It would have been sucide to head out to sea; the tide just washes up to the north so I thought I'd see if I could get to the Fitzmaurice for some fresh water.'

For the next four days, Mr Ansell and his dogs, one of which was injured in the shipwreck, by now very thirsty, floated around the estuaries before paddling up the entrance to the river.

On the fifth day, Mr Ansell landed the dinghy and made camp on the bank of the river.

'I thought I'd sit it out there and wait until the wet came in October. Then I'd have a chance to follow the wet season waterholes down to the Vic, along as I didn't get too weak. I built a sort of treehouse,' Mr Ansell said.

'A few saplings in the fork of a tree so I could camp off the ground and get away from scorpions and crocodiles. All the time I was there I shared the tree with a big tree snake – he used to come down and wonder who the hell I was,' he said.

Mr Ansell said most of his ammunition went down with the boat but he saved his rifle and a handful of bullets.

'I shot wild buffalo for food. The first week I shot four but in the last week (he was marooned for eight weeks) I only shot one – I getting pretty weak by then.

I skinned them and cut off meat for food – I cut off strips a few feet long then hung them to dry out for three or four days. I ate them boiled or dried. The dogs and I ate together.'

To supplement his rather boring diet, Mr Ansell feasted on a few wild berries.

Mr Ansell's biggest worry came from the huge crocodiles with whom he shared his bush home and who were drawn out of the water and up the bank by the scent of his dogs.

He said he shot one 16-foot crocodile when it tried to eat his dogs which were tethered at the campsite.

He cut off its head and kept it for a souvenir.

'There were a lot of them about but I didn't want to waste ammunition and besides, I didn't want the smell of dead crocs bringing more around. But salties (Mr Ansell's pet name for saltwater crocodiles) love dog and this bloke went straight for my pups.'

Mr Ansell said that the whole time he was missing he knew no one was looking for him because he had told his girlfriend he would be gone for at least two months.

(739 words)

Figure 9.1

are ready to write your Twitter post and file 20 words for the RSS feed. As previously stated, writing for Twitter can be seen as a form of headline writing because of the 140-character limit.

Consider these two 140-character Tweets based on Figure 9.1:

4 cowboys riding through the remote outback to visit their ancestral home made an amazing discovery when they met a man who had been lost all alone in the wild for 60 days.

Real life Crocodile Dundee found by chance alive and well in crocodile-infested outback 2 months after being shipwrecked killed buffalo with his bare hands for food.

Both these sentences are 140 characters and both are accurate in terms of the facts contained in Figure 9.1. The first version sets a scene, but runs out of words before getting to the salient fact – that the man was in good health. The second version includes the chance discovery, illustrates the danger of the environment, introduces how he came to be lost and provides insight into how he survived. Reference to the movie character Crocodile Dundee, who was famous for his bush skills, adds colour and context in just four words. While both versions are 140 characters, the first is 33 words and the second only 26, even though it contains more information.

To write the RSS feed, to be used as a breaking news ticker on a website and/or for broadcast, you need to edit the information in the Tweets down to 20 words. For example:

Man found by chance alive in crocodile-infested outback 2 months after ship-wreck killed buffalo with his bare hands for food.

ONLINE REPORT

Now you have a sentence that is the core of the story, whether you are writing for online or social media, print or broadcast. As you turn to writing the next version of the story, for online, you not only look to the text but to any other resources available. Based on the decisions you make about the crux of the story, you will need to reorder the paragraphs to bring the most newsworthy aspects of the story to the beginning. These paragraphs, found at the end of the story in Figure 9.1, are moved to the beginning of the story.

Now consider Figure 9.2. The paragraphs have been reorganized to emphasize the most interesting and/or important facts but the story does not flow easily and the rearrangement of paragraphs leaves gaps in the story. In this case, a new introduction is needed to encapsulate the main point. His quotes need to be in context and used to build the story of his ordeal. Figure 9.3 illustrates how this can be achieved by restructuring the story. It emphasizes the most interesting part of the story and indicates to the reader that the rest of story will contain details of the man's ordeal. From the version in Figure 9.3, you can construct a story for online. The version in Figure 9.3 is longer than the previous two, which is problematic because the print story must be cut to 500 words. Sometimes a story gets longer before it gets shorter.

So you can imagine their surprise when here of all places, they meet up with Kununurra buffalo catcher Rod Ansell aged 22 years.

The group had headed down to the Fitzmaurice River for much needed water when they encountered Mr Ansell living in a makeshift bush camp.

He told them he had left his home in the remote Western Australian township two months ago for a couple of months fishing in the Queens Channel of the Victoria River, near the border between Western Australia and the Northern Territory.

Mr Ansell said that the whole time he was missing he knew no one was looking for him because he had told his girlfriend he would be gone for at least two months.

Mr Ansell's biggest worry came from the huge crocodiles with whom he shared his bush home and who were drawn out of the water and up the bank by the scent of his dogs.

He said he shot one 16-foot crocodile when it tried to eat his dogs which were tethered at the campsite.

He cut off its head and kept it for a souvenir.

'There were a lot of them about but I didn't want to waste ammunition and besides, I didn't want the smell of dead crocs bringing more around. But salties (Mr Ansell's pet name for saltwater crocodiles) love dog and this bloke went straight for my pups.'

Mr Ansell said most of his ammunition went down with the boat but he saved his rifle and a handful of bullets.

'I shot wild buffalo for food. The first week I shot four but in the last week (he was marooned for eight weeks) I only shot one – I getting pretty weak by then. I skinned them and cut off meat for food – I cut off strips a few feet long then hung them to dry out for three or four days. I ate them boiled or dried. The dogs and I ate together.'

On the fifth day, Mr Ansell landed the dinghy and made camp on the bank of the river.

'I thought I'd sit it out there and wait until the wet came in October. Then I'd have a chance to follow the wet season waterholes down to the Vic, along as I didn't get too weak. I built a sort of treehouse,' Mr Ansell said. 'A few saplings in the fork of a tree so I could camp off the ground and get away from scorpions and crocodiles. All the time I was there I shared the tree with a big tree snake – he used to come down and wonder who the hell I was' he said.

But tragedy struck on the first day of his holiday when Mr Ansell's 18-foot boat which was towing a 12-foot dinghy drifted into the tide and up the estuaries that formed the entrance to the Fitzmaurice, which also empties in the Queen's Channel.

It was sunset when Mr Ansell and the two dogs he had brought with him for company had a terrible shock.

'It was pretty quite, then something heaved up under the boat and threw me and the pups and all my stuff into the water.' he said today.

Mr Ansell said he retreived the dinghy and emptied out a tin of powdered milk from his supplies and used it to bale water out of the dinghy until he was satisfied that it was floating properly.

'I had been drifting all this time and didn't quite know where I was. It would have been sucide to head out to sea; the tide just washes up to the north so I thought I'd see if I could get to the Fitzmaurice for some fresh water.'

For the next four days, Mr Ansell and his dogs, one of which was injured in the shipwreck, by now very thirsty, floated around the estuaries before paddling up the entrance to the river.

To supplement his rather boring diet, Mr Ansell feasted on a few wild berries.

The four cowboys had been travelling for days in the forbidding landscape of the far north.

The trip was hot, dry and dusty but the four persevered because one of their number was fulfiling a long-held dream to visit his Aboriginal tribal homeland.

They rode cautiously because they know that in this desolate place the only inhabitants were deadly snakes, scorpions and crocodiles.

To be injured here or lose your horse means certain death.

(742 words)

Figure 9.2

A man found by chance after he was lost for two months in crocodile-infested Northern Australia has told how he lived in a tree with a giant snake and hunted wild buffalo for food.

He also survived an attack by a 16-foot crocodile and kept its head as souvenir.

Four cowboys happened upon Kununurra buffalo catcher Rod Ansell, 22, while on a trip to a remote Aboriginal tribal homeland.

Mr Ansell told the men he was shipwrecked shortly after he headed out on a fishing trip when a giant crocodile overturned his boat. He said he knew no one would be looking for him because he had told his girlfriend he would be gone for at least two months.

Mr Ansell said most of his ammunition went down with the boat but he saved his rifle and a handful of bullets.

'I shot wild buffalo for food. The first week I shot four but in the last week (he was marooned for eight weeks) I only shot one – I getting pretty weak by then. I skinned them and cut off meat for food – I cut off strips a few feet long then hung them to dry out for three or four days. I ate them boiled or dried. The dogs and I ate together.'

Mr Ansell's biggest worry came from the huge crocodiles with whom he shared his bush home and who were drawn out of the water and up the bank by the scent of his dogs.

He said he shot one 16-foot crocodile when it tried to eat his dogs which were tethered at the campsite.

He cut off its head and kept it for a souvenir.

'There were a lot of them about but I didn't want to waste ammunition and besides, I didn't want the smell of dead crocs bringing more around. But salties (Mr Ansell's pet name for saltwater crocodiles) love dog and this bloke went straight for my pups.

'I thought I'd sit it out there and wait until the wet came in October. Then I'd have a chance to follow the wet season waterholes down to the Vic, along as I didn't get too weak. I built a sort of treehouse,' Mr Ansell said.

'A few saplings in the fork of a tree so I could camp off the ground and get away from scorpions and crocodiles. All the time I was there I shared the tree with a big tree snake – he used to come down and wonder who the hell I was,' he said.

He told them he had left his home in the remote Western Australian township two months ago for a couple of months fishing in the Queens Channel of the Victoria River, near the border between Western Australia and the Northern Territory.

But tragedy struck on the first day of his holiday when Mr Ansell's 18-foot boat which was towing a 12-foot dinghy drifted into the tide and up the estuaries that formed the entrance to the Fitzmaurice, which also empties in the Queen's Channel.

It was sunset when Mr Ansell and the two dogs he had brought with him for company had a terrible shock.

'It was pretty quite, then something heaved up under the boat and threw me and the pups and all my stuff into the water.' He said today.

Mr Ansell said he retreived the dinghy and emptied out a tin of powdered milk from his supplies and used it to bale water out of the dinghy until he was satisfied that it was floating properly.

'I had been drifting all this time and didn't quite know where I was. It would have been sucide to head out to sea; the tide just washes up to the north so I thought I'd see if I could get to the Fitzmaurice for some fresh water.'

For the next four days, Mr Ansell and his dogs, one of which was injured in the shipwreck, by now very thirsty, floated around the estuaries before paddling up the entrance to the river.

On the fifth day, Mr Ansell landed the dinghy and made camp on the bank of the river.

continued

To supplement his rather boring diet, Mr Ansell feasted on a few wild berries.

The four cowboys who found Mr Ansell had been travelling for days in the forbidding landscape of the far north.

The trip was hot, dry and dusty but the four persevered because one of their number was fulfiling a long-held dream to visit his Aboriginal tribal homeland.

They rode cautiously because they know that in this desolate place the only inhabitants were deadly snakes, scorpions and crocodiles.

To be injured here or lose your horse means certain death.

The group had headed down to the Fitzmaurice River for much needed water when they encountered Mr Ansell living in a makeshift bush camp.

(795 words)

Figure 9.3

With just 100 words as a limit, the online story needs to make the best use of the other resources available in the format, such as audio, real-time vision, and still images. Taking into account the resources of Figure 9.5 (below), there are details you can omit from your text report as they are covered in supplementary material. The aerial vision of the remote area negates the need to describe it. As the online version will be followed by a more nuanced version in print, this version should focus on the highlights of the story, directing readers to the print version for more information. Consider the audio described in Figure 9.5. If you choose to use it, you need not repeat information from the audio in the story. What parts of the audio would you use? Would you use a photo of the man who was lost? Would it matter if the photo was out of date? Should you identify it as such? Consider Figure 9.6 which is exactly 100 words and uses the additional material. What has been omitted from the text?

A man found by chance after he was lost for two months in crocodile-infested Northern Australia has told how he lived in a tree with a giant snake and hunted wild buffalo for food.

He also survived an attack by a 16-foot crocodile and kept its head as souvenir.

Four stockmen happened upon Kununurra buffalo catcher Rod Ansell, 22, while travelling to a remote Aboriginal tribal homeland.

Mr Ansell told the men he was shipwrecked shortly after he headed out on a fishing trip, when a giant crocodile overturned his boat. He said he knew no one would be looking for him because he had told his girlfriend he would be gone for at least two months.

To protect himself from crocodiles and other predators, Mr Ansell took shelter at night in the fork of a tree.

continued

'I built a sort of treehouse with a few saplings in the fork of a tree,' he said.

'All the time I was there I shared the tree with a big tree snake – he used to come down and wonder who the hell I was.'

Mr Ansell said most of his ammunition went down with his boat but he saved his rifle and a handful of bullets.

'I shot wild buffalo for food. The first week I shot four but in the last week I only shot one – I was getting pretty weak by then.

'I skinned them and cut off meat for food – I cut off strips a few feet long then hung them to dry out for three or four days. I ate them boiled or dried. The dogs and I ate together.'

Mr Ansell also shot a 16-foot saltwater crocodile when it was drawn to his camp by the scent of his dogs, which were tethered at the campsite.

'There were a lot of them about but I didn't want to waste ammunition and besides, I didn't want the smell of dead crocs bringing more around. But salties love dog and this bloke went straight for my pups,' he recalled.

He cut off its head and kept it for a souvenir.

He told them he had left his home in the remote Western Australian township two months ago for a couple of months fishing in the Queen's Channel of the Victoria River, near the border between Western Australia and the Northern Territory.

But tragedy struck on the first day of his holiday when Mr Ansell's 18-foot boat which was towing a 12-foot dinghy drifted into the tide and up the estuaries that formed the entrance to the Fitzmaurice, which also empties into the Queen's Channel.

It was sunset when Mr Ansell and the two dogs he had brought with him for company had a terrible shock.

'It was pretty quiet, then something heaved up under the boat and threw me and the pups and all my stuff into the water,' he said today.

Mr Ansell said he retrieved the dinghy and emptied out a tin of powdered milk from his supplies and used it to bail water out of the dinghy until he was satisfied that it was floating properly.

'I had been drifting all this time and didn't quite know where I was. It would have been suicide to head out to sea; the tide just washes up to the north so I thought I'd see if I could get to the Fitzmaurice for some fresh water.'

For the next four days, Mr Ansell and his dogs, one of which was injured in the shipwreck, by now very thirsty, floated around the estuaries before paddling up the entrance to the river.

On the fifth day, Mr Ansell landed the dinghy and made camp on the bank of the river. 'I thought I'd sit it out there and wait until the wet came in October. Then I'd have a chance to follow the wet season water holes down to the Vic, as long as I didn't get too weak.'

To supplement his meagre diet, Mr Ansel ate wild berries.

The four stockmen who found Mr Ansell had been travelling for days in the forbidding landscape of the far north.

The trip was hot, dry and dusty but the four persevered because one of their number was fulfilling a long-held dream to visit his Aboriginal tribal homeland.

They rode cautiously because they know that in this desolate place the only inhabitants were deadly snakes, scorpions and crocodiles.

To be injured here or lose your horse means certain death.

The group had headed down to the Fitzmaurice River for much needed water when they encountered Mr Ansell living in a makeshift bush camp.

(771 words)

Figure 9.4

1. **Bushman1.jpg (File photo of lost man)**

2. **Bushman.mp3 (Audio of reporter in Darwin)**

The Aboriginal stockmen said the man was in good spirits and told them he had been shipwrecked two months earlier.

The stockmen said the man had plenty of food, with strips of buffalo meat drying around the fire. He told them he had shot wild buffalo and skinned them with a hunting knife. The remains of a large crocodile were also found at the camp.

The lost man told he killed the croc when it attacked his camp and kept its head as a souvenir.

The man at the centre of the story was taken to hospital before being released. He is reluctant to talk about his experience.

3. **Outback.dvd (Vision of far north Western Australia)**

5 minutes of aerial footage.

Figure 9.5   Other resources

PRINT REPORT

As you prepare the most comprehensive report, now that you have the elements in order, next examine the copy again, looking for jargon, slang, spelling errors, excessive adjectives and clichés. You should remove passive voice, clumsy sentence structure and repetition.

Consider the changes evident in Figure 9.4. Repetition such as 'he was marooned for eight weeks' has been removed. Also rewritten was the paragraph beginning 'Mr Ansell's biggest worry came from the huge crocodiles with whom he shared his bush home.' The reference to worry is unnecessary and it is hardly accurate to say he 'shared his home' with crocodiles. The anecdote about the crocodile is rewritten to make it more concise and powerful.

The information about how Mr Ansell lived has also been rewritten to link his comment about building a treehouse to his description of it. Repetition about why he lived in a tree is edited out of the direct quote. In another direct quote, Mr Ansell refers to 'crocs'. Is it clear that this is an abbreviation of the word 'crocodile'? If it is, there is no need to change it. He also refers to 'salties', which is a far less common abbreviation and needs to be explained. However, it is not appropriate to describe the term as 'a pet name'. This is resolved by introducing the name saltwater crocodiles before the direct quote. What about expressions such as 'water holes' and 'the wet'? In Australia, where the story is set, these terms are commonly understood but an expression such as 'the wet' should be in inverted commas. In other parts of the world, such terms need clarification. Does 'the Vic' need clarification? The Victoria River is mentioned in the story but you need to decide if readers will understand the connection. Is the name of the Channel 'Queens' or 'Queen's'? You would need to consult an atlas.

(Bushman1.jpg) A man found by chance after he was lost for two months in crocodile-infested Northern Australia has told how he lived in a tree with a giant snake and killed buffalo for food. Rod Ansell, 22, also survived an attack by a 16-foot crocodile and kept its head as souvenir.

Four stockmen found the man while visiting their remote tribal homeland (outback.wmv). Ansell told the men he was shipwrecked shortly after starting a fishing trip when a crocodile overturned his boat. He knew no one would be looking for him because he had told friends he would be gone for months. (bushman.mp3).

Figure 9.6

A number of spelling errors have also been corrected. Can you find them? Other terms, such as 'rather boring', have been changed for a more appropriate one, such as 'meagre', or a simpler expression, such as when 'their number' becomes 'them'. Unessential adjectives have been removed and tenses changed (e.g. 'know' becomes 'knew'). What about the word 'travelling'? In some countries this word is spelled 'traveling' – check the correct spelling. 'Cowboy' is a word that has meaning in the Western world but in Australia these people are called 'stockmen'. Choose the appropriate word for the country in which the story will be published. Figure 9.4 also illustrates the changes after punctuation has been corrected.

THE BUTCHER'S ART IN ACTION

At 771 words, the version of the story in Figure 9.4 is too long, so now that you are satisfied the other problems have been 'fixed' you must attend to the second part of the task, which is cutting the story to 500 words for print. Begin by cutting whole paragraphs that are not essential. For example, the reason why the cowboys (stockmen) were in the place where Ansell was found is not essential to the story – the important thing is that he was found by chance. With this information edited out, the story is reduced to 656 words. The fact that his diet included wild berries is also non-essential information.

Next identify sentences that can be shortened or simplified. As part of this process 'told them he had' becomes 'Mr Ansell'. The phrase 'township two months ago for a couple of months fishing' is repetitive and redundant. Similarly, the sentence 'But tragedy struck on the first day of his holiday when Mr Ansell's 18-foot boat, which was towing a 12-foot dinghy, drifted into the tide and up the estuaries that formed the entrance to the Fitzmaurice, which also empties in the Queen's Channel' is overwritten and clumsily constructed. Was it a tragedy if nobody died? The sentence describing the shipwreck includes 'colour', such as the fact that he emptied a tin of powdered milk so he could use it to bail out the dinghy. Such detail may be interesting in a longer piece but is not essential. Equally, that he was thirsty hardly needs stating, nor does the dog's injury unless this is central to a later part of the tale. Is it necessary to include that he landed the dinghy before making camp on the bank?

Now the story has been reduced to 556 words. Once you are satisfied that all non-essential information has been removed, you must turn your attention to individual sentences with a view to making them shorter. Examine each sentence and remove every possible word.

> Scrutinise every part of your sentence and ask, 'What does it go with?' or 'What does it support?' or 'What information does it give about some other part?' or 'What is it referring to?' All variations of the master question, 'How does it fit into the sentence's logical structure?' (Fish, 2011: 21)

Return one last time to your verbs. Are they the strongest words you can accurately use? Do the verbs add to the context of the story? Many years ago, the author worked for a chief sub-editor who insisted that news briefs were exactly 25 words. I didn't believe it at first, but it is true any story can be told in 25 words and still make sense.

Figure 9.7 shows the story at exactly 500 words. What has changed? Most sentences have been edited. The sentence describing the shipwreck is more concise. Two sentences about the things he retrieved in the shipwreck become one. That he ate buffalo boiled or dried is removed because while it is interesting, it is not essential. More interesting is the imagery created by the sentence 'The dogs and I ate together.' Finally, a description of what happened in the first five days after the shipwreck is edited into a simple sentence. How would you have edited the story? Would you have taken different decisions, made different choices? Why?

A man found by chance after he was lost for two months in crocodile-infested Northern Australia has told how he lived in a tree with a giant snake and hunted wild buffalo for food.

He also survived an attack by a 16-foot crocodile and kept its head as souvenir.

Four cowboys happened upon Kununurra buffalo catcher Rod Ansell, 22, in a remote, uninhabited area they seldom visited.

Mr Ansell told the men he was shipwrecked when a giant crocodile overturned his boat. He said he knew no one would be looking for him because he had told his girlfriend he would be gone for at least two months.

To protect himself from crocodiles and other predators, Mr Ansell took shelter at night in the fork of a tree.

'I built a sort of treehouse, a few saplings in the fork of a tree,' he said.

'All the time I was there I shared the tree with a big tree snake – he used to come down and wonder who the hell I was.'

'I shot wild buffalo for food. The first week I shot four but in the last week I only shot one – I getting pretty weak by then.

'I skinned them and cut off meat for food – I cut off strips a few feet long then hung them to dry out for three or four days. The dogs and I ate together.'

Mr Ansell also shot a 16-foot saltwater crocodile when it was drawn to his camp by the scent of his dogs, which were tethered at the campsite.

There were a lot of them about but I didn't want to waste ammunition and besides, I didn't want the smell of dead crocs bringing more crocs around. But salties love dog and this bloke went straight for my pups,' he recalled.

continued

He cut off its head and kept it for a souvenir.

Mr Ansell had left his home in remote Western Australia to go fishing in the Queen's Channel of the Victoria River, near the border between Western Australia and the Northern Territory.

Around sunset on the first day his 18-foot boat, which was towing a 12-foot dinghy, drifted with the tide into estuaries at the entrance to the Fitzmaurice River.

'It was pretty quiet, then something heaved up under the boat and threw me and the pups and all my stuff into the water,' he said today.

Mr Ansell said he retrieved the dinghy, his dogs and some gear, including his rifle and a handful of bullets.

'I had been drifting all this time and didn't quite know where I was. It would have been suicide to head out to sea; so I thought I'd see if I could get to the Fitzmaurice for some fresh water.

'I thought I'd sit it out there and wait until the wet came in October. Then I'd have a chance to follow the wet season water holes down to the Vic, along as I didn't get too weak.'

(500 words)

Figure 9.7

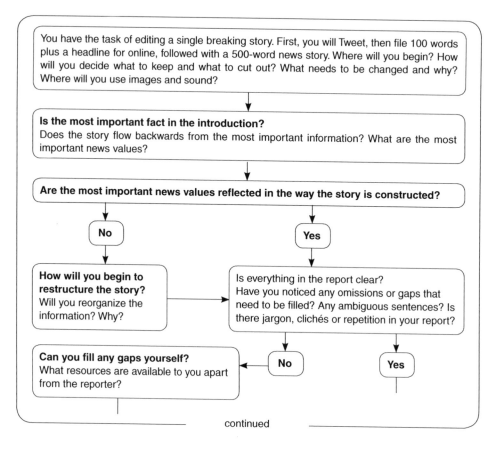

You have the task of editing a single breaking story. First, you will Tweet, then file 100 words plus a headline for online, followed with a 500-word news story. Where will you begin? How will you decide what to keep and what to cut out? What needs to be changed and why? Where will you use images and sound?

Is the most important fact in the introduction?
Does the story flow backwards from the most important information? What are the most important news values?

Are the most important news values reflected in the way the story is constructed?

No

Yes

How will you begin to restructure the story?
Will you reorganize the information? Why?

Is everything in the report clear?
Have you noticed any omissions or gaps that need to be filled? Any ambiguous sentences? Is there jargon, clichés or repetition in your report?

Can you fill any gaps yourself?
What resources are available to you apart from the reporter?

No

Yes

continued

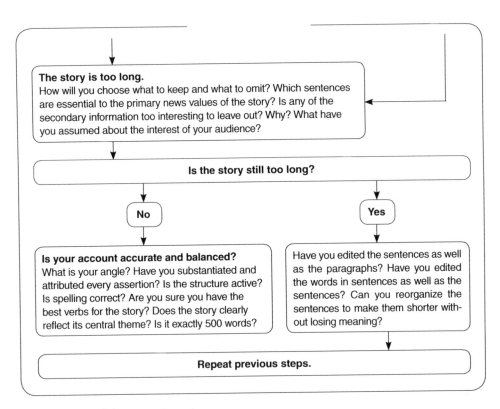

Figure 9.8   Editing news in action

CONCLUSION

Words still have primary importance as the means by which members of society communicate with each other. In today's media environment, where there have never been so many competing voices, writers need more than ever to understand how to organize words and sentences to maximum effect.

On one level, sub-editing is a production tool used by journalists to ensure that reporting fits the style, length and news priorities of the publishing organization. Editing is also the process by which writers polish and refine the messages they create. Developing editing skills and processes for evaluating the strengths of various parts of your writing is important from the very start of your career. The better the editor you are, the more effectively you can see your writing as the sum of its parts, the better writer you will be. As a reporter, you should apply the same process to your work as copy editors do, before you submit the story. Never assume that others will pick up your mistakes or that you can abdicate responsibility for errors.

Most of the time, the writer does not have the opportunity to negotiate changes with the copy editor. However, sometimes the editing process is a collaboration between a writer and the person who commissions the work. This aspect of editing is explored through consideration of a magazine article in the next chapter. One final piece of advice – *always proofread your writing twice.*

FURTHER ACTION

1   Think of a headline for Figure 9.7 of about 25 characters (letters and spaces). Now cut the number of characters in half and see if you can distil the message.

2   Edit Figure 9.1 without further reference to the edited version. How does your edited version differ from the published one?

3   Choose any news story and edit to exactly 25 words.

4   Take a piece of your own writing and cut it by 20 per cent.

FURTHER READING

Fish, S.E. (2011) *How to Write a Sentence and How to Read One.* New York: Harper Collins.

Gibson, M.L. (1989) *The Writer's Friend.* Ames, IA: Iowa State University Press.

Layton, R. (2011) *Editing and News Design: How to Shape the News in Print and Online Journalism.* Melbourne: Palgrave Macmillan.

Perry, R. and Ansell, R. (1980) *To Fight the Wild.* Sydney: Pegasus Books.

10

TAKING NEWS FURTHER

You have had a non-commissioned magazine article accepted by *FHM*, an internationally successful magazine for men. Before publication, however, the editor wants you to amend the piece in several ways. First, he suggests a change from the first-person voice. Then the editor asks you to provide more information about the subject's early adventures. Then he tells you the piece is too long and must be cut by 800 words. Finally, the editor also edits the piece to fit the magazine layout adopted. What processes will you use to tailor the story to the publication?

Ernest Hemingway, the American journalist and author, was a wordsmith in the true sense of the word. His writing is simple and spare, uses mostly words of one or two syllables and yet is among the most powerfully evocative in modern literature. Hemingway's work demonstrates that the power of the written word comes not so much from the words themselves but the way they are arranged, the rhythm in the writing and flow of ideas. Journalism written in the simplest language can move readers profoundly – to tears of joy or sadness, to anger and it can even move them to act. Adam argues that the use of plain language in journalism is a limit imposed by the public:

> Whatever else might be said about the language of journalism, it is fair to say that it is disciplined by its public and empirical character. It may strive to represent scientific ideas or the abstract notions of philosophy, but it does not adopt the vocabularies of those disciplines. It always uses a vocabulary that can be understood in the street or the marketplace. Furthermore, it is always explicit in its references; it is laced with nouns, adjectives and proper names; it is concrete, powerfully descriptive and light on, though not devoid of, metaphors and similes. That does not mean it is devoid of beauty. It may well be beautiful. (Adam, 1993: 32)

It should come as comfort to aspiring journalists that seamless prose did not come easily even to, who laboured over draft after draft of his work, whether it was fact or fiction. He is reported to have written to his attorney in despair, saying: 'I have a diamond mine if people will let me alone and let me dig up the stones out of the blue mud and then cut and polish them' (cited in Didion, 1998: 76).

In an article published on the centenary of Hemingway's birth, Joan Didion wrote about Hemingway's style:

> This was a man to whom words mattered. He worked at them, he understood them, he got inside them. When he was 24 years old and reading submissions to *Transatlantic Review* he would sometimes try rewriting them, just for practice. ... You care about punctuation or you don't, and Hemingway did. You care about the 'ands' and 'buts' or you don't, and Hemingway did. (Didion, 1998: 74)

Didion's essay considered whether Hemingway would have been happy to have published writing that he considered incomplete or inferior. While her argument is strong, it is also true that there is much to learn from imperfect writing. Good journalism is especially compelling because it is real. Real people, real experiences – journalists participate in real events and seek to make some sense of them by identifying the characters, the themes and the drama in real events. This chapter explores the self-editing processes undertaken by writers in negotiating with an editor the final version of a story. It provides a methodology by which you can strip your own writing back to its parts and critically reflect on the decisions underlying the style, tone and content of the text. It does this by exploring the processes underlying an actual piece of journalism published in three countries in 1999 and 2000 (Sheridan Burns, 1999b). Systematic consideration of five drafts of the article, from an incomplete idea to the published piece, reveals how the writer's theme is disseminated. Reflecting on the organization of text and use of language demonstrates how editing affects media messages.

BACKGROUND TO THE ARTICLE

The catalyst that led the author to write the magazine article discussed in this chapter was two news events. The event concerned the man at the centre of the news event described in Chapter 9. Both events were pretty sensational. In the first event the man was in his 20s and used bush skills to survive for 60 days in crocodile-infested bush. In the second, some years later, the same man was shot dead after he ambushed police waiting at a roadblock to apprehend him. He had shot and killed one officer from nearby bushes, the first hint the police had he was there. The other police officer returned fire and the assailant was killed.

There was more to the story. The policeman was the first to be killed in the Northern Territory of Australia in more than 40 years. The wanted man was well known and once respected in the community. He was a skilled outback bushman who would probably never have been found by police. More than that, his heroic adventures as a young man (see Chapter 9) had inspired the international movie success, *Crocodile Dundee*. The author was fascinated by the story, which seemed at odds with the public persona of the dead man – articulate, likable, laconic and very, very capable. A man in control of his destiny. While the facts of the criminal events immediately preceding the deaths were still *sub judice*, the author set out to answer the question 'How could someone so good go so bad?'

Award-winning feature writer, David Leser, wrote about the challenges of writing character profiles in the introduction to his book of essays *The Whites of Their Eyes*. He said that a profile is much more than a description of the events of someone's life and what they have to say about it:

> A good profile has to embrace the idea that there are few people who can withstand a relentless scrutiny; that all of us are riven by complexities and contradictions. (Leser, 1999: preface)

So it was that the author took on the challenging task of drawing a profile of the dead bushman. It was important from the outset that the narrative did not portray him as a romantic figure, because he had gratuitously murdered a policeman. It was equally important that the subject was not portrayed as a monster or someone who had dramatically 'gone bad'. The writer was attracted to the underlying story about how someone who could survive in the wild for eight weeks, could not survive the pressures of the modern world. Another aspect was the author's prior knowledge of the character's story. Years previously, the author read a book written, in the first person, by the dead man (Perry and Ansell, 1980). To the author, the quiet self-assurance revealed by the person who wrote the book was wildly incompatible with the character of the 'cop killer' presented in the media. The process of making an idea into a piece of published journalism had begun.

Before moving into the drafting process, the author had to decide which publication, or style of publication, was appropriate for the story. This is because the style, tone and structure of the piece will be affected by this decision. As a freelance journalist, the author knew from experience that to write a piece and then try to find an audience for it can be frustrating and fruitless. At *FHM*, the editorial team interrogates a feature idea before a writer is commissioned under a detailed brief. That way the magazine's formula is adhered to, the writer has better direction, and the editing is minimal. It is therefore the writer's duty to know a publication's style and convince the editor that he or she will be appropriate. In this case, the author chose *FHM* because she wanted her message to reach the 18–35 male demographic targeted by the magazine. The author approached the editor with the idea, and he agreed that the topic was appropriate and to read a draft.

> The subject of this piece also fits into the style of *FHM*'s 'True Life' section because the story has drama and a true crime ring to it. It also had the important sub-text that all men, no matter how capable, are human. All men are equally capable of the horrendous, the heroic and the pathetic. This fits in with the magazine's values and influences the decision to publish it. (Ridgway, 1999)

THE DRAFTING PROCESS

To begin to write you need a good supply of facts, quotes and a handful of anecdotes or stories to illustrate your information and make it more interesting. Your story needs more substance than merely information about a subject and your interviewees' reflections on that subject. It seeks to provide insight and bring a person or situation to life, in all its complexity. The first stage in building a framework for *insight* is to identify a theme for the article. The theme is the underlying message conveyed through the artful organization of the parts of a story. Typically, your theme is something that can be stated in general terms and encapsulated in one sentence, for example 'The death of one man is also the death of an Australian bush myth'. You do not necessarily *say* that in those words in your article – the theme you choose should emerge through the selection and arrangement of your specific, concrete details. Your aim in choosing a theme is to think about all the facts, quotes and anecdotes and get them into focus; to bring disparate parts into relationship with each other to offer a new perspective.

The techniques used in journalism are also those used by other storytellers. Journalism also features plot, characterization, action, dialogue, sequencing, dramatization, causation, myth, metaphor and explanation. The difference is that journalism is constructed in simple language and explicit terms, and the journalist is always the narrator who guides the reader through the story.

The journalist takes the reader on a journey, dropping clues as to the meaning of it all along the way. Tom Wolfe said of journalism: 'It's really reporting *scenes*, that's what you look for constantly. You are waiting for things to happen in front of your eyes, because it's really the scene that brings the whole thing to life – that's where you get the dialogue' (Wolfe, 1975: 5). Through scenes, the characters in journalism gradually reveal personality traits, habits, feelings, attitudes and ideas that present them in a new or different light.

A Sydney journalist wrote a piece about a homeless man who briefly shot to fame as the smiling face of poverty in a TV ad campaign. When the man was found dead on the streets from the effects of alcoholism just a fortnight later, the journalist told the story of the man's life beginning with the words:

> John Young's fifteen minutes of fame lasted two weeks, but he couldn't remember a second of it. (Perrin, 1995)

In telling Charlie's story, which was real, he wrote eloquently and vividly about the way society deals with issues of human justice. His article benefits from a compelling introduction, which some would argue is the most important part of the structure. Sometimes the ending comes to a writer first, but the starting point is always a sentence or phrase that captures not just the theme of the piece but also its style and tone. Once the theme is established, you have a framework on which to build the story. Thinking it through, planning it in your head, is the hardest part of the task for many writers, but so is getting the rhythm right.

The real skill in editing is knowing what to leave out to make the picture clearer. Hemingway drew an analogy between writing and an iceberg, because no matter how big the story is that the writer tells, there is always so much readers do not ever see.

Quotes are a very powerful way of getting your story across. When you quote someone, the reader reads not just what they said, but the *way* it is said, giving clues about the speaker's personality. The problem with quotes is that they are all context – there is no narrative to hold them together. Like *cinéma-vérité*, quotes alone take you closer to reality, but the reality is a more chaotic one. Anecdotes are an essential partner to quotes because they can be woven into the narrative structure. By telling an anecdote without commenting on it, you let readers draw their own conclusions. But by selecting one anecdote over another you *guide* the way the reader interprets what you tell.

All journalism is written to a 'style', which directly reflects the style of the target publication. In the case of the article discussed in this chapter, the readership is a demographic of men aged between 18 and 35. This affects the way the writer answers the question 'What is most interesting to the reader?' and thereafter everything from the theme and structure to the choice of individual words. All writing is capable of being reworked, restructured, sub-edited and made better.

The straightforward language of journalism means that the poetry is most often in the verbs. For example, it's the difference between:

'Wait,' she began,

'Wait,' she roared, and

'Wait,' she breathed.

Journalists use language to add levels of complexity to their writing. Consider the difference between being 'marched' and 'paraded'. Both convey a loss of individual control, but only the latter conveys a loss of dignity. Deft use of language and grammatical devices is the way writers add depth and colour to their writing.

WORKING WITH WORDS

Consider the published article examined in this chapter. Before consulting the drafts (Figures 10.2–10.4), read the published piece (Figure 10.1). Does the introduction stimulate your interest in the topic? Why? Is the life described in the article interesting and engaging? Can you relate to any of the characters? Does the article have a clear theme, and if so, what is it? Journalism seeks to provoke a reaction or emotional response in the reader, so ask yourself: 'How does the story make me *feel*?' Try to find the source of your reactions. Are there any anecdotes, quotes or parts of the narrative that resonate with you? Do you think the writer has told the story objectively? Should the writer be objective? Or should the writer follow Deamer's advice, and 'feel anger or sorrow or empathy' for the subject (Whitington, 1978)? Is your overall impression that the story is fair? Are important facts missing? Where in the text can you find the source of your opinion? Now consider the story in terms of the developing drafts (Figures 10.2–10.4) and seek to trace the story from the writer's idea to the editor's cut.

THE LEGEND AND THE FALL

Rod Ansell, 1987 'Territorian Of The Year', and the man who inspired Paul Hogan's 'Crocodile' Dundee finished up a dead cop killer. Why?

THE FIRST TIME THE WORLD HEARD of Rod Ansell was '77 and back then he was a modern-day Robinson Crusoe. The bloke who was said to have survived for eight weeks in the wilds of the Northern Territory, without fresh water and plagued by crocodiles. In '80 Ansell was big news again when he published a book, To Fight The Wild, illustrating that adventure, and urbanites were fascinated by his story. It was incredible to think that such a man existed at the end of the 20th century. Anyone else would have been dead on the first day, when a giant crocodile flipped his boat. But Ansell was so matter-of-fact about it. He explained why in his book:

'All the blokes up in this country, who work with cattle, ringers, stockmen, bull-catches, whatever, all of them, have really narrow shaves all the time. But they never talk about it . . . I think the opinion is that if you come through in one piece, and you're still alive, then nothing else really matters. It's like going out to shoot a kangaroo. You don't come back and say you missed by half-an-inch. You either got him or you didn't. So that is how I looked at it. Until the paper got hold of the story, and that changed a lot of things.'

In '84 he was paraded on The Michael Parkinson Show – the episode Paul Hogan officially claims inspired his movie character 'Crocodile' Dundee. Parkinson smirked through the interview, making much of the fact Ansell didn't wear shoes. Hilarity followed the disclosure that he'd slept on the floor of his fancy hotel suite, preferring the carpet to a bed. He said the floor was closer to reality.

At the time he lived with his wife and kids on Melaleuca Station, 140km east of Darwin, a 'buffalo block' allocated by the Northern Territory government in '84. They slept under a tarpaulin and cooked by campfire. It took four years to finish the homestead, working as time and money allowed.

'But what do you do all evening, without TV?' Parkinson asked condescendingly, urging his guest to perform 'one of your tricks'.

The bushman obliged by picking up a five-cent coin between his teeth, while doing a pushup with one arm behind his back. More hilarity and winking followed between audience and host – not one of whom could have picked up that coin, let alone lasted five minutes up the Fitzmaurice.

The last time his name came up was in August '99. The photographs were similar, frozen in time, but the headlines were different.

'Real Life "Crocodile" Dundee killed in shootout' and 'Cop Killer's Last Hours' rang out. It was alleged he'd shot and killed police Sergeant Glen Huitson at a roadblock when stopped in relation to two other murders.

Rod Ansell's life had ended in ignominy. Somehow he went from quintessential Aussie bushman to the sort of bloke who'd shoot a stranger – and a policeman at that.

When he first got back after being lost up the Fitzmaurice in '77, Rod Ansell didn't tell anyone about his amazing survival. In his book, he wrote 'I could see no point in saying: "Oh by the way, Mum, I got stranded in the bush for a couple of months." No point at all. A bit like yelling "Fire!" after the house burnt down.' As it was, the story was so incredible it was bound to get out.

continued

In May that year Ansell had set out, with two pups as companions, to go fishing. He wasn't specific about his plans. He told his girlfriend he was heading for the Victoria River with his boat and dinghy and would be gone a couple of months.

At 22 he was an experienced bushman, having moved to 'the land of lots of time' at 15 from country Queensland. The tide turned against him on the first day. As he limped the boat toward shore against the current, 'something big' capsized the boat. He clambered into the dinghy and grabbed the pups and what gear he could as everything else floated away. Simultaneously bailing and rowing for his life, Ansell headed up the Fitzmaurice River instead. Three days later he was on the bank, almost 200km from the nearest settlement.

He had just started to unload the dinghy when a 16-foot (4.8m) crocodile attacked at close range. 'Took no notice of me,' Ansell recalled dryly. 'Just came straight in, broad daylight and all. I snatched the rifle and blasted her . . . the dogs must have been too much of a temptation, laid on like that.' Ansell kept the croc's head as a souvenir; he had an oar, a rifle, 27 bullets, two knives, a steel and a stone. There was a swag, tarpaulin and three tins – one empty and the one less than half-full of sugar. He salvaged two shirts, a pair of shorts, jeans, a belt and jacket. He had lost his boots, which he seldom wore, and it would be years before he wore boots again.

Over the weeks, Ansell shot wild cattle and buffalo, both for the meat and their blood, which had to substitute for water. He knew how to slit their throats, drain the meat and dry it so it would last. He made a unique bag to hold his hunting gear.

'I saw a young bull on my way back to camp. I shot that, then cut the scrotum off. When the testicles had been taken out I dropped the knives and things into the empty pouch of the scrotum and tied it around my waist with a strip of greenhide.'

He used the gunpowder from a bullet to prime his fire and slept in the fork of a tree away from crocodiles, sharing the branches with a brown snake. 'He didn't take much notice of me after he got used to me, and I left him alone,' he wrote.

He made a rope from a cowhide by cutting two narrow strips in an ever-increasing circle, then twisting the strands together. 'It would come in handy if I broke a leg and couldn't hunt, or if I ran out of ammunition. I could use it to trap a beast.'

Ansell marked the sunrise each day with a notch in the tree, philosophical about his chance of rescue. He reasoned he'd have to wait for the tide to return to Victoria Channel. He'd have to make his bullets last, because he was now too weak to run down a bull, or to walk out of there.

He didn't miss people, he recalled. 'It's best to be by yourself . . . maybe it's got something to do with being in tune with the land, something like that . . . Although the thought did cross my mind that if I hadn't been like that I would never have ended up in such a situation in the first place.'

He passed the lonely days writing poetry. 'Well, committing it to memory really,' he wrote, 'seeing I had nothing to write on.' The poetry, like the bushman, was unpretentious. He recalled his embarrassment when his mates found out about it. They were aghast. 'Their reaction was "Getaway! You're having me on!"' he wrote.

He spent his nights in the tree, watching dingoes kill. 'Very cruel hunters, dingoes,' he mused, (but) 'the sound of the pack howling on a moonlit night is one of the most beautiful things you can hear in the bush.'

After five weeks a plane came. He saw it, chased it, watched it fly away. It started to get him down. 'With no one to talk to, you begin to lose your feeling of who you are. It's probably like the thing about time: with nothing to relate time to, it would be like living in a vacuum, so keeping track of the days became important,' he wrote.

Impossibly, there was discovery and rescue. Four stockmen from the station 200km away happened upon him by chance. Ansell certainly wasn't expecting them. His two months was up, but if people were looking, and found his boat, they'd go up the Victoria River where he was originally headed, not the Fitzmaurice where he ended up.

continued

But they came. Ansell heard the sound of horse bells floating down the river and paddled towards it. He hitched the boat and ran along the horse tracks until he saw a man. He told the story of their meeting.

'I said "G'day" and he said, "Where'd you spring from?"

"I've had a bit of bad luck and my boat tipped about seven weeks ago."

"Do you know what day it is?"

"I never know what day it is,"' replied Ansell.

He returned in no mood to brag.

'I didn't tell anyone what had happened. Not at first. I hadn't talked about it because I really didn't think it was that important. Maybe I shouldn't have got stranded in the first place.'

Ansell's story hit the headlines in August '77, and he relived his experience in a film called To Fight The Wild, then he wrote the book because, he said, he needed the money to pay debt incurred while he was lost on the river. The book led to celebrity interviews like the aforementioned Parkinson debacle and other unwelcome trips to the city. And it came at a cost Ansell never anticipated. Unlike Hollywood's (and Hogan's) 'Crocodile' Dundee, he lost the respect of his peers by going public.

'Proving the point about the story being true or not wouldn't matter that much. Because the people it would affect, who affect me, are the people who live where I work, and know me. And people up here have a phobia about appearing on the media. So that was detrimental to my standing in their eyes . . . they thought it was a terrible thing to do.'

It was a rejection from which there was no return. After the fuss, Ansell went back to Melaleuca Station. Journalist Chips Mackinolty, who met him in the '80s, said he was 'articulate and likeable, if somewhat intense.' Others were less charitable. Ansell knew people found him hard to get along with. He wrote that having a quick temper, and 'being a little bloke', he learned actions speak louder than words. 'I can't see the sense in arguing about something,' he said.

If the '80s started with promise – in '87 he was named Territorian of the Year – things went from bad to worse when the Ansells destroyed 3,000 head of the buffalo on their property to comply with the Territory disease control program. Three neighbouring owners, including the Sultan of Brunei, each got $100,000 government loans in compensation. The Ansells didn't. They said it was because they criticised the plan, the government said their claim didn't measure up. The marriage collapsed and in '90 Ansell stood for parliament, still fighting stock eradication. He lost.

In June '91 the Ansells were forced to sell up. 'It's not just me that's gone under, it's an entire industry,' he told reporters.

'He basically walked away from it,' said the current manager of Melaleuca Station. When Paul Hogan found international movie success, Ansell took him to court seeking royalties. He lost again.

In truth, 'Crocodile' Dundee wasn't really his story. For a start, Hogan ditched the poetry and introspection that were central to the man who wrote To Fight The Wild. 'Crocodile' Dundee was friendly and well-liked. Ansell preferred his own company and others preferred it that way too. More importantly, Hogan's character took his native self-reliance into the modern world and came out on top. Ansell, the 'real Dundee' did not.

In '92 he was convicted of stealing cattle from a neighbouring property and assaulting the station owner. He said he'd mistakenly set up a yard two kilometres within the boundary of the neighbour's 40,000 square kilometre station. He was given a two-year bond and fined $500. He vowed to fight on. 'I've got two boys growing up. I've always told them: "If you live your life straight and stand up, you'll be all right." And I won't be able to say that unless I get this sorted out.'

Since his death, reports have circulated that Ansell was a changed man. Some said he was involved with harder drugs. Rumours abound. An old acquaintance told The Australian he was shocked by their last encounter.

continued

'He'd shaved his head and put cowboy boots on. Rod always wore no shoes and he had long hair. And he knew who I was and I knew who I was looking at but instead of saying "How you going, Halsey?" as he'd normally do, he said nothing.'

The coroner will decide, on the balance of probabilities, what led Rod Ansell onto the track he took. What is certain is that the police had been looking for him for 12 hours after shootings at two properties. But they didn't expect to find him armed at a roadblock in broad daylight, as the NT Assistant Police Commissioner John Daulby explained. 'I am at a loss to say anything about the motive. If this person wanted to secrete himself he could easily have done that. He was a bushman.'

Journalist Paul Toohey described the death scene in The Australian.

'Pathetically gaunt, Rod Ansell wore an expression of utmost misery. It wasn't that he was dead . . . It wasn't that Ansell's life had turned wretched suddenly on the Tuesday morning. He had been that way for years.'

He was a far cry from the man once described as 'an unassuming achiever, someone who embodies the spirit of the Territory'. Ironically, it's an epithet that fits Glen Huitson – a heroic young father simply doing his job in a part of Australia where a policeman hadn't been killed in 47 years. Three others ended up in hospital. And then there's Constable Jim O'Brien, the country copper, who saw a mate cut down and was forced to kill Ansell himself.

At any time in those last hours Ansell could have stopped his car and shot himself, but he didn't. Such was the journey of the poetry-writing bushman. He may have fought the wild and won but in the end he was irretrievably lost in his own heart of darkness, driving deliberately towards a police roadblock as a means to his end.

Figure 10.1   Published article in *FHM*

The real life Crocodile Dundee and me went back a long way.

The first time I heard his name was in 1977, but it wasn't Crocodile Dundee back then, it was 'modern day Robinson Crusoe'.

I was a cadet reporter then and it was a big news story. Some bloke was said to have survived for eight weeks in the wild, without fresh water and plagued by crocodiles. In fact, it was claimed, he had not just survived, he had thrived.

The first time I heard his voice was in 1981 and I was sitting on my living room floor with one leg in plaster to the hip, using the ABC radio morning book reading to drown out the roar of traffic on Sydney's Willoughby Road.

Over the weeks that followed I became fascinated by the story described in *To Fight The Wild*. It was incredible to think that such a man could still exist near the end of the twentieth century.

A man who so matter-of-factly described how he had lived in a tree with a green tree snake, caught buffalo with his bare hands, slaughtered and eaten them. Everyone I knew would have been dead on the first day, when a 16-foot crocodile flipped his boat. But he was cool, so cool about it. He explained why in the preface of his book.

'All the blokes up in this country, who work with cattle, ringers, stockmen, bull catchers, whatever, all of them, have really narrow shaves all the time. But they never talk about it . . .

I think the opinion is that if you come through in one piece, and you're still alive, then nothing else really matters. The event is over . . . It's like going out to shoot a kangaroo. You don't come back and say you missed by half an inch. You either got him or you didn't. So that is how I looked at it. Until the papers got hold of the story, and that changed a lot of things.'

continued

I first saw him in 1984 on the *Michael Parkinson Show*, the episode Paul Hogan officially claims inspired his character, Crocodile Dundee.

And I squirmed as Parkinson smirked his way through the bushman's story, making much of the fact that he didn't wear shoes. Much hilarity followed the disclosure that the bushman had slept on the floor of his fancy hotel suite, preferring the carpet to a too-soft bed.

The bushman responded laconically. He was still in his twenties then, his unwanted adventure a thing of the past. He was, that night, an innocent abroad in a different jungle.

'But what do you do all evening, without TV?' Parkinson asked urbanely, urging his guest to show the audience 'one of your tricks'.

The bushman obliged by picking up a five-cent coin between his teeth, while doing a push up with one arm behind his back.

More hilarity and winking between audience and host.

Go on Parkinson, I thought, you do it.

The last time I saw him was in the newspapers, just recently. The photographs were the same, frozen in time, but the headlines were different – 'Real Life Crocodile Dundee killed in Shootout' and 'Cop Killer's Last Hours' and 'A Myth Ends in Bullets and Tears'.

We never actually met, Rod Ansell and I, and I couldn't say I knew him. But that's the point.

Rod Ansell's extraordinary story ended in ignominy and the needless death of another human being. Somewhere along the line, he went from a barefoot poet who liked his own company to the sort of person who'd shoot a man because he's a policeman.

But his fifteen minutes of fame were the stuff of legend.

When he first got back, Rod Ansell didn't tell anyone about his amazing survival, for fear of upsetting his mother (and she was). In the preface to the book, he wrote: 'I could see no point in saying: "Oh by the way Mum, I got stranded in the bush for a couple of months." No point at all. A bit like yelling "Fire!" after the house has burnt down.'

But the story was so incredible, it was bound to get out. In May 1977, Ansell set out, accompanied by two eight-week-old pups, to go fishing. He wasn't too specific about his plans, he wasn't sure himself, but he told his girlfriend Lorraine, that he'd be gone a couple of months.

He was barely out of his teens, but he was bush savvy, having moved to the Territory at age 15 from country Queensland and he was 'living in the land of lots of time', where the vagaries' nature of the landscape and weather often protracted travel.

But he was barely a day into his journey when the tide turned against him. As he limped toward shore and shelter, something heaved up from under the boat and turned it over. Ansell retrieved the dinghy from the wrecked boat and the pups from the water before the tide came back for him.

As the dinghy and all his gear were swept out with the tide, Ansell grabbed what he could as it all floated by. Finally he was marooned up the Fitzmaurice River, almost 200 kilometers from the nearest permanent human settlement. Simultaneously bailing out the boat and rowing for his life, Ansell headed for shore. Three days later he was on the bank, where he started to unload the dogs, one of which had a broken leg. Out of nowhere came a 16-foot crocodile.

'Took no notice of me,' Ansell recalled, 'but just came straight in, broad daylight and all. I snatched the rifle and blasted her . . . the dogs must have been too much of a temptation, laid on for her like that.' Ansell kept the croc's head as a souvenir.

Apart from the dogs, he had one oar, a rifle, 27 bullets, two knives, a steel and a stone. There was a swag of blankets and tarpaulin, with two swag straps, one in two sections connected by the swivel chain from a set of hobbles. Three tins, including the empty pea tin and the one less than half full of sugar. Two shirts, one pair of shorts, jeans and a jacket, a belt. He had lost his boots, which he seldom wore, and it would be years before he wore boots again.

continued

Over the weeks that followed, Ansell shot wild cattle, both for the meat and their blood, which had to substitute for water. He knew how to slit their throats, drain the meat, slice it and dry it so it would last. He used the gunpowder from a bullet to prime his fire. He slept in the fork of a tree, away from crocodiles drawn by the scent of dog, sharing his space with a big green snake. He made a rope by tearing a hole in the center of a cowhide and cutting a narrow strip in an ever-increasing circle. He marked the sunrise each day with a notch in the tree.

From the first moment, Ansell was philosophical about his chances of rescue – in fact his only hope, he thought, was to wait for the tide to float back into Victoria Channel. And he knew he'd have to make his bullets last, because he was way too weak to run a bull down on foot, or to walk out of there. He didn't miss people, he recalled. 'It's best to be by yourself . . . maybe it's got something to do with being in tune with the land, something like that . . . All that kind of thing standing me in good stead on the Fitzmaurice. Although the thought did cross my mind that if I hadn't been like that I would never have ended up in such a situation in the first place.'

He passed the days writing poetry. 'Well, committing it to memory really,' he wrote, 'seeing I had nothing to write on.' He spent his nights in the tree, watching the dingoes kill. 'Very cruel hunters, dingoes,' he mused, (but) 'the sound of the pack howling out in the wild country on a clear moonlit night is one of the most beautiful things you can hear in the bush.'

Five weeks into his odyssey, a light plane came his way. He saw it, chased it, and watched it fly over the horizon.

He wrote in *To Fight the Wild* that it started to get him down. 'With no-one to talk to, you begin to lose your feeling of who you are. It's probably like the thing about time: with nothing to relate time to, it would be like living in a vacuum, so keeping track of the days became important.'

Finally, impossibly, there was discovery and rescue by three Aboriginal stockmen and their white cattle manager. Ansell wasn't expecting them by any means. He knew his two months was almost up, but it was still too soon for his girlfriend to have raised the alarm. If they were looking for him, and found his boat, they'd go up the Victoria River, not the Fitzmaurice.

But they came. Ansell heard the sound of horse bells floating down the river and paddled towards it. He hitched the boat and ran along the horse tracks. Incredibly, he saw a hat attached to a man on a horse. He tells the story of their meeting.

'I said "G'day" and he said, "Where'd you come from?"
"I've had a bit of bad luck and my boat tipped about seven weeks ago."
"Do you know what day it is?"
"I never know what day it is."'

And so Ansell was returned to civilization, but in no mood to brag of his escape.

'I didn't tell anyone, not even Lorraine, what had happened. Not at first. I hadn't talked about it because I really didn't think it was that important. Maybe I shouldn't have got stranded in the first place, but these things happen.'

Back in Western Australia, Ansell's story hit the headlines in August 1977. First he was approached for a feature film about his experience, called *To Fight The Wild*. From that he wrote the book, published in 1980, because he needed the money. He had breached cattle catching contracts while lost in the wild and came back to debts.

The publication of the book gave him new celebrity and led to interviews like the one on the Parkinson program and trips to the city he never enjoyed. But it came at a cost Ansell had never anticipated. Unlike Crocodile Dundee, he lost the respect of his peers by going public. Even being named Territorian of the Year in 1988 didn't help. It was a crushing blow.

'Proving the point about the story being true or not wouldn't matter that much. Because the people it would affect, who affect me, are the people who live where I work, and know me. And

continued

people up here have a phobia about appearing on the media. So that was detrimental to my standing in their eyes, they thought it was a terrible thing to do.'

It didn't get any better. The 1980s were a hard time, even for hard, resilient bushmen. He watched Paul Hogan turn his story into international movie success and took him to court for royalties, but lost. Hogan's character took his simple bush skills to the concrete jungle of the modern world and came out on top. The real Crocodile Dundee did not.

Later his livelihood, catching wild cattle and bulls, was destroyed by a Queensland government scheme to slaughter feral stock in a bid to eradicate domestic livestock diseases. 'It's not just me that's gone under, it's an entire industry,' he argued bitterly. He took on the government about the buffalo cull, and lost there too – he claimed he was ripped off in his compensation. He stood for parliament as an independent and lost again.

The bushman had a property, Melaleuca, but he wasn't a farmer. 'He basically walked away from it,' says the current manager.

'He had a mimosa problem which he didn't do anything about and it exploded and took over the floodplain. It went from a good station to a next to useless station.'

Ansell didn't handle the changes. He was accustomed to never complain and never explain, to run his own race. He was always hard to get along with, he admitted. Having a quick temper, and being a little bloke, he said, he learned actions speak louder than words. 'I can't see the sense in arguing about something,' he wrote in *To Fight the Wild*.

He lost the property, his wife and kids in the early 90s and went bush. At the time he was killed, he'd been living in an Aboriginal outcamp on a remote station. In 1992 he was convicted of stealing cattle and assaulting a station owner. An old colleague told *The Australian* that the Ansell he last saw was a changed man.

'He's shaved his head and put cowboy boots on. Rod always wore no shoes and he had long hair. And he knew who I was and I knew who I was looking at but instead of saying "How you going Halsey", as he'd normally do, he said nothing.'

The coroner will decide, on the balance of probabilities, what led Rod Ansell to take the track he did. What is certain is that the police had been looking for him for 12 hours after shootings at two properties. But they didn't expect to find him at a roadblock in broad daylight, as the NT Assistant Police Commissioner John Daulby explained.

'I am at a loss to say anything about the motive. If this person wanted to secrete himself he could easily have done that. He was a bushman.'

Journalist Paul Toohey described the scene in *The Australian*.

'Pathetically gaunt, his grimy face and feet (bare as usual) suggesting a heavy ingrained dirt that could never be scrubbed clean, Rod Ansell wore an expression of utmost misery . . . It wasn't that Ansell's life had turned wretched suddenly on that Tuesday morning. He had been that way for years.'

In his wake he left a policeman dead and three other people in hospital. He was a far cry from the man once described as 'an unassuming achiever, someone who embodies the spirit of the Territory.'

Such was the journey of the poetry-writing buffalo catcher who liked to be alone, from Territorian of the Year to alleged drug-addled cop killer. From an oddity called the modern-day Robinson Crusoe, to a hero called Crocodile Dundee, to a redundant buffalo catcher, failed farmer and family man and finally driving towards the police roadblock as a means to his end.

Figure 10.2   First draft

The first time most Australians heard his name was in 1977, but it wasn't Crocodile Dundee back then, it was 'Modern-day Robinson Crusoe'. Some bloke was said to have survived for eight weeks in the wilds of the Northern Territory, without fresh water and plagued by crocodiles. In fact they reckoned he had not just survived, he had thrived.

In 1980, Rod Ansell was big news again when he published a book, *To Fight The Wild*, and city folk were temporarily fascinated by his story. It was incredible to think that such a man could still exist near the end of the twentieth century.

This man calmly described how he lived in a tree with an eight-foot snake, caught buffalo with his bare hands, slaughtered and ate them. He should have been dead on the first day, when a giant crocodile flipped his boat. But he was so matter-of-fact. He explained why in his book.

'All the blokes up in this country, who work with cattle, ringers, stockmen, bull catchers, whatever, all of them, have really narrow shaves all the time. But they never talk about it . . . I think the opinion is that if you come through in one piece, and you're still alive, then nothing else really matters. The event is over. It's like going out to shoot a kangaroo. You don't come back and say you missed by half an inch. You either got him or you didn't. So that is how I looked at it. Until the papers got hold of the story, and that changed a lot of things.'

In 1984 he was paraded on The Michael Parkinson Show; the episode Paul Hogan officially claims inspired his movie character, Crocodile Dundee.

Parkinson smirked urbanely through the interview, making much of the fact Ansell didn't wear shoes. Hilarity followed the disclosure that he'd slept on the floor of his fancy hotel suite, preferring the carpet to a bed.

The bushman responded laconically. He was an innocent abroad that night but he didn't seem to mind.

At the time he lived with his wife and kids on Melaleuca Station, 140km east of Darwin, a 'buffalo block' allocated by the Northern Territory government in 1984. They slept under a tarpaulin with swags and mosquito nets and cooked by campfire. It took four years to finish the homestead, working as time and money allowed.

'But what do you do all evening, without TV?' Parkinson asked condescendingly, urging his guest to perform 'one of your tricks'.

The bushman obliged by picking up a five-cent coin between his teeth, while doing a push up with one arm behind his back.

More hilarity and winking between audience and host – not one of whom could have picked up that coin, let alone last five minutes up the Fitzmaurice.

The last time his name came up was in the newspapers, just recently. The photographs were the same, frozen in time, but the headlines were different – 'Real Life Crocodile Dundee killed in shootout', 'Cop Killer's Last Hours' and 'Crocodile Dundee's murderous rampage'.

Rod Ansell's extraordinary life ended in ignominy and the indefensible death of another human being. Somehow he went from the quintessential Aussie bushman to the sort of bloke who'd shoot a man because he was a policeman.

But his fifteen minutes of fame were the stuff of legend.

When he first got back, Rod Ansell didn't tell anyone about his amazing survival, for fear of upsetting his mother (and she was). In the book, he wrote: 'I could see no point in saying: "Oh by the way Mum, I got stranded in the bush for a couple of months." No point at all. A bit like yelling "Fire!" after the house has burnt down.' As it was, the story was so incredible it was bound to get out.

In May 1977 Ansell had set out to go fishing, with two pups for company. He wasn't too specific about his plans – he wasn't sure himself. He told his girlfriend he was heading up the Victoria River with his boat and dinghy and he'd be gone a couple of months.

continued

Barely out of his teens, he was an experienced bushman having moved to the Territory at 15 from country Queensland. He was used to 'living in the land of lots of time' where the vagaries of landscape and weather often protracted travel.

Barely a day into his journey, the tide turned against him. As he limped the boat toward shore against the current, something capsized the boat. Ansell had barely retrieved the dinghy and the pups before the tide came back for them.

As the dinghy and his gear went out on the tide, Ansell grabbed what he could as it all swept by. Simultaneously bailing out the dinghy and rowing for his life, Ansell headed for the shore of the Fitzmaurice River. Three days later he was on the bank, almost 200 kilometres from the nearest permanent human settlement.

He had just started to unload the gear and the dogs, one of which had a broken leg, when out of nowhere and at close range a 16-foot crocodile attacked.

'Took no notice of me,' Ansell recalled dryly, 'but just came straight in, broad daylight and all. I snatched the rifle and blasted her . . . the dogs must have been too much of a temptation, laid on like that.' Ansell kept the croc's head as a souvenir.

He had one oar, a rifle, 27 bullets, two knives, a steel and a stone. There was a swag of blankets and tarpaulin, two swag straps and three tins – one empty and the one less than half full of sugar. He salvaged two shirts, a pair of shorts, jeans, a belt and jacket. He had lost his boots, which he seldom wore, and it would be years before he wore boots again.

Over the weeks, Ansell shot wild cattle and buffalo, both for the meat and their blood, which had to substitute for water. He knew how to slit their throats, drain the meat, slice it and dry it so it would last. He made a new oar to replace the one that was lost

by ....
He used the gunpowder from a bullet to prime his fire.

He slept in the fork of a tree, away from crocodiles, sharing his space with a green snake because he knew it wouldn't hurt him.

Insert quote ....
He made a rope by tearing a hole in the centre of a cowhide and cutting a narrow strip in an ever-increasing circle. He marked the sunrise each day with a notch in the tree.

From the first, Ansell was philosophical about his chance of rescue. He reasoned he'd have to wait for the tide to return to the Victoria Channel. He'd have to make his bullets last, because he was now too weak to run a bull down on foot, or to walk out of there.

He didn't miss people, he recalled. 'It's best to be by yourself . . . maybe it's got something to do with being in tune with the land, something like that . . . All that kind of thing standing me in good stead on the Fitzmaurice. Although the thought did cross my mind that if I hadn't been like that I would never have ended up in such a situation in the first place.' He passed the days writing poetry. 'Well, committing it to memory really,' he wrote, 'seeing I had nothing to write on.' The poetry, like the bushman, was unpretentious. The bush talked to him, and he talked back.

I have flouted the wild,
I have followed her here
Fearless, familiar, alone;
Yet the end is near
And the day will come
When I shall be overthrown

He recalled his embarrassment when his mates found out about the poetry. When it came out, they were aghast. 'Their reaction was "Get away! You're having me on!"' he wrote.

He spent his nights in the tree, watching dingoes kill. 'Very cruel hunters, dingoes,' he mused, (but) 'the sound of the pack howling out in the wild country on a clear moonlit night is one of the most beautiful things you can hear in the bush.'

continued

After five weeks a light plane came. He saw it, chased it, watched it fly over the horizon. He wrote in To Fight the Wild that it started to get him down. 'With no-one to talk to, you begin to lose your feeling of who you are. It's probably like the thing about time: with nothing to relate time to, it would be like living in a vacuum, so keeping track of the days became important.'

Impossibly, there was discovery and rescue. Three Aboriginal stockmen, one of who owned the nearest station, and their white cattle manager happened upon him by chance. Ansell certainly wasn't expecting them. He knew his two months was up, but it was too soon for his girlfriend to raise the alarm. If they were looking for him and found his boat, they'd go up the Victoria River, not the Fitzmaurice.

But they came. Ansell heard the sound of horse bells floating down the river and paddled towards it. He hitched the boat and ran along the horse tracks. Incredibly, he saw a man on a horse. He told the story of their meeting.

'I said "G'day" and he said,
"Where'd you spring from?"
"I've had a bit of bad luck and my boat tipped about seven weeks ago."
"Do you know what day it is?"
"I never know what day it is."'

Ansell was returned to civilisation but in no mood to brag.

'I didn't tell anyone . . . what had happened. Not at first. I hadn't talked about it because I really didn't think it was that important. Maybe I shouldn't have got stranded in the first place, but these things happen.'

Ansell's story hit the headlines in August 1977. Then he was asked to re-live his experience in a film called To Fight The Wild. From that he wrote the book because he said he needed the money. He had broken cattle catching contracts while lost and came back to debts.

The book led to celebrity interviews like the one on Parkinson and trips to the city he never enjoyed. And it came at a cost Ansell had never anticipated. Unlike Crocodile Dundee, he lost the respect of his peers by going public.

'Proving the point about the story being true or not wouldn't matter that much. Because the people it would affect, who affect me, are the people who live where I work, and know me. And people up here have a phobia about appearing on the media. So that was detrimental to my standing in their eyes . . . they thought it was a terrible thing to do.'

It was a crushing rejection from which there was no return.

After the fuss, Ansell went back to Melaleuca Station. Journalist Chips Mackinolty wrote of meeting him in the 1980s. 'He was buffalo-catching in central Arnhem Land. It was a tough life by any standard, working seven days a week from dawn to dusk alongside the Aboriginal stockmen who would later employ him. There were few chances for a beer around the campfire, but when that happened he was an articulate and likeable man, if somewhat intense.'

Others who knew him then were less charitable about his temperament, especially when it came to guns. Ansell accepted that people found him hard to get along with. He was a man who didn't complain and didn't explain. He wrote in To Fight the Wild.

That having a quick temper, and being a little bloke, he learned actions speak louder than words. 'I can't see the sense in arguing about something,' he said.

The 80s had started with promise – in 1987 he was named Territorian of the Year – but things went from bad to worse. To comply with the Territory government's stock disease control program the Ansells destroyed 3000 head of the buffalo on their property, expecting to be compensated like the other graziers who had been forced to destock. Three neighbouring owners, including the Sultan of Brunei, each got $100,000 government loans to compensate for their losses. The Ansells didn't. They said it was because they had publicly criticised the plan, the government said

continued

their claim didn't measure up. Joanne Ansell told The Sun-Herald that their sons lived in fear of having to leave their home after a visit from a government veterinarian.

'He sat down with us over a cup of tea and said it was not his concern if we were forced off our property. He said "People go broke all the time," and shrugged his shoulders,' she said.

They battled on – Joanne started a boat hire business to bring in cash, but to no avail.

It has since been said that Ansell also grew cannabis on his property, as cash-strapped farmers have been known to do. Ansell is reported to have been a long-term heavy user but it didn't feature in his telling of his story. If he pined for drugs when lost in the wild, he didn't mention it.

The marriage collapsed but the couple tried to hold on to the property. In 1990 Ansell stood for parliament as an Independent, still fighting stock eradication. He lost. In June 1991 the Ansells were forced to sell up after 15 years. 'I've finished bashing my head up against a brick wall,' he told reporters. 'It's not just me that's gone under, it's an entire industry.'

'He basically walked away from it,' says the current manager of Melaleuca Station.

'He had a mimosa problem which he didn't do anything about and it exploded and took over the floodplain. It went from a good station to a next to useless station.'

When Paul Hogan found international movie success, Ansell took him to court seeking royalties. He lost again. In truth, Crocodile Dundee wasn't really his story. For a start, Hogan ditched the poetry and intense introspection that were central to the man who wrote To Fight The Wild. Crocodile Dundee was friendly, easy-going and well-liked. Ansell was always his own man.

More importantly, Hogan's character was able to take his native self-reliance into the modern world and come out on top. The real Crocodile Dundee did not.

When he was killed, he'd been living rough in an Aboriginal outcamp on a remote station.

Insert quotes re aboriginal people.

In 1992 he was convicted of stealing buffalo from a neighbouring property and assaulting the station owner. Ansell maintained he was genuinely mistaken in setting up a temporary yard two kilometres within the boundary of 40,000 square kilometre Mainaru Station. He insisted that the buffalo had been driven in from Arnhem Land. He was given a two-year bond and fined $500. At the time, he vowed to clear his name.

'I've got two boys who are growing up. I've always told them: "If you live your life straight and stand up, you'll be alright." And I won't be able to say that unless I get this sorted out.'

Since his death, reports have circulated that Ansell was a changed man. Rumours abound about what really happened and why. Some said he was involved with hard drugs. Several days after his death Ansell's girlfriend turned up in Brisbane, apparently on the run from him herself. Police said she was not a suspect.

A man who said he'd known him for years told The Australian he was shocked by their last encounter. 'He'd shaved his head and put cowboy boots on. Rod always wore no shoes and he had long hair. And he knew who I was and I knew who I was looking at but instead of saying "How you going Halsey", as he'd normally do, he said nothing.'

The coroner will decide, on the balance of probabilities, what led Rod Ansell to take the track he did. What is certain is that the police had been looking for him for 12 hours after shootings at two properties. But they didn't expect to find him at roadblock in broad daylight, as the NT Assistant Police Commissioner John Daulby explained.

'I am at a loss to say anything about the motive. If this person wanted to secrete himself he could easily have done that. He was a bushman.'

Journalist Paul Toohey described the scene in The Australian.

'Pathetically gaunt, his grimy face and feet (bare as usual) suggesting a heavy ingrained dirt that could never be . . . scrubbed clean, Rod Ansell wore an expression of utmost misery. It wasn't that he was dead . . . It wasn't that Ansell's life had turned wretched suddenly on that Tuesday morning. He had been that way for years.'

continued

He was a far cry from the man once described as 'an unassuming achiever, someone who embodies the spirit of the Territory.' Ironically, it's an epithet that fits the policeman he allegedly killed – a heroic young father recently commended for selflessly saving lives. He was simply doing his job in a part of Australia where a policeman hadn't been killed in 47 years. Three others ended up in hospital. And then there's the other country copper who saw a mate cut down and was forced to kill.

At any time in those last fateful hours Rod Ansell could have stopped his car and shot himself, but he didn't.

Such was the journey of the poetry-writing bushman shipwrecked up the Fitzmaurice from Territorian of the Year to alleged cop killer.

From an oddity called the modern-day Robinson Crusoe, to a hero called Crocodile Dundee, to a redundant buffalo catcher, failed husband and dispossessed grazier.

And finally, irretrievably lost in the heart of darkness, a desperate man driving deliberately towards a police roadblock as a means to his end.

Figure 10.3   Second draft

The first time the world heard of Rod Ansell was in 1977, but he wasn't called Crocodile Dundee back then, he was 'Modern-day Robinson Crusoe'.

Some bloke was said to have survived for eight weeks in the wilds of the Northern Territory, without fresh water and plagued by crocodiles. In fact they reckoned he had not just survived, he had thrived.

In 1980, Ansell was big news again when he published a book, *To Fight The Wild*, and urban Australians were temporarily fascinated by his story. It was incredible to think that such a man could still exist near the end of the twentieth century.

This man calmly described how he lived in a tree with an eight-foot snake, caught buffalo with his bare hands, slaughtered and ate them.

Anyone else would have been dead on the first day, when a giant crocodile flipped his boat. But he was so matter-of-fact about it. He explained why in his book.

'All the blokes up in this country, who work with cattle, ringers, stockmen, bull catchers, whatever, all of them, have really narrow shaves all the time. But they never talk about it . . . I think the opinion is that if you come through in one piece, and you're still alive, then nothing else really matters.

'It's like going out to shoot a kangaroo. You don't come back and say you missed by half an inch. You either got him or you didn't. So that is how I looked at it.

'Until the papers got hold of the story, and that changed a lot of things.'

In 1984 he was paraded on *The Michael Parkinson Show* – the episode Paul Hogan officially claims inspired his movie character, Crocodile Dundee.

Parkinson smirked urbanely through the interview, making much of the fact Ansell didn't wear shoes. Hilarity followed the disclosure that he'd slept on the floor of his fancy hotel suite, preferring the carpet to a bed.

The bushman responded laconically. At the time he lived with his wife and kids on Melaleuca Station, 140km east of Darwin, a 'buffalo block' allocated by the Northern Territory government in 1984. They slept under a tarpaulin with swags and mosquito nets and cooked by campfire. It took four years to finish the homestead, working as time and money allowed.

continued

'But what do you do all evening, without TV?' Parkinson asked condescendingly, urging his guest to perform 'one of your tricks'.

The bushman obliged by picking up a five-cent coin between his teeth, while doing a push up with one arm behind his back.

More hilarity and winking followed between audience and host – not one of whom could have picked up that coin, let alone lasted five minutes up the Fitzmaurice.

The last time his name came up was in the newspapers again, just recently. The photographs were the same, frozen in time, but the headlines were different – 'Real Life Crocodile Dundee killed in shootout', 'Cop Killer's Last Hours' and 'Crocodile Dundee's murderous rampage'.

Rod Ansell's extraordinary life ended in ignominy and the indefensible death of another human being. Somehow he went from the quintessential Aussie bushman to the sort of bloke who'd shoot a man because he was a policeman.

But his 15 minutes of fame were the stuff of legend.

When he first got back, Rod Ansell didn't tell anyone about his amazing survival, for fear of upsetting his mother (and she was). In the book, he wrote: 'I could see no point in saying: "Oh by the way Mum, I got stranded in the bush for a couple of months." No point at all. A bit like yelling "Fire!" after the house has burnt down.'

As it was, the story was so incredible it was bound to get out.

In May 1977 Ansell had set out to go fishing, with two pups for company. He wasn't too specific about his plans – he wasn't sure himself. He told his girlfriend he was heading up the Victoria River with his boat and dinghy and he'd be gone a couple of months.

At 22 he was an experienced bushman, having moved to the Territory at 15 from country Queensland. He was accustomed to 'living in the land of lots of time' where the vagaries of landscape and weather often protracted travel.

Barely a day into his journey, the tide turned against him. As he limped the boat toward shore against the current, 'something big' capsized the boat. Ansell had barely retrieved the dinghy and the pups before the tide came back.

As the dinghy and his gear went out on the tide, Ansell grabbed what he could as it all swept by. Simultaneously bailing out the dinghy and rowing for his life, Ansell headed for the shore of the Fitzmaurice River. Three days later he was on the bank, almost 200 kilometers from the nearest permanent human settlement.

He had just started to unload the gear and the dogs, one of which had a broken leg, when out of nowhere a 16-foot crocodile attacked at close range.

'Took no notice of me,' Ansell recalled dryly. 'Just came straight in, broad daylight and all. I snatched the rifle and blasted her . . . the dogs must have been too much of a temptation, laid on like that.' Ansell kept the croc's head as a souvenir.

He had an oar, a rifle, 27 bullets, two knives, a steel and a stone. There was a swag of blankets and tarpaulin, two swag straps and three tins – one empty and one less than half full of sugar. He salvaged two shirts, a pair of shorts, jeans, belt and jacket. He had lost his boots, which he seldom wore, and it would be years before he wore boots again.

Over the weeks, Ansell shot wild cattle and buffalo, both for the meat and their blood, which had to substitute for water. He knew how to slit their throats, drain the meat, slice it and dry it so it would last. He made a bag to hold his hunting gear.

'I saw a young bull on my way back to camp. I shot that, then cut the scrotum off. When the testicles and everything had been taken out I dropped the knives and things into the empty pouch of the scrotum and tied it around my waist with a strip of greenhide.'

He used the gunpowder from a bullet to prime his fire and slept in the fork of a tree, away from crocodiles, sharing the branches with a brown snake. 'Maybe he ate different gear, I don't really know,' Ansell wrote. 'But he didn't take much notice of me after he got used to me, and I left him alone.'

continued

He made a rope by tearing a hole in the centre of a cowhide and cutting two narrow strips in an ever-increasing circle then twisting the strands together.

'It would come in handy if I sprained an ankle or broke a leg and couldn't hunt, or if I lost the gun or ran out of ammunition. I could use it to trap a beast,' he wrote.

Ansell marked the sunrise each day with a notch in the tree, philosophical from the first about his chance of rescue. He reasoned he'd have to wait for the tide to return to the Victoria Channel. He'd have to make his bullets last, because he was now too weak to run a bull down on foot, or to walk out of there.

He didn't miss people much, he recalled. 'It's best to be by yourself . . . maybe it's got something to do with being in tune with the land, something like that . . . All that kind of thing standing me in good stead on the Fitzmaurice. Although the thought did cross my mind that if I hadn't been like that I would never have ended up in such a situation in the first place.' He passed the days writing poetry. 'Well, committing it to memory really,' he wrote, 'seeing I had nothing to write on.' The poetry, like the bushman, was unpretentious. The bush talked to him, and he talked back.

I have flouted the wild,
I have followed her here
Fearless, familiar, alone;
Yet the end is near
And the day will come
When I shall be overthrown

He recalled his embarrassment when his mates found out about the poetry. They were aghast. 'Their reaction was "Get away! You're having me on!"' he wrote.

At night, in the tree, he watched dingoes kill. 'Very cruel hunters, dingoes,' he mused, (but) 'the sound of the pack howling out in the wild country on a clear moonlit night is one of the most beautiful things you can hear in the bush.'

After five weeks a light plane came. He saw it, chased it, watched it fly over the horizon. He wrote in *To Fight the Wild* that it started to get him down. 'With no-one to talk to, you begin to lose your feeling of who you are. It's probably like the thing about time: with nothing to relate time to, it would be like living in a vacuum, so keeping track of the days became important.'

Impossibly, there was discovery and rescue. Three Aboriginal stockmen, one of whom owned the nearest station, and their white cattle manager happened upon him by chance. Ansell certainly wasn't expecting them. His two months was up, but it was too soon for his girlfriend to raise the alarm. If they were looking for him and found his boat, they'd go up the Victoria River, not the Fitzmaurice.

But they came. Ansell heard the sound of horse bells floating down the river and paddled towards it. He hitched the boat and ran along the horse tracks. Incredibly, he saw a man on a horse. He told the story of their meeting.

'I said "G'day" and he said, "Where'd you spring from?"

"I've had a bit of bad luck and my boat tipped about seven weeks ago."

"Do you know what day it is?"

"I never know what day it is."'

Ansell was returned to civilisation but in no mood to brag.

'I didn't tell anyone . . . what had happened. Not at first. I hadn't talked about it because I really didn't think it was that important. Maybe I shouldn't have got stranded in the first place, but these things happen.'

Ansell's story hit the headlines in August 1977. Then he was asked to relive his experience in a film called To Fight The Wild. From that he wrote the book because he said he needed the money. He had broken cattle catching contracts while lost and came back to debts.

continued

The book led to celebrity interviews like the one on Parkinson and trips to the city he never enjoyed. And it came at a cost Ansell had never anticipated. Unlike Crocodile Dundee, he lost the respect of his peers by going public.

'Proving the point about the story being true or not wouldn't matter that much. Because the people it would affect, who affect me, are the people who live where I work, and know me. And people up here have a phobia about appearing on the media. So that was detrimental to my standing in their eyes . . . they thought it was a terrible thing to do.'

It was a rejection from which there was no return.

After the fuss, Ansell went back to Melaleuca Station. Journalist Chips Mackinolty wrote of meeting him in the 1980s. 'He was buffalo-catching in central Arnhem Land. It was a tough life by any standard, working seven days a week from dawn to dusk alongside the Aboriginal stockmen who would later employ him. There were few chances for a beer around the campfire, but when that happened he was an articulate and likeable man, if somewhat intense.'

Others who knew him then were less charitable. Ansell accepted that people found him hard to get along with. He was a man who didn't complain but then he didn't explain either. He wrote in To Fight the Wild that having a quick temper, and 'being a little bloke', he learned actions speak louder than words. 'I can't see the sense in arguing about something,' he said.

If the 80s had started with promise – in 1987 he was named Territorian of the Year – things went from bad to worse. To comply with the Territory government's stock disease control program the Ansells destroyed 3000 head of the buffalo on their property, expecting to be compensated like the other graziers who had been forced to destock. Three neighbouring owners, including the Sultan of Brunei, each got $100,000 government loans to compensate for their losses. The Ansells didn't. They said it was because they had publicly criticised the plan, the government said their claim didn't measure up. Joanne Ansell told The Sun-Herald that their sons lived in fear of eviction after a visit from a government veterinarian.

'He sat down with us over a cup of tea and said it was not his concern if we were forced off our property. He said "People go broke all the time," and shrugged his shoulders,' she said.

They battled on – Joanne started a boat hire business to bring in cash – but to no avail.

The marriage collapsed but the couple tried to hold on to the property. In 1990 Ansell stood for parliament as an Independent, still fighting stock eradication. He lost. In June 1991 the Ansells were forced to sell up after 15 years. 'I've finished bashing my head up against a brick wall,' he told reporters. 'It's not just me that's gone under, it's an entire industry.'

'He basically walked away from it,' says the current manager of Melaleuca Station.

'He had a mimosa problem which he didn't do anything about and it exploded and took over the floodplain. It went from a good station to a next to useless station.'

It has since been said that Ansell farmed cannabis on his property, as cash-strapped farmers have been known to do. He is reported to have been a long-term heavy user but it didn't feature in his version of his life. If he pined for drugs while lost in the wild, he didn't mention it.

When Paul Hogan found international movie success, Ansell took him to court seeking royalties. He lost again. In truth, Crocodile Dundee wasn't really his story.

For a start, Hogan ditched the poetry and introspection that were central to the man who wrote To Fight The Wild. Crocodile Dundee was friendly, easy-going and well liked. Ansell preferred his own company and others often preferred it that way too.

More importantly, Hogan's character was able to take his native self-reliance into the modern world and come out on top. The real Crocodile Dundee did not.

When he was killed, he'd been living rough in an Aboriginal outcamp on a remote station. He spoke the Urapanga language fluently and was reportedly a fully initiated white man.

Cheryl White told The Australian she last saw her childhood friend a week before he died.

'He walked his brumbies through Arnhem Land. That's all he's ever done since he lost his property. He did a lot of cattle work with the Aborigines.'

continued

In 1992 Ansell was convicted of stealing cattle from a neighbouring property and assaulting the station owner. He maintained he was genuinely mistaken in setting up a temporary yard two kilometres within the boundary of 40,000 square kilometre Mainaru Station. He insisted that the cattle had been driven in from Arnhem Land. He was given a two-year bond and fined $500. At the time, he vowed to clear his name.

'I've got two boys who are growing up. I've always told them: "If you live your life straight and stand up, you'll be alright." And I won't be able to say that unless I get this sorted out.'

Since his death, reports have circulated that Ansell was a changed man. Some said he was involved with hard drugs. Days after his death Ansell's girlfriend turned up in Brisbane. Police said she was not a suspect. Rumours abound.

A man who said he'd known him for years told The Australian he was shocked by their last encounter. 'He'd shaved his head and put cowboy boots on. Rod always wore no shoes and he had long hair. And he knew who I was and I knew who I was looking at but instead of saying "How you going Halsey?" as he'd normally do, he said nothing.'

The coroner will decide, on the balance of probabilities, what led Rod Ansell to take the track he did. What is certain is that the police had been looking for him for 12 hours after shootings at two properties. But they didn't expect to find him at a roadblock in broad daylight, as the NT Assistant Police Commissioner John Daulby explained.

'I am at a loss to say anything about the motive. If this person wanted to secrete himself he could easily have done that. He was a bushman.'

Journalist Paul Toohey described the scene in The Australian.

'Pathetically gaunt, his grimy face and feet (bare as usual) suggesting a heavy ingrained dirt that could never be scrubbed clean, Rod Ansell wore an expression of utmost misery. It wasn't that he was dead . . . It wasn't that Ansell's life had turned wretched suddenly on that Tuesday morning. He had been that way for years.'

He was a far cry from the man once described as 'an unassuming achiever, someone who embodies the spirit of the Territory.' Ironically, it's an epithet that fits the policeman he allegedly killed – a heroic young father was simply doing his job in a part of Australia where a policeman hadn't been killed in 47 years. Three others ended up in hospital – and then there's the other country copper, who saw a mate cut down and was forced to kill.

At any time in those last fateful hours Rod Ansell could have stopped his car and shot himself, but he didn't. Such was the journey of the poetry-writing bushman shipwrecked up the Fitzmaurice from Territorian of the Year to alleged cop killer. From an oddity called the modern-day Robinson Crusoe, to a hero called Crocodile Dundee, to a redundant buffalo catcher, failed husband and dispossessed grazier. He may have fought the wild and won but in the end he was irretrievably lost in this own heart of darkness, driving deliberately towards a police roadblock as a means to his end.

Figure 10.4   Final draft

THEME AND STRUCTURE

The writer of this article set out to explore more than the idea that the machismo of the bushman, so admirable in a mythical sense, has no place in a modern society where no man is free to live by his own rules. This theme may be put succinctly with the phrase 'He conquered the wild but was lost in today's society'. Is the writer successful or does the shape of the narrative paint the central character as one-dimensional, a hero or a villain? Responses to the publication of this article included that it demonized the central figure as 'some bitter and dangerous monstrosity' and 'treated the subject with respect, despite his indefensible actions'.

The writer also set out to explore how private people become public property through events not of their own choosing and often pay a terrible price. She was fascinated by the idea that she had somehow formed a view of this man's character over a decade or more without ever having access to the subject. Moreover, that even those people close to the dead man were perplexed by his violent end. Did the writer succeed?

It may be argued that the piece is successful on the first count but that the second aspect, more interesting to the writer, is lost. The focus of the article is on events more than 20 years earlier, which represented a turning point for the main character. A simplistic view is that this part of the man's life was the most sensational, and that readers in the demographic are too young to remember his exploits. Was the published account simply a chronology of his celebrity status as it changed from fame to misfortune? Or did it tell a tough, hard story about human nature? Did you attribute malice to the writer, or think she had been unfair to Ansell? Perhaps, then, the writer had achieved her goal by moving a reader struggling to reconcile sympathy for the central character with the brutality of his final acts.

THE EDITING PROCESS

In the earliest drafts, the writer is still seeking to develop the theme from a first idea to a piece that will appeal to the target audience. In fundamental ways, the theme in the first draft is quite similar to the published piece. First and final drafts begin with a description of how Ansell became famous – from the 1977 trip to his book and film. All drafts include the story of the actual fishing trip as this re-ignites in the audience what captured the 'world' about him in the first place.

The most significant change is the move in the first two drafts (Figures 10.2 and 10.3) from the first-person voice to a third-person narrator. As indicated at the start of the chapter, the direction to change came from the editor. Was he correct? The first person voice offers a different means of viewing Ansell's character but is difficult to sustain, given that the writer was not personally acquainted with the character. It also adds another layer of complexity to a story that travels a long timeline punctuated with dramatic events. It may also be argued that removing the narrator as a player in the narrative keeps the focus on the central character. Early drafts are in a human-interest voice, following the 'bush legend' story for the most part and asking 'what went wrong?' These drafts include the central character's poetry, indicative of a sensitive, thoughtful man. The poetry is later edited, reduced and eventually cut. Does the story suffer as a result?

As the drafts progress, more facts are added to give the story greater substance. The writer initiates some of these changes; others come at the direction of the editor. For example, the snake that shares Ansell's tree home changes from a green snake to a brown snake, which is more dangerous. This is not sensationalizing; it is simply a case of the writer checking back with the source – in this case the book about the central character's adventure. Another example is an early query from the editor.

> If he was going up the Victoria River, how did he end up in the Fitzmaurice? I'm also confused as to the tide: why did it rush out when he capsized then rush back in (when the croc got the dog) and then appears to rush out for two months. If it came in and out every day why didn't he just get in the bloody boat and float away with it? (Ridgway, 1999)

Another significant inclusion as the drafts progress is more information about Ansell's poor social skills and his notion that actions speak louder than words. This addition is crucial to help readers understand the complexities in a person who was at once 'articulate and likable' but also preferred his own company and could be hard and uncompromising. The writer changes 'sort of bloke who'd shoot a man because he was a policeman' to 'shoot a stranger' to avoid speculating on the killer's motivation. The writer also adds information about the character's wife and anecdotes provided by others to 'flesh out' the character she is describing.

The writer grapples with a character who, on the face of it, is someone to be admired yet who ruthlessly murders an innocent person. In the process, it may be argued that the article is transformed from a soft, human-interest piece to a 'true crime' story, with a corresponding shift in focus, language and tone. As the piece becomes longer, the style of the target publication is reasserted. The editor's insight, by email, is at once constructive and blunt:

> It's a bit bleeding heart ... I favor leaving the early stuff and trimming back the recounts later on where he goes to court, loses the farm, gets bitter and twisted, battles on, other journos' recounts of meetings etc. (Ridgway, 1999)

A criticism that may be levelled at the published piece is that it promises to answer the question 'Why?' but spends little time considering the events that led directly to a violent end.

STYLE AND LANGUAGE

The author's decision to target the planned article at *FHM* magazine is the most significant influence on the style, tone and language of the article. The young readership may not be at all familiar with the early life of the subject, and had perhaps not yet thought beyond the sensational facts of the crime. The challenge was to develop her theme in a way that would engage this demographic. Another significant influence on the structure of the article was the time frame in which it was produced. The first draft was written before the police inquiry was completed. Because of this, the writer was unable to report with confidence on the actual events leading to the crime or reasons for it. In the event, an inquest into the policeman's death made no determination as to the killer's motives.

The introduction to a feature article must do more than attract the reader's interest. The opening sentences also establish the tone and style of the article and give the reader a sense of the journey he or she will undertake by reading on. The introduction in Figure 10.1 refers to 'the world' assigning a sense of importance to the central character, even if his name is not immediately recognizable. The link with literary figure Robinson Crusoe creates immediate responses in the reader about the character of Ansell. The more recent film reference to *Crocodile Dundee* broadens the appeal, because the film was an international success and would be known to the readers. The opening asks why Ansell 'ended up a cop-killer' but focuses on Ansell's escape as the turning point in his life. Is the connection between this experience and the events that ended his life clearly revealed by the structure of the article? Also important to the introduction of the article is the writer's description of the central character's appearance on television. This is the clearest indication of the writer's empathy for the subject, even if the story to follow is not flattering.

This description is also crucial to establishing the character as someone who suffered as a result of fame thrust upon him.

The writer also establishes her theme with the selection of quotes drawn from Ansell's book, *To Fight the Wild*. Two quotes in particular – the description of his first encounter with his rescuers and his feeling back then about the media – are central to the depiction of Ansell's character. Another quote, eventually cut from the final piece was drawn from media reports when he faced criminal charges. The quotes from the book let the character 'speak for himself' in a way that would not normally be available to a writer describing a dead character.

As the article changes through the drafting process, the use of language becomes more and more significant. Language is the tool writers use to persuade, discomfort and otherwise touch readers and language is very important to this piece. Devices used by the author include narrative development, adjectives, active verbs, repetition, irony, rhetorical questions, short sentences to punctuate longer ones, and strategic use of quotes. Word choice and language are extremely important because it is the words used to retell, describe, illustrate and project that shape the character in the audience's mind. This is solely up to the writer, even though the writer is dealing in 'facts'.

Consider the language used throughout the article. The writer describes Ansell as being 'paraded on *Parkinson*'. Would the message sent be different if he was described as 'guest starring on *Parkinson*'? He was described as being 'plagued by crocodiles'. How is this different from being 'annoyed' or 'threatened' by crocodiles. The imagery created in the way a writer brings words together is the way the writer holds an audience. The use of assonance, such as 'He had not just survived, he had thrived', effectively adds to the writer's character portrait. As the drafts progress, the writer also uses language to edit the work for length as well as structure. The examples below demonstrate how the writer simultaneously saves eight words and projects a greater fall:

Somewhere along the line he went from a barefoot poet who liked his own company to the sort of person who'd shoot a man because he was a policeman. (Figure 10.3)

Somehow he went from a quintessential bushman to the sort of man who would shoot a stranger because he's a policeman. (Figure 10.4)

The writer weaves her own observations about the character into the text. The writer's perspective is revealed in phrases such as 'his 15 minutes of fame were the stuff of legend', 'he talked to the bush and the bush talked back' and 'Rod Ansell could have stopped the car and shot himself, but he didn't'. Sometimes the reader is addressed directly in statements such as 'It was incredible to think such a man existed at the end of the twentieth century', and 'It would be years before he wore boots again'. These statements highlight the major images of the article and prepare the reader for the conclusion to follow.

The conclusion is a most important part of a feature article because it is there that the writer reaffirms the theme and draws together the various elements in the narrative. The conclusion to this article evokes vivid imagery, ties in the theme, and uses alliteration and assonance in drawing a conclusion to the story of Rod Ansell. It seeks to reinforce an image of the central character as an extraordinary bushman who was at home in the wild but ill-equipped for the modern world. The writer does this through the use of two literary analogies, references to Ansell's own book, *To Fight the Wild*, and *Heart of Darkness* (1983), Joseph Conrad's exploration of human nature. The organization of the final sentences portrays Ansell's life as a journey over which he had little control, whether he was winning or losing. It also seeks to reinforce that Ansell was appropriated by the media at various times but his true character was much more complex. The published version of the article removes this element. Does this make the ending more, or less, effective in your view, and why?

THE EDITOR'S CUT

While it may be argued that the writer's process in editing the article consisted of the refining and honing of ideas evident from the first draft, the changes in the published version are more dramatic. These are the changes made by the editor in the absence of consultation with the writer. The editor's changes may be significant and affect the length, structure and even the angle of the published work after it has left the writer for the last time. The editor also controls the layout of the published article, which makes its own contribution to the meaning conveyed by the text. It is at this point that the style of the publication has the most direct impact on the writer's work. In commercial media, the number of advertisements determines the number of editorial pages in a publication. The layout of the magazine is created by the Art Director, often in the absence of the text, and is based on the number and dramatic strength of photographs available to illustrate the piece in the magazine's style.

> *FHM* is a magazine run on a tight formula. ... Gone are the days of a writer, no matter how respected, calling an editor to say, 'I've got 3000 words, will you run it as is?' The magazine takes the position that not all stories and themes broadly thought to be 'men's stuff' are right for it and its readers. If that were the case it would be identical to 100 other 'men's' magazines around the world, wouldn't it? As a result, the editorial team has a very definite way in which they present words and pictures to the reader. It's a subjective position from which every word in the magazine is committed to print. (Ridgway, 1999)

The layout and editing stage is crucial to the effectiveness of the published piece but is also the time when inaccuracies can inadvertently threaten the credibility of the writer's work. In this scenario, the editor has set out to cut about 400 words from the piece that has been submitted in order to fit the layout designed for the article, as well as refining the copy to suit the style of the publication. The selection of and positioning of photographs and choice of headlines and sub-headlines will impact directly on the impression created by the article before the reader engages the text. In this scenario, the editor has accepted the headline suggested by the writer, 'The Legend and the Fall', a reference to a popular movie with a similar name. The editor has added a sub-heading: 'Rod Ansell, 1987 Territorian of the Year, and the man who inspired Paul Hogan's "Crocodile Dundee" finished up a dead cop killer. Why?' The choice of words in this heading speaks volumes about the direct style of the publication.

The published version is less sympathetic to its subject than the first draft, written by the writer in the first flush of an idea and without reference to the facts. The story is less about the subject's fall from grace and more about the 1977 adventure that first brought him to public attention. Does this diminish the theme chosen by the writer? Does the published article offer the same insight into the character of the subject, his life and times? In the first draft, the writer is in no position to focus on the mysterious events surrounding his death and the shootings (one fatal) that preceded it. These facts were simply not known at the time of writing. Another change by the editor is to insert more 'hard facts', such as the name of the dead policeman, and introduce details of the later crimes earlier in the story. In doing so, however, the editor inadvertently inserts a factual error increasing the number of people killed by Ansell from one to three. Consider the difference between the writer's copy (Figure 10.4) and the published version (Figure 10.1):

> There is no doubt police were looking for him after two shootings the previous day. (Figure 10.4)

> It was alleged he shot and killed PC Glen Huitson at a roadblock when stopped in relation to two murders. (Figure 10.1)

Other changes have been motivated by the need to make the overall article shorter. For example, the number of headlines quoted in the opening is reduced from three to two, and the phrase 'shoot a stranger because he was a policeman' has been edited to 'shoot a stranger and a policeman at that'.

The second example illustrates how subtle changes can significantly affect meaning. The writer wrote 'because he was a policeman', because the gunman fired at the roadblock from some distance away and without knowing which policeman he was firing at. The editor changed the meaning of the sentence to suggest it was somehow more remarkable to shoot a policeman. Similarly, in changing the sentence beginning 'He published a book, *To Fight the Wild ...*' to include the words 'illustrating his adventure', the editor suggests a mercenary motive not intended by the writer. The editor also edits the introduction and conclusion to the article, directly affecting the theme of the article. In removing the word 'called' from references to Ansell's public persona, the editor takes away the sense of his life being public property. The editor also removes the literary association with Robinson Crusoe as well as all reference to Ansell's family and their part in his life. Other sentences inserted by the writer, such as 'his 15 minutes of fame were the stuff of legend' and 'He had not just survived, he had thrived', have also been cut – reducing the writer's direction over the piece.

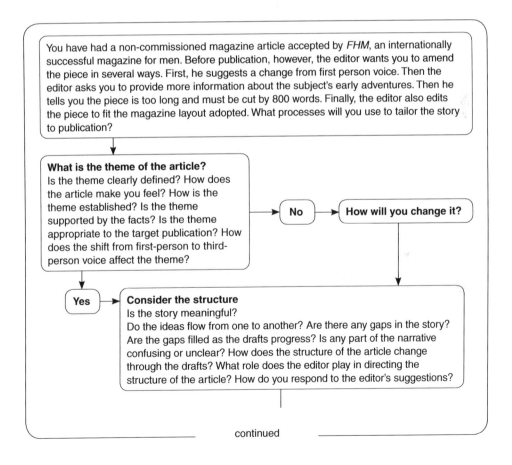

You have had a non-commissioned magazine article accepted by *FHM*, an internationally successful magazine for men. Before publication, however, the editor wants you to amend the piece in several ways. First, he suggests a change from first person voice. Then the editor asks you to provide more information about the subject's early adventures. Then he tells you the piece is too long and must be cut by 800 words. Finally, the editor also edits the piece to fit the magazine layout adopted. What processes will you use to tailor the story to publication?

What is the theme of the article?
Is the theme clearly defined? How does the article make you feel? How is the theme established? Is the theme supported by the facts? Is the theme appropriate to the target publication? How does the shift from first-person to third-person voice affect the theme?

No → **How will you change it?**

Yes → **Consider the structure**
Is the story meaningful?
Do the ideas flow from one to another? Are there any gaps in the story? Are the gaps filled as the drafts progress? Is any part of the narrative confusing or unclear? How does the structure of the article change through the drafts? What role does the editor play in directing the structure of the article? How do you respond to the editor's suggestions?

continued

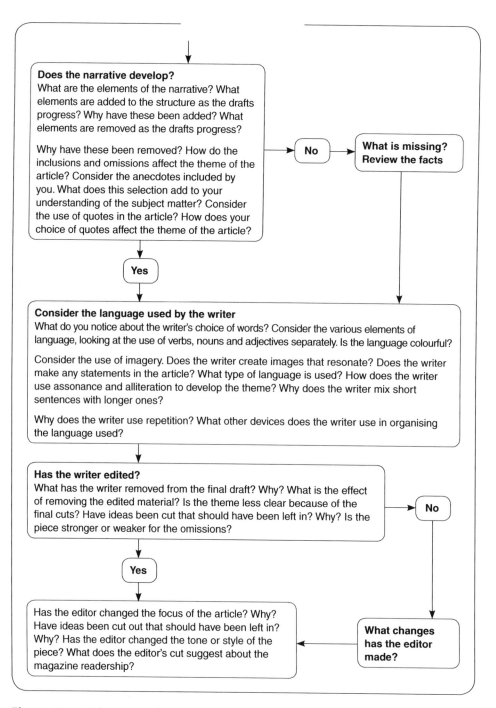

Figure 10.5   Taking news further

CONCLUSION

Has the editor made the piece stronger or weaker through his feedback during the editing process and his own editing? As illustrated elsewhere in this book, editing is a wholly subjective process, informed by the professional judgement and experience of the person doing the editing. Examining the process reveals that the theme comes first followed by a structure for organizing the narrative. Then the writer goes through a series of inclusions and omissions of information until the narrative is complete. From this point, the writer's focus shifts to language – the expression of images and selection of verbs, nouns and adjectives. Language is further refined through the final editing processes, where first the writer and then the editor reduce the length of the final piece. In the final edit, the editor brings an outsider's perspective to what the writer has sought to do and makes professional value judgements underpinned by his own understanding of the publication's style and readership.

FURTHER ACTION

1   Choose a magazine article that you have enjoyed reading. Examine it closely in terms of the language used by the writer. What do you notice? Is there any powerful imagery? How is it done?

2   Consider the submitted draft of this article in this chapter (Figure 10.4). Now edit 400 words from the text, just as the *FHM* editor did. Compare your edit to that of the *FHM* editor. How do they differ? What underpinned your decisions?

3   Try to capture the essence of the story in a 140-word Tweet. Is it difficult? Why?

4   Choose any magazine. Using the layout, content, advertising and writing style as a guide, write a 100-word profile of the target reader.

5   Read the newspapers closely. Choose a news story as inspiration for a feature article on a related topic.

FURTHER READING

Leser, D. (1999) *The Whites of Their Eyes: Profiles*. Sydney: Allen & Unwin.
Phillips, L.W. (ed.) (1984) *Ernest Hemingway on Writing*. New York: Touchstone.
Ricketson, M. (2004) *Writing Feature Stories: How to Research and Write Newspaper and Magazine Articles*. Sydney: Allen & Unwin.

BIBLIOGRAPHY

Adam, S.G. (1993) *Notes Towards a Definition of Journalism: Understanding an Old Craft as an Art Form*. St Petersburg, FL: The Poynter Institute for Media Studies.

Altschull, J.H. (1984) *Agents of Power: The Role of the News Media in Human Affairs*. New York: Longman.

Associated Press (2000) 'Poll: Four in 10 US journalists say they've softened tone'. News Report circulated on wire service, 5 January.

Aylsen, B., Sedorkin, G. and Oakham, M. (2011) *Reporting in a Multimedia World* (2nd edn). Sydney: Allen & Unwin.

Bacon, W. (1999) 'What is a journalist in a university?', in T. Flew, J. Sternberg and C. Hippocrates (eds), *Media Wars*. Brisbane: Key Center for Culture and Policy, pp. 79–91.

Barr, T. (1977) *Reflections of Reality*. Melbourne: Rigby.

Benkler, Y. (2011) 'Giving the networked public sphere time to develop', in R.W. McChesney and V. Pickard (eds), *Will the Last Reporter Please Turn Out the Lights: The Collapse of Journalism and What Can be Done to Fix It*. New York: The New Press, p. 225.

Betancourt, L. (2009) *The Journalist's Guide to Twitter*, www.mashable.com/2009/05/14/twitter-journalism.

Black, J., Steele, B. and Barney, R. (eds) (1997) *Doing Ethics in Journalism* (3rd edn). Boston, MA: Allyn & Bacon.

Bok, S. (1978) *Lying: Moral Choice in Public and Private Life*. New York: Random House.

Boud, D. and Feletti, G. (eds) (1991) *The Challenge of Problem Based Learning*. London: Kogan Page.

Brady, J. (1977) *The Craft of Interviewing*. Cincinnati, OH: Writer's Digest.

Breen, M. (ed.) (1999) *Journalism: Theory and Practice*. Sydney: Macleay Press.

Breit, R. (1998) 'Legal pitfalls on the internet', in S. Quinn (ed.), *Newsgathering on the Net*. Winchelsea, Victoria: Precision Press.

Candlin, E.F. (1970) *Teach Yourself Journalism*. London: Teach Yourself Books.

Carey, J. (1998) Email transcript of interview with David McKnight, published on Jeanet discussion group.

Carlyon, L. (1982) *Paper Chase: The Press under Examination*. Melbourne: Herald & Weekly Times Ltd.

Chomsky, N. and Herman, E. (1988) *Manufacturing Consent*. New York: Pantheon Books.

Christians, C., Rotzoll, K. and Fackler, M. (1987) *Media Ethics: Cases and Moral Reasoning*. New York: Longman.

Cohen, B.C. (1963) *The Press and Foreign Policy*. Princeton, NJ: Princeton University Press.

Conrad, J. (1983) *Heart of Darkness*. Harmondsworth: Penguin.

Cudlipp, H. (1980) *The Prerogative of the Harlot: Press Barons and Power*. London: The Bodley Head.

Deitz, M.L. (2010) *Watch This Space: The Future of Australian Journalism*. Melbourne: Cambridge University Press.

Didion, J. (1999) 'Last words: those Hemingway wrote, and those he didn't', *The Australian Magazine*, July 17–18.

Eggerking, K., Scott, P. and Sheridan Burns, L. (1998) *Media and Indigenous Australians*. Curriculum Project. Brisbane: University of Queensland.

Elliot, D. (1986) *Responsible Journalism*. Beverly Hills, CA: Sage.

Epstein, E.J. (1974) *News from Nowhere*. New York: Random House.

Epstein, E.J. (1977) *Between Fact and Fiction: The Problem of Journalism*. New York: Random House.

Evans, H. (1972) *Newsman's English*. Oxford: Heinemann.

Ewart, J. (1997) 'Journalists, readership and writing', *Australian Studies in Journalism*. Brisbane: University of Queensland, pp. 83–103.

Fanning, E. (1998) 'News breaks and standards crash', *Walkley Magazine*, July: 12.

Fish, S.E. (2011) *How to Write a Sentence and How to Read One*. New York: Harper Collins.

Flew, T., Sternberg, J. and Hippocrates, C. (eds) (1999) *Media Wars*. Brisbane: Australian Key Center for Culture and Media Policy.

Forde, S. (1999) 'Reinventing the public sphere: the Australian alternative press industry'. Unpublished PhD dissertation, Griffith University, Queensland.

Gaunt, P. (1990) *Choosing the News: The Profit Factor in News Selection*. New York: Greenwood Press.

Gibson, M.L. (1989) *The Writer's Friend*. Ames, IA: Iowa State University Press.

Grattan, M. (1998) *Editorial Independence: An Outdated Concept?* Brisbane: University of Queensland, Department of Journalism.

Greenwall, H.J. (1957) *Northcliffe: Napoleon of Fleet Street*. London: Wingate.

Gurevitch, M. (1990) *Culture, Society and the Media*. London: Routledge.

Hacker, S. and Seshagiri, A. (2011) *Why Twitter Matters*. Berkeley. CA: Knight Digital Media Centre, http://multimedia.journalism.berkeley.edu/tutorials/twitter/.

Hall, S. (1992) 'Discourse and power', in S. Hall (ed.), *Formations of Modernity*. London: Polity Press.

Hartley, J. (1996) *Popular Reality*. London: Arnold.

Hedges, C. (2011) 'The disease of objectivity', in R.W. McChesney and V. Pickard (eds), *Will the Last Reporter Please Turn Out the Lights: The Collapse of Journalism and What Can be Done to Fix It*. New York: The New Press.

Henningham, J. (1998) 'Australian journalists' attitudes to education', *Australian Journalism Review*, 20 (1): 77–90.

Hirst, M. (2010) *News 2.0: Will Journalism Survive the Internet?* Sydney: Allen & Unwin.

Hodgson, F.W. (1998) *New Sub-Editing* (3rd edn). Oxford: Butterworth-Heinemann.

Hunter Institute of Mental Health (2008) *Response Ability*. Resources for Journalism Education. Newcastle, NSW: HIMH.

Jervis, R. (1987) *News Sense*. Adelaide: Adelaide Newspapers Pty Ltd.

Keen, A. (2007) *Cult of the Amateur: How Today's Internet is Killing Our Culture and Assaulting Our Economy*. London: Nicholas Brealey Publishing.

King, J. (1997) 'Principles, professionalism and philosophy', *Australian Journalism Review*, 19 (1): 19–34.

Kingsbury, D. (1998) *The Politics of Indonesia*. Melbourne: Oxford University Press.

Koch, T. (1990) *The News as Myth: Fact and Context in Journalism*. New York: Greenwood Press.

Koch, T. (1991) *Journalism for the 21st Century*. New York: Praeger.

Kolb, D. (1984) *Experiential Learning: Experience in the Source of Learning and Development*. Englewood Cliffs, NJ: Prentice-Hall.

Langer, E.J. (1989) *Mindfulness*. Reading, MA: Perseus Books.

Lasica, J. (2009) *Wall Street Journal's Social Media Policy*, www.socialmedia.biz/social-media-policies/wall-street-journals-social-media-policy.

Layton, R. (2011) *Editing and News Design: How to Shape the News in Print and Online Journalism*. Melbourne: Palgrave Macmillan.

Lebacqz, K. (1986) *Six Theories of Justice: Perspectives from Philosophical and Theological Ethics*. Minneapolis, MN: Augsburg Publishing House.

Lehmann, N. (2006) 'Amateur Hour: journalism without journalists', *The New Yorker*, 7 August, www.newyorker.com/archive/2006/08/07/060807fa_fact1#ixzz1YSOJwEK0.

Leser, D. (1999) *The Whites of Their Eyes: Profiles*. Sydney: Allen & Unwin.

McAdams, M. (2011) *Social Media Guidelines for Journalists*. http://mindymcadams.com/tojou/2011/social-media-guidelines-for-journalists/ (May 16 2011).

McChesney, R.W. and Nichol, J. (2011) 'Down the news hole', in R.W. McChesney and V. Pickard (eds), *Will the Last Reporter Please Turn Out the Lights: The Collapse of Journalism and What Can be Done to Fix It*. New York: The New Press.

McChesney, R.W. and Pickard, V. (eds) (2011) *Will the Last Reporter Please Turn Out the Lights: The Collapse of Journalism and What Can be Done to Fix It*. New York: The New Press.

McGregor, C. (1983) *Soundtrack for the Eighties*. Sydney: Hodder & Stoughton.

McGuiness, P.J. (1999) 'Media studies, journalism and the Zeitgeist, *Quadrant*, March: 2–5.

McManus, J. (1994) *Market-Driven Journalism: Let the Citizen Beware*. Thousand Oaks, CA: Sage.

McQuail, D. (1994) *Mass Communication Theory* (3rd edn). London: Sage.

Malcolm, J. (1989) 'The journalist and the murderer', *The New Yorker*, March: 38–73.

Malcolm, J (1990) *The Journalist and the Murderer*. New York: Knopf.

Marshall, I. and Kingsbury, D. (1996) *Media Realities: The News Media and Power in Australia*. Melbourne: Longman.

MEAA (1997) *Code of Ethics for Australian Journalists*. Sydney: Media, Entertainment and Arts Alliance, Australia.

Meadows, M. (1992) 'A sense of deja-vu – Canadian journalism ponders its future', *Australian Journalism Review*, 14 (2), July–December.

Meadows, M. (1997) 'Taking a problem-based learning approach to journalism education', *Asia Pacific Media Educator*, 3 (July).

Mencher, M. (1991) *News Reporting and Writing*. New York: W.C. Brown.

Nichol, J. and McChesney, R.W. (2011) 'The death and life of great American newspapers', *The Nation*, June 16 2011, www.thenation.com.

Nystrand, M. (1986) *The Structure of Written Communication: Studies in Reciprocity between Writers and Readers*. Orlando, FL: Academic Press.

Oakham, K.M. (1998) 'Kick it Karl: a jump start for journalism education', *Australian Journalism Review*, 20 (2): 24.

O'Donnell, P. (1999) 'Professional communicators or multimedia information traffickers?' Unpublished paper presented to the Journalism Education Association Annual Conference, Melbourne.

Paletz, D.L. and Entman, R.M. (1982) *Media*Power*Politics*. New York: The Free Press.

Papworth, L. (2009) *At War: Journalism vs Social Media Rules of Engagement*. www.laurelpapworth.com.

Patterson, P. and Wilkins, L. (1994) *Media Ethics: Issues and Cases* (3rd edn). Dubuque, IA: McGraw-Hill.

Pavlik, J. (1998) 'Journalism ethics and new media', *Media Ethics*, 9 (2): 1–3.

Pearson, M. (1992) 'Identifying key competencies for journalists', Paper presented to the Journalism Education Association Annual Conference, Newcastle, NSW.

Pearson, M. (1994) 'Re-thinking quality in journalism education', *Australian Journalism Review*, 16 (2).

Perrin, A. (1995a) 'Man who was bank's TV face dies of neglect', *Sydney Morning Herald*, 10 January, p. 3.

Perrin, A. (1995b) 'Smiling face of poverty dies', *Sydney Morning Herald*, 10 January, p. 3.

Perry, R. and Ansell, R. (1980) *To Fight the Wild*. Sydney: Pegasus Books.

Phillips, L.W. (ed.) (1984) *Ernest Hemingway on Writing*. New York: Touchstone.

Ricketson, M. (2004) *Writing Feature Stories: How to Research and Write Newspaper and Magazine Articles*. Sydney: Allen & Unwin.

Ridgway, N. (1999) Email correspondence between the author and the editor of *FHM* magazine.

Ryle, G. (1960) *Dilemmas*. Cambridge: Cambridge University Press.

Samaritans (UK) (2000) 'Guide to reporting of suicide and mental illness', www.samaritans.org.uk.

Schön, D.A. (1983) *The Reflective Practitioner: How Professionals Think in Action*. New York: Basic Books.

Schön, D.A. (1986) *Educating the Reflective Practitioner*. New York: Basic Books.

Schultz, J. (1994) *Not Just Another Business: Journalism, Citizens and the Media*. Sydney: Pluto Press.

Sellers, L. (1979) *The Simple Sub's Book*. London: Permagon Press.

Sheridan, L. (1977) 'Some first impressions', in *Staff News*. Sydney: John Fairfax & Sons Pty Ltd.

Sheridan Burns, L. (1995) 'Philosophy or frontline: a survey of journalism educators about teaching ethics', *Australian Journalism Review*, 17 (1): 1–10.

Sheridan Burns, L. (1996a) 'Blocking the exits: focus on the decision in ethical decision-making', *Australian Journalism Review*, 18 (1): 87–99.

Sheridan Burns, L. (1996b) 'From knowing how to being able', *Teaching Review*, 1 (1): 87–97.

Sheridan Burns, L. (1997) 'Problem-based learning: is it new jargon for something familiar?' *Australian Journalism Review*, 19 (1): 59–72.

Sheridan Burns, L. (1999a) 'The President's column', *Australian Journalism Review*, 21 (2): 4.

Sheridan Burns, L. (1999b) 'The legend and the fall', *FHM*, October. Sydney: Emap Publications.

Sheridan Burns, L. and Hazell, P. (1997) *Response ... Ability: Curriculum Materials for Journalism*. National Youth Suicide Prevention Strategy University Curriculum Project, Hunter Area Mental Health, Newcastle, www.responseability.org.au.

Sheridan Burns, L. and Hazell, P. (1999) 'Youth suicide and the media's response ... ability', *Asia Pacific Media Educator*, 6: 57–71.

Sheridan Burns, L. and McKee, A. (1999) 'Reporting Indigenous issues: some practical suggestions for journalists', *Australian Journalism Review*, 21 (2): 103–16.

Shirky, C. (2008) *Here Comes Everybody: The Power of Organising without Organisations*. New York: Penguin.

Silk, M. (1991) 'Who will rewire America?' *Columbia Journalism Review*, May–June: 45–8.

Spitzberg, B.H. and Cupach, W.R. (1988) *Handbook of Interpersonal Competence Research*. New York: Springer.

Splichal, S. and Sparks, C. (1994) *Journalists for the 21st Century*. Norwood, NJ: Ablex Publications.

Starr, P. (2009) 'Goodbye to the age of newspapers (hello to a new age of corruption)', *The New Republic*, 4 March. Reproduced in R.W. McChesney and V. Pickard (eds), *Will the Last Reporter Please Turn Out the Lights: The Collapse of Journalism and What Can be Done to Fix It*. New York: The New Press.

Stephens, M. and Lanson, G. (1986) *Writing and Reporting the News*. Orlando, FL: Holt, Rinehart & Winston.

Tapsall, S. (1998) 'Spreadsheets and databases', in S. Quinn (ed.), *Newsgathering on the Net*. Winchelsea, Vic.: Precision Press.

Tapsall, S. and Varley, C. (2001) *Journalism: Theory in Practice*. Melbourne: Oxford University Press.

Thomas, R. (1999a) 'The benefits of learning news writing through new methods'. Paper presented to Best Practices in Journalism Education international web conference, Penn State University, Philadelphia, 25 March–7 April.

Thomas, R. (1999b) 'Learning news writing: a process intervention in a product setting'. Unpublished Master of Arts thesis, The University of Auckland, New Zealand.

Underwood, D. (1993) *When MBAs Rule the Newsroom: How Markets and Managers are Shaping Today's Media*. New York: Columbia University Press.

Usher, N. (2011) 'Professional journalists hands off citizen journalism', in R.W. McChesney and V. Pickard (eds), *Will the Last Reporter Please Turn Out the Lights: The Collapse of Journalism and What Can be Done to Fix It*. New York: The New Press, pp. 264–77.

Walsh ,M (2010) *Futuretainment:Yesterday the World Changed, Now it is Your Turn*. London: Phaidon.

Warren, A. (1995) *The Media Report*. ABC Radio National, 21 December.

White, S.A. (1992) *Reporting in Australia*. Melbourne: Macmillan.

Whitington, D. (1978) *Strive to be Fair: An Unfinished Autobiography*. Canberra: Australian National University Press.

Windschuttle, K. (1999) 'Cultural studies versus journalism', *Quadrant*, 15 (3): 11–20.

Wolfe, T. (1975) *The New Journalism*. London: Pan Books.

INDEX

17529534R00109

Made in the USA
Middletown, DE
27 January 2015